D1830330

PHILOSOPHICAL ESSAYS

Owing to the antiquity and rarity of this book, certain pages are regrettably absent, and readability is compromised due to the blurring of the original text. If you possess any insights regarding the availability of these missing sections, kindly inform us. Your assistance is crucial in ensuring the completion of this significant work for the benefit of future generations.

PHILOSOPHICAL ESSAYS

BY

SURENDRANATH DASGUPTA

C.I.E., M.A., Ph.D. (Cal. et Cantab.),
D.L.itt., (Hony Rome), I.E.S.,
PRINCIPAL SANSKRIT COLLEGE, CALCUTTA

GYAN

Published by

Gyan Publishing House
5, Ansari Road
Daryaganj, New Delhi-110002
Phone: 011-47034999, 9811692060
E-mail: books@gyanbooks.com

Distribution Network
gyanbooks.com
India, USA, Canada, UK, Australia

© Publisher

All rights reserved. No part of this work may be reproduced, stored, adapted, or transmitted in any form or by any means, electronic, mechanical, photocopying, micro-filming, recording or otherwise, or translated in any language, without the prior written permission of the copyright owner and the publisher.

ISBN: 978-93-6208-285-5 (PB)
First Published, 1941

2nd Impression 2024

Printed at: Gyan Press, Delhi.

The book is sold subject to the condition that it shall not, by way of trade or otherwise, be lent, resold, hired out, or otherwise circulated without the prior publisher's written consent.

PHILOSOPHICAL ESSAYS
Author: SURENDRANATH DAS GUPTA

PHILOSOPHICAL ESSAYS

BY

SURENDRANATH DASGUPTA,
C.I.E., M.A., Ph.D., (Cal. et Cantab.),
D.Litt., (Hony. Rome), I.E.S.,
PRINCIPAL, SANSKRIT COLLEGE, CALCUTTA

PUBLISHED BY THE
UNIVERSITY OF CALCUTTA
1941

To

HIS EXCELLENCY

SIR JOHN ARTHUR HERBERT, G.C.I.E.,

THE GOVERNOR OF BENGAL

AND

THE CHANCELLOR OF THE CALCUTTA UNIVERSITY

as a tribute of respect.

CONTENTS

	Preface	vii
1.	Idealism in Gentile	1
2.	International Morality	28
3.	Approach to Metaphysics	63
4.	Some Aspects of Buddhist Philosophy ...	82
5.	Croce and Buddhism	117
6.	General Introduction to Tantra Philosophy	151
7.	Yoga Psychology	179
8.	Philosophy of Vasubandhu in Viṃśikā and Triṃśikā	198
9.	Dogmas of Indian Philosophy ...	208
10.	Implications of Realism in the Vedānta	234
11.	Message of Buddhism	255
12.	Yoga Theory of the Relation of Mind and Body	276
13.	Epistemology of the New School of Logic in Bengal	321
14.	Māyā of Śaṅkara and his Followers ...	332
15.	Meaning of Culture	350
16.	A Hindu View of Religion	374

PREFACE

Most of these papers were read before International gatherings, either in this country or abroad. Some of them, however, appeared in learned journals, and there are one or two which appear here for the first time. They have been written at different times and treat of subjects which are widely different. As such no unity of thought can be claimed. But it is hoped that the unconventional manner in which many of the subjects have been approached may stimulate the interests of abler scholars for reaping a better harvest. My best thanks are due to my pupils, Prof. Miss S. Mitra, Śāstrī, M.A. and Dr. Satindra N. Mukherjee, M.A., Ph.D., and Dr. S. B. Dasgupta, M.A., Ph.D., Lecturer, Calcutta University, for very kindly revising the proofs. My best thanks are also due to my friend, Dr. Syamaprasad Mookerjee, M.A., D.Litt. (Hon.), Bar.-at-Law, President, Post-Graduate Council in Arts for the kind interest that he took in the work which eventually led to its publication by the Calcutta University.

IDEALISM IN GENTILE

The word 'Idealist' is sometimes used, in a popular manner, to denote one whose mind is chained by certain ideas, which one sets before him as the norms of one's action, keeping oneself blind to other sagacious considerations. Brutus is called an 'Idealist', since he stabbed Cæsar, only because he thought he was a tyrant. He could not think of the personality of Cæsar as a whole, the effects that would be produced by his death, the condition of the Roman people at the time, his personal considerations for him as a friend, and the good that Cæsar might produce were he allowed to live. An idealist in this sense is a mere visionary, who, instead of taking into consideration all circumstances and conditions, and the bearing of the moral principles in the varying fields, in which they are applied, abstracts the moral principles from the concrete reality, in connection and in correlation with which alone they may be said to be imperative. When Kant withdraws his moral maxims from the field of experience and accepts them only as the form of the Law, and considers reverence for such a law as the only sentiment that should be present in the performance of a moral action, his moral philosophy becomes as abstract as Geometry. In the ancient epics of India there are many instances of action according to certain set principles. Rāma went to forest, because father's wishes are to be respected; and he banished his wife, because the wishes of the people are to be respected. Yudhiṣṭhira courted his banishment, because the laws of the game of dice were inexorable; Bhīṣma courted his death, because of his principle that his arrows should not hurt a woman; and Draupadī took five husbands, because a mother's wishes have to be respected. All these instances show that actions according to certain set principles are visionary and abstract and that such actions are sometimes more immoral than moral. Such ideals may come from within or may be picked up from customary practices, or from scriptures. But in any case they defeat their purpose, because they are not in consonance with the whole, with reference to which alone they may claim to have their imperative character. The scriptural code of conduct prescribed for a Hindu or a Christian suffers from the same defects.

But, however these may be, the popular connotation of the word 'idealist' shows, that idealism means the reference of a person in his entirety to certain ideas which must determine his actions. The cardinal ideas in such idealists are not mere inert ideas, admissions of mind or cognitions, but they have a determinative function, a potential activity which ultimately guide and determine the person in his active capacity.

The word 'idealism' is also sometimes used to denote an optimism as a basis of action. Thus we say that a true man of action must have some idealism. We mean thereby that, though there may be failures, miseries and sufferings, and though there may be circumstances, conditions and obstructions, which for the time being may appear inexorable, invincible and impregnable, yet the man of action must get himself seated upon the bed-rock of an unflinching faith in a possibility of a betterment of things which should goad him to action even through destruction. Demogorgon in *Prometheus Unbound* of Shelley echoes this form of idealism when he says:—

> "To suffer woes which Hope thinks infinite ;
> To forgive wrongs darker than death or night ;
> To defy Power, which seems omnipotent ;
> To love, and bear ; to hope till Hope creates
> From its own wreck the thing it contemplates ;
> Neither to change, nor falter, nor repent ;
> This, like thy glory, Titan, is to be
> Good, great and joyous, beautiful and free ;
> This is alone Life, Joy, Empire, and Victory."
>
> (ACT. II.)

Idealism in this sense means a supreme faith in the ideal which is realising itself and is bound to realise itself, more and more completely, even though obstructions in their multifold forms may, at the present moment, seem to check and defy its exalted career. The word 'idealism' is very closely associated in the above sense with an ideal of truth, love, or goodness, as far outweighing the powers of evil and misery over which it dominates. The ideal is subjective, and yet not wholly subjective, because it actualizes itself in the objective world, and even when it cannot so actualize, the firmness of the faith and the serenity of self-reconciliation with it achieves for it a development and transformation of personality which never submits itself to evil, but always defies it in an unflinching manner and makes the person a king of himself. Thus Prometheus says in another passage:—

> "Pity the self-despising slaves of Heaven
> Not me, within whose mind sits peace serene.
> As light in the sun, throned:
>
> * * *
>
> Pain is my element as hate is thine;
> Ye rend me now: I care not.
>
> * * *
>
> Yet am I king over myself, and rule
> The torturing and conflicting throngs within."
>
> (ACT. I.)

This idealism implies a dynamic personality which has set itself on certain ideals through the self-evolving value sense of faith in which he faces all evil and obstruction and dominates over them even through his own destruction. Another type of this idealism permeates practically through most systems of Indian Philosophy which believe in a possible ultimate extinction of sorrow as 'emancipation' which all men are destined to attain through a long course of births and rebirths, and the moral strife implied therein, such that ultimately the good overcomes the evil and man attains perfection and goes beyond good and evil.

Idealism in its true sense implies a spontaneous progressive movement as induced by ideals that live and form the very inmost being of the person himself. As a matter of fact, one may go even farther and say that 'being' with reference to an ideal constitutes one's very personality which can be defined only as a spontaneous self-evolution, a transformation of all objectivity into subjective demands for reaching a goal which though seemingly outside itself is in essence the very inside of spiritual movement. This idealism defines personality as a spontaneous movement in which the value and the movement become identified ; and which extends the limits of personality in accordance with the spiritual movements that draw itself forward,—yet living within itself, defying the notions of space and time in its eternity. In this sense the ideal becomes identical with personality which again is the same as the spontaneous movement in accordance with the ideal. The ideal thus is not something outside or posited as a being as opposed to the Person, or as something which is external to it, which it has to reach but which it has not reached. But the personality itself is defined both by its connotation and its denotation by the ideal, and as such it is different from the empirical ego which is only a contingent abstraction from the life of the personality and as such is as external to it as anything else. Personality in this sense would mean a concrete self-evolving spontaneity which integrates in itself past, present and the future. The Prometheus that is presented to us in Shelley's work is not Prometheus limited by space and time. It is the Prometheus typifying the ideal of faith, hope, love and freedom that not only defies and destroys evil but outlives Demogorgon's external necessity and is unlimited and infinite in itself as it represents an uncurbed progressive will in whose nature all separate discreet acts and aspects have dissolved and melted themselves. Such a personality may well be understood in the concept of an integrated self-evolution of a unity of ideals which cannot be limited by anything else external to it or by any abstracted being or by any aspect which may be torn off from its inside.

Idealism and value are thus very closely connected. The sense of value and the value itself, may also be regarded as identical in nature only with the qualificatory provision that the sense of value is a cognitive abstraction from value itself. Value understood in this sense is a dynamic spontaneity which like the ray of the sun is invisible and indescribable in itself but which shows itself only through specific reflections by which it splits up its nature and shows itself through abstracted forms. In the field of physical science all attempts to define the nature of light have up till now failed miserably. The mathematical descriptions of the nature of light are but abstract numerical equations just as the physical perceptions of light are but unique sense-abstractions of its nature. The reality of light, therefore, exists as a dynamic principle but baffles our grasp. Value also represents the reality of the dynamic personality of which we have been speaking but it is only in its emergent forms of abstraction that its nature can be grasped, intuited or described. The multiplicity of values is thus only an abstraction. The certainty and the reality of personality as described herein coincides exactly with the concept of dynamic value as herein described. Kant's conception of value or the moral ideal is also formless, but this formlessness is the formlessness of abstraction which stands opposed to the empirical ego as a command or imperative which it must obey, but which is in a sense outside of it. Kant has made no efforts to show the intrinsic relation subsisting between the empirical ego and the transcendental law, and has given no reason as to why the empirical ego should obey demands of the so-called transcendental ego.

The word 'ideal' even in its popular sense of a goal has a meaning only in relation to a progressive movement and is in itself only an abstraction from the very nature of movement. It is conceived as being something outside the movement, only because the movement as such cannot be conceptually realised. The realisation of movement by an intuitive absorption is also only a partial grasp of it, for the movement as such involves (when conceptually abstracted) elements and relations and their interrelations which are not intelligible by any intuitional grasp as such. The movement as such is not intellectually comprehensible, nor also intuitively intelligible as a pure duration, as Bergson thinks; for what is understood by Bergson's pure duration is only an element of the intellectual, though he positively denies it to be such. Bergson says that reality is mobility. It is not things made, but things in the making; not self-maintaining stages, but only changing states exist. The consciousness we have of our own self in its continual flux, introduces us to the interior reality on the model of which we must represent other realities. All reality, therefore, is tendency, if we agree to mean by tendency an incipient change of direction. Bergson thinks that by violent mental effort one can get himself away from the various states and relations and place himself in the very nature of the flowing pulsation in which the perceiver himself together with everything else in the world are dissolved, as it were, into a pure flow of mobility,—a river divested of its waters and intuited as a mere flow. Things are but abstractions when taken apart from the all-engulfing flow. It is this unintermitted flow that is the nature of reality and we can know it through intuition of our own person with which the reality of the world is coterminus. For intuition reveals the fact that we have nothing but flowing—a flowing duration which extends through all and everything without any break: and this want of break is duration. Bergson says that we can realise the nature of this reality by intuition and not by abstraction, as is the case with all intellectualism. But a little reflection will show that Bergson's intuition is nothing more than abstract imagination. The violent effort of which he speaks is the effort of imagination to divest the mind for the time being from all aspects of our experiences and to concentrate it only on the aspect of the flow just as the ordinary intellectualist, a follower of Plato for example, would abstract only the universal types of our experiences—the ideas as the only realities. Intuition ought to mean a concrete vision akin to perception, at least if it is to be differentiated from intellectual abstraction. We have, however, seen that Bergson's intuition is nothing more but an abstract imagination which pins itself upon the flowing aspect of our experience as distinguished from the static aspects. By a peculiar confusion of thought he thinks that this flowing aspect is given to us by our intuitive vision as a fundamental reality, in consequence whereof he is led to believe the static aspects as mere abstraction.

The mystery behind the flowing and the static lies in the fact that the relation behaving either as relata or as relations show themselves in their multifold emergent forms. There is no mere flow from which the relations and the relata are only abstracted as petrified objects. If they are abstracted from it, that is, if they were not in the very nature of the flow, they would be all false and we should be landed in pure illusionism of thought and perception. Even if they are half-truths their whole truth must be in the very nature of that flow in which they are welded together. If that is so, the flow is not the only reality, for the flow holds within itself all that is said to be abstracted from it as its partial appearances—as congealed facts. The mere flow in itself is as much an abstraction as all that is said to be abstracted from it. The flow thus has no reality in itself apart from all that flows. The very word 'flow' means the emergents of varied forms, relations or appearances, taken together in a whole from which the elements cannot be detached except by abstraction. The flow, the pure act, the movement is transcendental in the sense that it cannot be intuited by any known means of cognition as a basic reality which stands alone by itself. It, therefore, goes beyond our experience, so much so that Plato in Greece, his seniors, the Upaniṣadic sages in India, and their follower, Śaṅkara, denied the reality of all movement. The Buddhists on the other hand as well as the crypto-Buddhists such as the *Yoga-vāśiṣṭhins* pinned their faith on the mere flowing nature of all our experiences and things represented by them. But having failed to demonstrate the nature of such a pure act of the mind, or a pure flow, a pure passing movement they ended in denying all reality as such. If the mere movement, the mere passing away was the most impressive and the most dominant characteristic of our experiences, and if there was nothing to hold them together, then there would be no reality, there would be only the passing phenomena like images in Banquo's glass ; specific priority would be the only definition of causation and since nothing existed as the permanent pivot of the world, the ultimate truth would be one of nihilism. It is for this reason that while the *Laṅkāvatāra* describes our experiences as the only realities and discards the objectivity and the materiality as existing outside and regards the experiences as being generated by the spontaneous activity of the spirit of the Mind, it is unable ultimately to define the nature of the mind or the spirit as such. For if such an entity existed it would not be movement, and by the very nature of Buddhistic hypothesis nothing else but movement could be regarded as the dominant fact. The *Laṅkāvatāra,* therefore, ultimately denies the reality of the Mind and shrinks itself to the position that the assumption of Mind is only a convenient expression for the surging out of mental phenomena from their beginningless pre-determinants. We have here a doctrine of spiritual creation without a creator, and a view of movement as the successive and integrated passing away of phenomena to phenomena, or of phenomenal wholes to phenomenal wholes. As a matter of fact, the phenomenal wholes also have no reality as they are but products of an imaginative synthesis without an objective counterpart.

To supplement these defects some schools of

Indian Philosophy have accepted the doctrine of spiritual creation as an emanation of movement as spiritual reality. The upholders of these doctrines started from the position of an incessant spiritual creation from within as explaining the entire universe of our experience; but by the logical necessity of thought they could not rest merely in the fact of an integrating process of spiritual creation, and were obliged to accept the transcendental existence of a spiritual reality, tranquil and undisturbed in itself as the ultimate ground of the ceaseless processes of spiritual creation. They thought that unless such a ground was admitted they would be swallowed up in the Buddhistic outlook of pure nihilism, and would be unable to assert anything as real. The passage from the tranquil transcendental to the process of ceaseless creation thus remains unexplained. In the case of Buddhism where a ceaseless process of phenomena rising and dying away is admitted, the movement or activity is to be taken in abstraction from that which moves; for the Buddhists do not admit that anything persists, and therefore they cannot also admit that anything moves. The so-called movement is thus merely an abstraction referring to the vacuity preceding and succeeding any moment of phenomenon. Since any phenomenon dies the very moment it rises into being, its nature cannot also be described as anything more than the movement of vacuity with a characteristic appearance. The so-called movement of phenomena rising into being and dying away thus becomes a process of vacuous movement where vacuity and movement cannot be distinguished from each other. The ultimate ethical goal of Buddhism, therefore, cannot hold for itself anything more than this vacuity. The highest value of the system therefore, the *Nirvāṇa,* cannot also be ontologically characterised as anything more than pure extension of vacuity, and the subsidiary values leading to the highest value have also to be characterised in terms of negation as detachment from desire, greed or grasping ; and the highest wisdom is also regarded as the superior knowledge of the essencelessness of the universe. When Buddhism admits sympathy and love as principles of value, these only follow as subsidiary corollaries from detachment from self, and not from independent positive principles. It is clear from this that Buddhism really fails to give a proper concept of the nature of movement which is a fundamental doctrine of its philosophy. For not only movement is here reduced to mere vacuity but even the terms or entities that move are but illusory appearances of vacuous forms. There is not only no statical essence but there is no dynamic essence as well. It is for this reason that passage from Buddhism to Vedānta and from Vedānta to Buddhism became so easy in the history of the development of these two systems. The Vedānta admits the characterless essence, which it calls pure Spirit, but denies movement, and explains the latter and all characterless forms emerging therefrom as nothing more but vacuous forms, pretending to have a reality only through their incxplainable association with the pure static essence, the spirit. Thus the theory of spiritual genesis, which is a fundamental doctrine of both Buddhism and the Vedānta fails to give an account of the spiritual creation, spiritual movement, or the spiritual act.

The Nyāya regards movement as a separate category which is associated with substance by an inalienable inherent relation and thereby refuses to give any philosophical explanation of the substance, the quality and the movement. They are like three sticks which are bound together in a particular manner, and are responsible through their collocations for all the happenings. In Plato there is no account of becoming as such, but there are only the 'ideas' which are in themselves immutable. Nature exists in reality so far as they are communicable in the shape of these ideas. The element of matter or of movement is pure non-being in Plato. Aristotle denies the Platonic transcendence of ideas and holds that it is by movement alone that ideas are realised in matter. But even for him the very expression that 'thought thinks' implies that what is thought is already a realised reality which as such can be defined and idealised in a system of fixed and unchangeable concepts. The nature thus has only meaning with him as static forms of the intellect. Thus Gentile says in his *Teoria Generale dello Spirito come Atto puro*, "Il divenire aristotelico, in quanto non è, nè può essere divenire del pensiero, resta ma pura esigenza: pensanto, non è divenire ; come divenire, non si puo pensare."

Hegel pointed out that the dialectical thinking of the real was impossible if it was separated from the act of thinking and merely regarded as a presupposition of it. According to him, reality could not be conceived dialectically unless it was also conceived as thought. But in the actual working of his system Hegel seems to dissociate the dialectical character of thought from the concepts which he makes evolve through it. The deduction of the categories of his 'logic' illustrates it. Becoming is an identity of Being and Non-being, because the Being which is not, becomes. Thus, starting from pure being, which is devoid of every determination and is the last abstraction of thought, Hegel passes over to the concept of becoming on the ground that being is as unthinkable as non-being, and therefore self-identical with each other. But if the absolute indeterminateness of being is equivalent to nothing there is really no unity of being and non-being which constitutes becoming. There is no opposition or contradiction ; no thesis and antithesis which are to be resolved in the higher synthesis of becoming, for if being is identical with non-being, it becomes a supposition of identity from which no movement can emerge. If being is both identical and different from non-being, then they are not absolutely indeterminate, for in the absolutely indeterminate no distinctions can be drawn. And Gentile rightly says, "In tal caso l'essere come puro essere sarebbe estranes al non-essere come puro non-essere, e non ci sarebbe quell'incontro e quel cozzo dei due, da cui Hegel vuolè che sprizzi la scintilla della vita. In conclusione, siamo, da una parte e dall'altra, innanzi a due cose morte, le quali non concorrono in un movimento." As a matter of fact, one can go still farther and say that when being and non-being are taken together as two abstract and absolutely indeterminate categories, it is impossible to understand how one may be opposed to the other. Opposition involves a movement and a counter-movement, and as such the two dead categories cannot involve the two different types of movement that are involved in the conception of opposition. The concept of movement is given neither in 'being', nor in 'non-being' and must, therefore, be conceived as extraneous to it. The meaning of movement thus falls entirely outside the categories and is initiated from outside, and is not explained in the deduction of the categories. The real being must belong to the concrete thought which in its non-being, in its self-positing, and in becoming defines and explains itself and not to the abstract being with which the category starts. Dialectic does not belong to thought but the thought itself is dialectic. This point has been very clearly brought out by Gentile when he says, "L'essere, che Hegel dovrebbe mostrare identico al non-essere nel divenire, che solo è reale, non è l'essere che egli definsce come l'assoluto indeterminato (l'assoluto indeterminato non può essere altro che l'assoluto indeterminato!) ; ma l'essere del pensiero che definisce e, in generale, pensa: ed è, come vide cartesio, in quanto pensa, ossia non essendo (perche, è, se fosse, il pensiero non sarebbe quello che è, un atto), e percio ponendosi, divenendo." The chief teaching of Gentile is that thought and act are identical. Action or movement does not belong to thought but it is thought itself—the thought that brings out of itself the manifold of ideas and is not something different from them nor is different from its self-creating spontaneity in which the many and the one, the present, past and the future are held together annulled and re-created. This is what he means by saying that the method or the process of the thought and the thought are the same, and the dialectic does not belong to thought, as Hegel supposed, but is identical with the thought. Thought, therefore, is not the nominative of becoming but the becoming itself. It is not the starting point of a race to be run, of an objective to be attained, of a goal to be realised, but being identical with what it seeks to achieve and what it achieves which again being identical with the seeking itself, it is not possible to blot it with a mark anywhere in its spontaneous process except by arbitrary abstractions from methodological interest.

In our discussion of the principle of movement with reference to an ideal goaded by the urge of a sense of value as defining the nature of idealism in one of the significance of the term, we passed in review various systems of thought, Eastern and Western, and we discovered that a gratuitous assumption of separation between being and movement is responsible for many confusions of thought and logic. The notion of movement is the notion of history, and the notion of philosophy and so far philosophy and history are identical. In Buddhism we have the notion of a progressive history which annuls the past, maintains itself in the present, and is dying away for the future. The integration of the universe in its past, present and future is present in one solitary moment of the present, yet this solitary moment has nothing abiding in it, for it is only a vacuous appearance, and the so-called movement, the march of history shrinks itself to a point which has position but no magnitude. Movement implies history and history implies relational reference and integration. Signor Gentile's thesis is that all relational integrations are a creation of an inner spontaneity which he calls the spirit. Whether this is so or not is a long question into which I should not like to enter in the present moment, but it certainly sounds a new note, more or less in the line of his famous compatriot Signor Croce, that the notion of movement cannot be external to thought. Nothing can emerge in thought that is not in itself an integration of relations. The fact that relations can become cognisable, is due to the peculiar phenomenon, which typifies the nature of thought as integrating relations. Thought enlarges itself to the extent, in which the integration is richer and more complex. The world of nature and the world of thought may be distinguished from each other, in this, that while detached relation-complexes taken from out of the life of the thought may be marked or labelled as this or that object, or this or that character, standing apart from thought, the life of thought is an ever-increasing process of integration in which all labels or marks are constantly changing their position and value. The word 'process', which is almost synonymous with movement, implies the phenomenon of wider and wider systems of synthetic relationship, when the function of each one of these relations contributes to the other a something, which, in its totality, marks off what we call a process or a movement. Movement thus is not something different from thought. It is not its quality or character, neither am I prepared to see eye to eye with Signor Gentile in holding that the action or the movement is a prior or a more fundamental fact of what constitutes the essence of thought. The act in itself as apart from the emergent relations is transcendental and there is no proof that it exists as apart from the relations or in any one of them. Yet the movement is immanent inasmuch as it shows itself in the widening synthesis of relations that constitutes the nature of thought. Relational complexes denoted by our thought as existing outside of it, as an object, may thus in one sense be regarded, as only a partial and lesser truth, inasmuch as in their separateness the potentiality of contribution arising out of a unitary complex is devoid of force or meaning. They may, therefore, be regarded in some sense as limbs and parts torn off from the living flow of thought. It is in thought alone that the relational-complexes are continually being intermingled and are continually looking forward and thus by their mutual contributory functions ascribe meaning to the whole. The self-reference and the other reference of relations mutually amongst themselves, in a way to introduce continuously other relations, is the soul of activity, or spontaneity that is implied in thought. When stress is laid on the fact of emergence as a process or activity, it appears as a transcendental something which cannot further be explained. But, as a matter of fact, to take this activity out of relation from all that with which it is integrally associated is to take it in abstraction. For, movement as defined by us as self-reference and other-reference of relations among themselves, is involved in the very nature of relations. Thought is thus nither being, nor non-being, nor becoming, nor the object, nor the subject—not that which is thought of or that which thinks, but a process which involves them all at one and the same time—a unity of self-reference and other-reference in which relations appear and contribute to the emergence of content-characteristics. Neither the process, nor the being can be regarded as any more primary than the other factors involved in it. If the movement or activity as such could be separated from the content-element, the content would be outside the movement and could not be expressed by it. The multiplicity of the content loses its character as such when it is seen in its proper aspect as a melted whole in the very being of the thought movement.

The Platonic or the Cartesian ideas may be regarded as positive in the sense that they are thinkable, and they are positive only with reference to the subject which posits them. But when taken merely from the point of view that they are posited by the subject, they are to be regarded merely as dead objects, and cannot be regarded as positive in the sense in which the self-emanating thought may be regarded as positive. That which is effected, finished and realised ceases to be thought and ceases to be real, because there is nothing to be done with it and it can do nothing. The Buddhists perceived the truth of this doctrine when they formulated the principle of positivity as that which effects something, which becomes, achieves or realises a purpose. The merely effected and finished product has no right to existence even, for when once effected it becomes divorced from the life of thought and becomes petrified. It is on this ground that they regarded all things as momentary and evanescent. They held that a moment, with its characteristic appearance, when produced, cannot farther be produced or related with movement, for, what is once done cannot be done again. It thus becomes detached from the life of thought, and thereby loses its right to exist. The universals, therefore, of Plato or the innate ideas of Locke have no right to being, as they are not involved in their dead positivity in the contributory process of the development of thought. These universals are never positive in so far as they fulfil their function in knowledge. True positivity is not something external to the self-relationing process of thought and presupposed by it. It is its own positive and real exposition of its own activity. It is equally true of the theory of empiricism, for, when empiricism opposes sensation or immediate experience to their concept, it is the subject which makes the concept its own by the very positing of it as an abstraction, construction or a presupposition. That which is posited for thought, is no longer thought, and that which is posited by it no longer exists for it, has gone out of it. When the Buddhists held that the world is recreated every moment, it is this definition of reality, the spontaneous reanimation into life by the enlivening process of thought that was implied by them. It was, therefore, that when the old school of Buddhism happened to admit the doctrine of momentarism, it transformed itself into a school of uncompromising idealism which appeared as nihilism in comparison with the schools of statical ideals that prevailed in India. The fire of thought always burns and leaves no ashes ; and in the very burning of it no one can put his finger and see this is and this is not. It is the very activity of the self-relationing thought process, which reveals itself in and through the terms of its relations, that is the true subject and support of our knowledge.

The individual and the universal are but two abstractions. Think the individual and in thinking it you universalize it: think the universal and in thinking it you individualize it. It is for this reason that the Buddhists on the one hand denied the being of universals as permanent individual or the subject of experiences. It is in the thought itself that the two terms show themselves in their immanent characters. From the universal which can be thought of but does not think and from the individual which can be intuited but does not intuite, one must turn to the concreteness of things in act, in which both of them, show themselves. When Descartes wanted to assure himself of his being, he did so by the argument, 'Cogito ergo sum'—I exist because I think, that is the existence of the thinker is assured in the process of thought and not what is posited by thought. The philosophy of the Vedānta wanted to abstract away all movement and take its ultimate refuge in a posited being, but it could not deny positivity to movement and its permanent association with the Ultimate Being. In doing this, it adopted a suicidal policy, as a result of which they precluded themselves from all knowledge regarding the nature of movement, which had yet to be regarded as positive in itself. The final mystery remains in the wrong abstraction of being from movement, which renders movement mysterious and the Ultimate Being indefinable and unspeakable except through its association with this mysterious category, the movement.

In the present view of the situation the dispute between the nominalists and realists vanishes, for, both the universal and the individual are real in the very identity of them both, such that nothing exists outside the universals, for it is they that individualise them, and nothing exists outside the individuals, because it is they, which show themselves as universals. Both of them are aspects of a self-relationing process. Signor Gentile rightly says, "Giacchè oltre l'universale del pensiero non c' e l'individuo essendo che l'universale stesso il vero individuo ; e fuori dell' individuo non c' è nè anche il nome di un universale, poiche l'individio stesso, nella sua genuina individualità, non può non essere, per lo meno, nominato, e investito de un predicato, e insomma della universalitla delà pensiero."

The Vedānta in its effort to deny any reality to movement and all that is implied in it seeks to demonstrate the unreality of the thought-process of our waking states on the analogy of the unreality of the dream-states and argues that just as the dream-processes are unreal as they are negated by waking processes, so the waking processes are unreal as they stand negated in a possible state of pure unchangeable consciousness as pure being. But it misses the fundamental point that dream-states are unreal not because they are negated by the waking experiences but because they belong to a universe of experiences which cannot be related with the waking experiences. The fundamental fact that makes reality, is that of relationing. The unrelational, therefore, stands as dead and therefore outside reality. The mystic states of communion and the like are more or less of a supra-relational order and involve experiences which may not be as relational as the experiences of the waking state but yet which involve a richness of experience which may be regarded as the throbbing of inarticulate relationing which has its roots in the character of the experiences in the ordinary life. The mystic experiences in the true sense can only be the outcome of a supernormally religious or moral life where the urges of relationing become too fast for expression and thus dissolve themselves in ineffableness.

The most fundamental notion of the activity involved in thought is this relating process in which the relata and the relations so contribute to one another by their mutual reference that a field is produced which further induces other fields into life and thus carries on the purpose or meaning which is the very structure of thought. The interchange of functions, the possibility of elements standing as wholes and wholes as elements is so great that it is impossible to speak of movement as different from that which moves, the ideal as being different from the person who seeks it, the value as being different from the effort that runs to achieve it. The ordinary pictorial form in which our language is constructed is entirely inefficient to give a graphic intention of the process of the inner life. Any philosophy that is constructed on the intellectualistic and atomistic type of linguistic expression is, therefore, bound to baffle its purpose. A geometrical figure remains what it is howsoever it may be placed, but every element of our thought-life has a distinctive tinge by the history of the processes that has gone before it and those that are yet to come out of it. Our mental processes may be regarded in an ordinary manner as standing between the past and the future but their meaning extends beyond the dim twilight-region of the past and the undiscovered region of the future now dark. They, therefore, assimilate the character of the past and the future and hold within themselves an eternity of value and meaning. The infinity is easily understood when we consider that there being nothing else but they, there is nothing anywhere which can limit their scope, meaning and extent. Movement is not prior to relations, for, movement itself is but a specific function of relations. Relations also are not prior to movement, because without movement there is no relation.

The ideal of movement is not something outside the movement but is contained in and through its very pulsation. The movement itself again is nothing but an ever-expanding field of mutually self-referring and self-creating relations. The call of the ideal is, therefore, nothing but the inherent call of one's own self-expanding personality. The expansion of the persons can only be in and through the relational integration and the expansion of other persons. That which curbs and misdirects or shortens the process of these self-expanding relational systems which form the personalities of man is sin. Sin is antagonistic to our nature inasmuch as it cuts short the self-expanding process by rousing obstructions to the onward movement of personality; that which helps the advancement of the continual process of the self-integrating personality is virtue and holiness. When we look at a moral law as a command of a superior voice to which our lower self must submit and yet unwilling to submit we have a concept of alienation which is inexplainable. On the other hand if we look at the moral law as the normal process of the self-expansion of personality and all transgressions as violations of this normal order we can well understand why we should desist from a prohibited course. The mere animal errors represent a universe of relations, the sphere of expansion of which is naturally limited by the appetites. The man, however, who is alive to his own special sphere of reason and the higher emotions may naturally find his progress impeded by the obstructions offered from the animal directions by which his progress of expansion must be barred. We call love a virtue and hatred a vice because hatred brings to the forefront the universes of the animal-man who is limited in the course of expansion by the brute necessities of the appetite and which, therefore, impedes the course of the self-expanding relationship which might otherwise have gone on. No appetite can be called a vice unless and until it impedes the course of the movement of spiritual life. Love is a virtue because it dissolves one person into another and so creates the other in himself that he realises him in himself and on the pretext of loving him is bent on a career of self-expansion. It is not a union in the ordinary sense where the unification is the goal, for true love is a course of self-creation where egotism, vanity, the animality and the smallness and narrowness shrink aside and under the fostering care of a happy emotion of Love the tree of life shoots forth its branches breathing love and light everywhere. The movement for the ideal is thus not a movement towards something which proceeds out of one's self but which in reality is a progressive self-illumination, an enlightened elaboration of one's own personality.

There is an old Indian adage that love transforms itself into knowledge; and some systems of Indian Philosophy assert that wisdom comes from Love, and they distinguish two kinds of knowledge, passive and dynamic. Love means the propulsion of desire. The object of desire can only be attained when it becomes a part of the person who desires it. Physical objects or objects of the desiring man as an animal can only be assimilated in the animal system. Such desires are thus extremely limited in the direction of the progressive expansion. When desire comes in the way of the fulfilment of man in the directions in which one person is opposed to another or set against the other we have the narrow individualities typified in egotism, vanity, selfishness, jealousy, hatred and the like. When one falsely identifies oneself with these emotions which are closely associated with the universe of man in the animal sphere, and desires to realise himself in these capacities, one naturally gets oneself opposed to other individuals of the same sphere. His desires being thus continually struck against the desires of others, there is a continual friction and the desiring man finds his desires refracted back to himself and becomes subject to constant misery and suffering. Desires in this sphere, thus, are always being largely frustrated. Only desires of a higher sphere can be designated as love. In this sphere a person does not desire to enlarge himself towards the direction of narrow limitations, but wishes to place himself in the very personality or the reality of the object or objects of his love. His dismissal of his lower spheres of existence leaves himself free in his higher sphere which becomes untrammelled and unrestricted by the obstructions of his biological and semi-biological selves: and it is in this sphere that we can designate desire as spiritual. Such desires can, therefore, be fulfilled to an infinite extent and are not likely to be obstructed by any extraneous cause. Our mental tranquility and peace are disturbed whenever our desires are obstructed from outside; and it is such obstructions that produce misery, suffering, and pessimism. The positive feeling that is associated with unobstructed desires may be designated as the emotional aspect of love. Such desires express themselves in feeling the spiritual unity that we have with other persons and with the world as a whole. They require no contribution from others, and are, therefore, spontaneous, unrestricted, and infinite. Such spontaneous love produces wisdom or rather is wisdom itself, for, it is a movement of an unfettered personality in the dynamic of its thought. Desires of this type can only move in the true affirmation of others in ourselves and only assimilation of them into us by a progressive expansion of our own spiritual universe. Pessimism results only from a narrow and fettered outlook of things. When the world is taken in its proper perspective, we have nothing to complain about it, for it then reveals itself in its true spirituality. Signor Gentile brings out the significance of this love in a very remarkable manner in his *Frammento di una gnoseologia dell' amore.*

INTERNATIONAL MORALITY

The practice of writers on moral philosophy has been to start with the mental or moral plane of an adult member of society. The facts of moral consciousness, to which appeal is generally made, generally refer to the moral experience of grown up men belonging to the society to which a writer himself belongs, or to societies which are akin to it. Such a procedure often overlooks the true bearing of moral experience in other fields. Among the writers of evolutionary morality we find constant references to the different kinds of moral experience, prevailing among different societies and nations in different parts of the world, and also to societies in different epochs of history with which we are ordinarily familiar. The problem of the growth of moral experience with the growth of reason or maturer experience, is thus left often in the dark. Random references to different kinds of experiences regarding good and evil among the primitive, or more or less savage people, can give but little idea regarding the manner or the meaning of the actual and possible growth of the content of our moral experience. Writers, again, like Kant deny the possibility of any growth of moral experience by the separation which they preach of the content of moral experience from its pure form as the moral law which only, according to them, determines the morality of our actions. If the contentless form of a moral law were the sole arbiter of the morality of actions, such a law, being universal in all men, irrespective of age, society, time or place, there could possibly be no growth of moral experience.

Kant defined moral good to consist in nothing else than the conception of the law itself, which certainly is only possible in rational beings in so far as this conception, and not the expected effect, determines the will. The conception of God as the supreme good is, according to him, also derived from the idea of moral perfection, which reason frames and connects inseparably with the notion of a free will. All moral conceptions have their seat and origin completely *a priori* in the reason; and they cannot be abstracted from any empirical or contingent knowledge. It is just this purity of their origin that makes them worthy to serve as our supreme practical principle. To be able to act according to the conception of laws or pure moral principles is to have a will. Will, thus, is the faculty to choose that only which reason, independent of any inclination, recognises as practically necessary, i.e., as good. If the ordinary will, however, does not in itself completely accord with reason (which is actually the case with man), then the actions, which objectively are recognised as necessary, are subjectively contingent; and the determination of such a will, according to objective laws imposed by the pure reason, is obligation. That which serves the will as the objective ground of its self-determination is the *end*; and if this is assigned by reason alone it must hold for all rational beings. Since all moral will is the free and spontaneous determination of pure reason, the end of every particular individual must be the same as the end of other individuals, for individuals only differ from one another in their contingent aspects. The moral end of every individual, therefore, coincides with the moral end of all other individuals. The moral imperative, therefore, necessarily means an injunction so to act as to treat humanity in one's own person or in that of any other, in every case as an end, never as a means. The unity of ends implied in it supplies the basis of Kant's conception of the kingdom of Ends. The will in itself which determines its end itself gives a law and, therefore, since both the ends and the law are given by it, it is absolutely free and independent of experience and free from the bondage of anything gained in experience. By 'kingdom' Kant understands the union of different rational beings in a system by comomn laws. But since all contingent and experimental elements have to be eliminated, all ends have to be conceived as combined in a systematic whole, as determined by the spontaneity of action engendered by the pure reason. Every individual being in such a kingdom is himself both the legislator and a subject under the domination of the law. All rational beings come under the law that each of them must treat itself and all others never merely as means, but in every case at the same time as ends in themselves.

The question that naturally arises out of the above estimate of Kant's doctrine of morality is regarding the nature of the pure reason, which is the source of the moral will. If this pure reason is absolutely *a priori* and independent of all experience, it should naturally so distinguish itself from experience of all kind as to appear the strongest, when it is unburdened by the shackles of experiences which often tend to oppose it. The struggle of moral will, leading to the moral sense of obligation, appears to present itself at its highest only in adult consciousness. The supremacy of the moral will appears also in greater and greater degree in persons who are themselves subject to the call of various interests depending on the attainment of vast experiences of pleasure and interest in various dimensions. A man whose interests are very limited has but occasion to show the strength of his moral will only feebly. Again, in the infant, where contingent experiences are at their lowest, there is hardly any intuition of the so-called pure reason, as functioning as the moral will. As a matter of fact, a young child has practically no consciousness of morality at all. The sense of morality grows with the development of the man in association with society. The young child lives in a universe mostly of appetites. The development of its personality goes on in proportion as his association with other fellow-beings continually grows. It may thus be inferred that whatever *a priori* element there may be in the intuition of pure reason showing itself in the functioning of the moral will, it reveals itself only in association with the social consciousness that he develops in his adult stage. It may also be noted that the moral consciousness shows itself more and more definitely and imperatively with the greater advance of social intercourse. The upholders of the theory of Evolutionary morals have demonstrated it to satisfaction that the sense of the "good" is not the same in similar situations among diverse nations in different periods of history. A study of experiences of the "good" among different people does not reveal the presence of the consciousness or reason functioning the will which may be regarded as universal or uniform. It is seen that various kinds of interests influence the notion of the "good". If, however, one would maintain that Kant's definition of the moral will has to be accepted as true in itself as apart from our judgments of good and bad, then such a definition would be of a parochial nature and ought not to detain any one in consideration of moral philosophy as a science; for in all discussions regarding moral science we are interested in delieneating the nature of our affirmation of any action as good or bad, such affirmation imply a notion of value, and the main interest of a moral philosopher is to analyse the concepts.

The structure of knowledge is such that nothing enters into it which cannot be expressed or conceived in terms of relationship. If the *a priori* intuition of pure reason were wholly different from all that are found in experience it would be impossible to establish any relation between it and the notions of experience, which would virtually mean that the pure reason is wholly alienated from the field of experience and this would baffle moral activities as a whole; for the transcendental pure reason must act in and through our experience. Kant himself says that the pure reason which is intuited as formal law determines the will as choice in the field of experience. The pure reason thus has to be admitted as working in and through experience by a spontaneous activity. Pure reason is said to have no form in itself but is regarded as the pure form of law. The pure form of the law as "thou shouldst" only expresses the notion of transcendent value which Kant regards as being one and unalterable and as working spontaneously and determining our choice. He further says that so far as our actions are chosen or determined by this unique universal and uniform sense of value they are to be called moral. If we look at Kant's problem from this point of view, it is difficult for us to agree with Kant, that such a notion of value should always remain transcendent yet practical. To be practical requires the notion of value to be immanent. The notion of value, therefore, must be immanent in our experience. The chief fault of Kant both in his *Critique of Pure Reason* and his *Critique of Practical Reason* has been the assumption of the transcendental factors which have been permitted to remain transcendent and yet are allowed to take part in experience in which their immanence is denied. It is for this reason that the transcendent principle remains purely as a contentless form unchanged and unchageable which in a mystical way is accepted to determine our choice. The other conception would have been to ascribe transcendence to notions of value in an entirely different manner. It would be possible for us to accept a notion of value as determining all our choices and yet to admit that the notion of value is not exhausted in any particular universe of choice. As the experiences are dominated and controlled by the notions of value, the notions of value themselves disintegrate and emerge back in luminary forms of other higher values. There is thus as much dialectic of values and experiences as of values themselves.

Kant, in keeping pure reason apart and unassociated with ordinary èxperience, stopped a further way of relating the two together, a condition which is required in all moral judgments. Such a transcendence of morality in a formal region is in conflict with an immanental view of values in experience. The value-sense, so far as it refers to an undefined and undefinable norm, naturally, however, refers to something transcendent and different from the mere assertive experiences. Our thoughts, ideas, and perceptions on their cognitive side refer to a norm, and it is called the norm of the "truth". Our actions refer to some ideal, and this is called the norm of the "good". Some of our emotions refer for their satisfaction to certain norms, which may be called the norm of the "beautiful". Thus the sense of value in its projected form shows itself not only in the department of our moral experiences, but also in all other departments of our cognitive, conative and emotive life. The reference to value characterises our experience, which expresses the underlying conviction in us, that our experiences are only worth their nature, only when they reveal in themselves certain appreciation of value. So long as our experiences are looked upon as detached from such a notion of value, they do not form an integral part of our personality and are regarded by us as more or less detached elements to be negated or discarded as accidental and out of harmony with ourselves. We no doubt pass through falsehood, but we do not wish to retain falsity as a part of ourselves. We no doubt commit evil actions, but we do not consider our nature as evil and often think of the evil as transitory states to be negated and passed over and thrown outside ourselves. This sense of value which presents itself in the three departments of our experiences, the cognitive, the conative and the affective, integrates in itself all our experiences, as the universal element ever-present in the flux. We may misperceive an object or misjudge a situation, but as soon as these errors are disclosed, we try to dissociate ourselves from them and take our shelter in such of our experience as are still believed to be true. Truth consists in the subsistence or non-subsistence or the affirmation or denial of one or more relationships between determinants and relational complexes or between them and relations or qualitative emergents to the extent, order, or manner in which such relationships subsist or do not subsist or exist or do not exist (restricting the words existence to objects of non-denotative experience and subsistence to objects of denotative experience or their presuppositions). Such a definition of truth does not explain the fact why what is felt as true should be valued and preserved and why what is perceived as false and untrue should be rejected. This assumption of the unworthiness of the untruth and the worthiness of the truth is the most fundamental and elementary nature of our mental development. The appreciation of value is something different from the relationships and their meanings. When we accept what is true and reject what is untrue we have a revelation of something that characterises the tendency of the movement of our thought-personality. Ethics begins with relations of personalities. No question arises as to why truths should be valued and the untruth despised, the good should be adored and the bad shunned, the beautiful should be sought and the ugly ignored just as we cannot say why pleasures should be aimed at and pain avoided. We have thus four distinct notions of value as truth, good, beauty and pleasure, as representing the intellectual, moral, æsthetic and biological which appear to be so ultimate and irreducible in terms of other concepts that they remain the last terms of explanation beyond which we cannot go. In this sense we can speak of them as unique and unrelational, but their nature as such is due to the fact that they are the methods of operation of the complex phenomena which constitute our personality. They contain within them some advancing goals which elude our grasp because they constitute the ultimate structure on which the web of our experiences is continually being spun. They thus contribute to the integrity, solidarity and the unity of our advancing personality. The continual flux of our experiences spinning apparently over nothing, through ceaseless changes of new relations appearing in different contexts and emerging forth in meaning of diverse purport have a bond of unity in the fourfold values which are the dialectic of the dynamic of our being and which run forth throughout the entire span of our conscious, semi-conscious or unconscious existence. The biological value which has its foundation in life as adjustment of acts to ends for the purpose of self-preservation and race-preservation holds in it the method that reveals the identity of the animal man with all other living beings. The other three values, though they appear to be different from one another and each unique in its own sphere, appear only at the human stage and distinguish it from other stages of living existence. Though each of these has its special features and modes of revelation they have such a fundamental affinity that they may be marked off as different determinations in different spheres of the same identical value-ideal. When we try to define what this value-ideal is, we fail to do so because in its formal nature as apart from the sphere in which it shows itself, it can hardly be said to have any existence at all. It is the goal which manifests itself in the working of the mind-complex in different aspects of its activity. It is present in every act of the mind-complex so far as it is not chained down to the biological aspects of life. It cannot be abstracted from the activity of the mind-complex and the spheres in which that activity shows itself because of the fact that it is manifested as the very nature of the activity itself in consonance with its sphere of self-maintenance. Kant's chief mistake consisted in the abstract separation of this value from the mind and the sphere of its activity. Taken apart from the relative sphere of its appearance it is an illusory abstraction.

When we seek truth we aim at a special consonance of relationship between two or more sets of relational orders, that is to say, the mind as a relational complex tends to affirm its unity in the various movements of its relational activity. This is, in fact, the self-realisation of the minds amidst apparent oppositions and obstructions. As such, the seeking of the truth is the setting free and the coming back of the spontaneous activity of the mind which is not satisfied until it has succeeded in discharging the functions of its spontaneity by weaving new types of relationship. It is, therefore, that the drive of the mind towards the goal of truth which is identical with its notion of value cannot be separated from its concrete sphere, for it itself is an emergent function of the concrete sphere. But as the spontaneity can never cease, the goal of truth can never be finally reached. It continues to reveal itself in ceaseless creational spontaneity.

The moral sphere in which we seek the good is only a special sphere of our search for the truth where we seek to relate ourselves with other persons in a bond of fellowship, in a recognition of their existence in ours, in looking into them as much as we perceive ourselves as our own ends. Such a self-reference to other persons is expressed in the moral sphere in a tripartite manner through knowledge, feeling and action. Kant's kingdom of ends is valid ; but not in the sense in which he accepts it but in the entire sphere of the concrete personality where the human personality in its self-affiliatory processes tends to overcome the superiority of the primary and more universal value of the biological sphere. A question of the man in the street as to whether a moral value does really curb the egotistic demands of the biological sphere is meaningless ; for whether or not the egotistic impulses are actually curbed by the superior value-sense is a matter of training and discipline. It is sufficient for our purposes if the normal man expects that in other persons the moral value ought to get precedence over biological values. It is from this point of view that Kant's maxim that "one should act according to a maxim which one can universalise at the same time" finds its significance. The universalisation does not refer to the formal law but to the moral activity in association with the entire sphere or conditions in which it appears. Given such and such a condition, given such and such a moral prompting, what should be my duty or the duty of any other person—that is the question. Under such circumstances, I contend that the universalisation of the superiority of the moral law would be acknowledged in one's own person as well as in those of others. Compare the utilitarian dictum-ideal of conduct "each person is to count himself as one and not more than one" with Green's ideal of conduct.

When Spencer defined 'good' as the adjustment of acts to ends and elaborated it in the physical, biological, psychological and social spheres and tried to show that the evolution of the conception of the 'good' indicated its gradual passage from the more homogeneous to the more heterogeneous, less co-ordinate to the more co-ordinate, less concrete to the more concrete, he proved that an action which is called more good involved more heterogeneity, concreteness and co-ordination in all the four spheres, i.e., the physical, the biological, the psychological and the sociological at the same time. His contention was that as human conduct evolved more and more to a higher and higher sphere it was possible that there should come a time when there would not be any conflict between what is socially good and what is physically or biologically good. He meant that in the course of evolution the disparate characters of the biological and physical values would be annulled and would show themselves in perfect unison with what is conceived as the socially good. Ordinarily there is a conflict between the individual and the society in certain spheres of action. This conflict is due to the fact that in the present state of society the biological good sometimes tends to differ from the social good. But Spencer thinks that, when evolved, the two values would show themselves as one and the conflict would be overcome. If Spencer's contention is right, as I believe it to be, the biological value ultimately manifests itself for its satisfaction in the same direction as the moral value. Two values may not be exactly identical but they would not point to two different poles ; and in tending to be morally good one would find a supreme satisfaction of what is biologically good in the highest degree. If this is so, the biologically good should have to be acknowledged as being in some sort of unity with the morally good, such that the former exists ultimately for the latter. Thus, just as the inorganic exists for life, so life and its values ultimately exist for the value as the moral good.

In our conception of the identity of the value as true and the value as the moral good we defined the moral good as a self-affiliatory process by which a person completely harmonises himself with all other persons of the world such that he can do nothing for himself and think nothing for himself which so far as it is possible for him, he would deny to others, i.e., in affirming himself in any particular manner he would also wish to affirm others in the same manner. When Mill defined the highest good as the greatest amount of happiness for the largest number of persons he committed the mistake of identifying the moral good with happiness. In so identifying he probably thought that he gave more concrete form to the idea of moral good than what I conceive here as almost indefinable. But in defining the moral good as happiness and in accepting different kinds of happiness, he really transferred the indefinability of the moral good to happiness. But he struck the right note of the self-affiliatory proccss of morality when he suggested that in case of the conflict between one individual and others one has to count himself as one and not more than one.

The fact that in the growth of life, the individual is at first associated with the biological impulses and values and the fact that the ordinary biological interests are often in conflict with those of others create separation and opposition between one individual and others of his community. When we deal with ancient hedonism we find that individual pleasure, defined both in its positive and in its negative aspects as absence of pain, is the standard of judgment. Excepting the cyrenaics, gradation or classification of pleasures as higher and lower is admitted by all Hedonists, which strikes at the root of pleasure as a definable entity and also the theory of pleasure as the ultimate standard. The transition of modern hedonism from individual pleasure to the pleasure of the greatest number is unwarranted in Mill, and can only be supported by supplementing the doctrines of social ethics such as is propounded by Leslie Stephen—that it is by seeking the well-being of the society as a whole that the well-being of the individual can be looked after. But if individual happiness be the goal the cases in which the individual well-being is not encouraged or is definitely opposed to, social well-being will remain unexplained and instances of heroic moral sacrifices of the individual for the society will not be accounted for by the theory.

Moral good thus may be thought to presuppose a social sphere for its achievement in which the individual acknowledges or posits the other members of the society as having equal rights and privileges for existence, enjoyment and advancement, with himself. In such a sphere each individual by his self-affiliating activity recognises the truth of others in himself and is prepared to give to others which he takes himself. But such a self-affiliation naturally presupposes a self-alienation from the biological side. One must also be able to dissociate in mind the spontaneous spiritual activity moving forward in the self-affiliatory process and thereby rise above such sheaths and obstructions that one constructed through one's daily intercourse with fellow-beings in society. Apart from the purely biological feelings and appetites that come as reflexes from the life of the body, our social intercourses help the production and growth of certain social crusts which come to us as an inferior social personality in which we associate ourselves with society not as spiritual beings but as separate social replicas of biological entities. The self-affiliatory spontaneity being of the nature of movement implies in itself an opposition to it as self-position, for without the self-position there would be nothing to account for the self-distinction without which self-unification would be impossible. Thus as the mind rises from the biological to the social plane the necessity of the social intercourse forces a man to create certain constructive elements by which he can assign his place in society as against and in contra-distinction with the position of other fellow-beings. Just as in the biological plane an animal must assert itself in order that it may live and help others to live, so in the social plane with the evolution of the social personality there is a self-affirmation of it which makes it possible for it to exist as a separate social unit. Vanity, sense of superiority, desire for fame, traditions, ambitions, ideals, self-assertions in multifold directions show themselves as characteristic qualities of such a self-affiliatory social unit. In a manner these may be regarded as the secondary instincts of a social animal. Just as in developed animal organisms the individual cells have an independent life to live but yet they cannot do so without the co-operation and co-existence of other living cells, so each individual social being has a double life, a life that he has to himself and a life that he leads in co-existence and co-operation with the lives of other selves. Yet the very independent life, which the cell or a man may be said to have as different from the life of other cells in the organism or of other men in the society, would not have been possible except for the co-presence of these other cells or men. The elements which constitute the life of an individual as a self-positing entity could never have shown themselves had it not been for the intercourse which he had with his fellow-beings; yet being the product of such an intercourse they may so enclose in a sheath, as it were, the self-developing individual that they may in their turn, obstruct the self-affiliatory processes for the very necessity of which they were created. This is what may be called the social dialectic, and this encased personality may be termed secondary social personality as different from the primary social personality of the self-developing individual. The secondary social personality may thus often work as an obstacle which together with biological personality must be transcended over to achieve the ends of the pure primary personality in the development of the virtues of the primary social personality as universal friendship, compassion, sympathy and the like through its self-affiliatory processes. It is possible thus to conceive that the pure personality may have to overcome the opposition of the biological personality as also that of the secondary personality in an abstract manner without emphasising the positive self-affiliatory process by which a definite and concrete affirmation and realisation of the primary social personality can be achieved. A large portion of Hindu ethics on its absolutistic side is directed towards the self-conquest of the pure personality over the biological personality and the secondary social personality. Freedom from passion, vanity, antipathy, greed and desires of all kinds is regarded to be the aim of the Yogins who have not so much something positive to strive for as to attain a culmination of the negative process of the conquest of the pure personality on the other two personalities. Such an abstract conquest thus though potentially super-social virtually remains indifferent to the realisation of the primary social personality and remains content in circumscribing the limits of pure personality to itself which is regarded as the goal of the self-realisation of the Yogins and Saints of similar class. The self-affiliatory processes thus remaining shut up within the bounds of the pure personality become contentless and thus generate the notion of a contentless static self or of vacuity such as *Nirvāṇa*. In some schools of Buddhist ethics, however, great emphasis has been laid on the development of the primary social personality and it has extended its bounds on all living beings. Such a widening of the limits has its natural difficulties in this that in putting oneself in the equal position with every living being the biological conflicts become insurmountable though in grandeur, magnificence of outlook it surpasses all possible ethical codes. The extension of social demands to animals where society is not present even in an implicit manner renders the attainment of the extended social goal almost impossible. If the demands of the man-eating tiger and that of a kind friend be put on the same level, disastrous consequences are bound to follow. The Buddhist motto of life that one should live for the good of living beings is an extension of the social principle to logical extremes and it, therefore, defeats its own purpose.

In the sphere of Hindu Scriptural ethics a distinction is drawn between the code of Scriptural duties limited to particular communities or particular stages of life and the broader and the more universal codes of ethics such as may be demanded for the realisation and fulfilment of the primary social personality. The former is called the *varṇa dharma* and the latter the *sādhāraṇa dharma* and the narrow code of Hindu ritualistic ethics would, in a case of conflict, give preference to what contributes to the social welfare of the country to that which would contribute to the welfare and well-being of the humanity as a whole. We thus see that while the Hindu ethics rises to a very high eminence by abstracting the activities of the pure personality within itself in some systems and while in certain systems of Buddhist ethics the self-affiliatory processes are given the widest latitudes in extending over all living beings, the sobriety and moderation by which alone pure personality could overcome the obstructions of the biological and the secondary social personality and emphasise the scope of its operation in the realisation of the aims and aspirations of the primary social personality, are largely lacking. Hindu and Buddhist ethics, therefore, though they rise to high eminence and magnificence of outlook, suffer from the defect of logical extremism and one-sidedness. The Scriptural Hindu ethics is consistently commonplace in emphasising the importance of narrower duties in preference to the broader ones.

It is not out of place here to mention that the present article is not written on the assumption of the existence of the soul-entity or the soul-substance as the statical entity. In most systems of Indian thought, where this assumption has played an important part, the connection of such an entity with thought as a whole as well as with volitions, desires and ideas have always remained unexplained. Various opinions have prevailed regarding the nature of the soul as the self. Some have conceived it as atomic ; some as all-pervasive, some as elastic ; some have regarded it as pure consciousness ; some as the unity of being, consciousness, and bliss ; some as devoid of any consciousness, feeling or volition. But in any case though the soul is regarded as the seat of all experiences, there is such a disparity of nature between the latter and the former, that the nature of their association has always remained practically unknown or unknowable. The present article is based on a view (which must remain an assumption until the writer has a chance of explaining it elaborately in his future writings) that the total personality of man is composed of the diverse relational groups (which may be regarded as elementary personalities) acting in unison and behaving in uniformity such that its composite nature is often lost sight of. These personalities are often identical in so far as they involve uniform self-relating processes each having its peculiar mode and each trying to influence the others. The final action, tendency and character of the whole person is determined by the comparative development and strength and the mode of the joint operation of the composite personalities. What we call the self or the individual is like the grouping together of many horses. When some of the horses are slack for the time being they may follow the lead of the one most active at the time. They may all be striving in different directions and draw the whole group in accordance with the sum-total of the different activities. The strength of the different directing personalities is neither equal, nor uniformly same such that one may exert itself at the expense of the others, for, being of the nature of relating activities, transformation of activities from one direction to another is possible up to certain varying limits. But they all being of the nature of relational activities, subordination of one type by the other is possible to an extent.

What we call the biological personality includes within it all the appetitive functions in their primary original state as we find in the case of animal life, showing itself in the self-preservative and race-preservative directions and also in their modifying manners due to their limitation and modification in diverse ways in the co-presence of other personalities. The biological personality in man may show itself primarily in a purely brutish manner and secondarily in a modified human and more complex manner due to the restrictions imposed on it and the modificatory influence contributed to it in the co-presence of other personalities with which it is associated. Thus when a hungry man rushes towards food we have an instance of the activity of the primary biological, but when the same person engages himself in the business speculation for hoarding money in the bank, this is an instance of the activity of the secondary biological personality. While the activities of the primary biological personality are limited by the needs of the body, as in the case of the animal, the activities of the secondary biological personality are almost infinite; for through reflection and re-reflection they can be advanced almost without limit. What I mean here by pure personality is the self-relationing activity which may in some sense be looked upon in an abstract manner as apart from the directing activities of the different specific personalities and representing in itself as some kind of surplus relational activity that works as a determinant of the various personalities. The pure personality, therefore, may be looked upon as having a central position from which it tends to bring to prominence the various higher aspirations which reveal themselves in the human selves. The pure personality, however, can only show itself in a concrete manner by enlarging the activities of the concrete social self as against the promptings of the lower biological self.

The sense of value thus of each personality within the composite-complex is apparently of a diverse character. The biological has a biological end in view which, therefore, serves for itself as the ultimate value. The secondary biological though naturally depending on the biological may itself often stand independently of it and may produce a distinct emergent value quite independent of the former. Even the ordinary biological sense of value contains within itself its opposite as is illustrated by the fact that the instinct of self-preservation is closely associated with that of race-preservation even in the very lowest forms of life. This may be called the dialectic of values and is deducible from the emergent nature of self-relationing complexes, i.e., the relational complexes spontaneously give rise to other complexes and each complex is associated with its own specific type of value. Value may thus be defined as the objective and relating activity of any specific type. Value should, therefore, be regarded as being inherent in the spontaneous nature of self-relating activity of the complexes. The order of its superiority may be determined by a gradation of fields of emergence of its new types provided always that they

O.P. 62/7

are not obstacles to the development of newer types and newer fields of emergence. The appearance of the value in the objective is reflected back on the on-rushing personality as an obligation. What is called conscience in ordinary language is thus an apperception of the situation of a relational complex in co-presence with an objective.

A mind-complex does not represent within it merely the reflections of the biological reflexes as one's biological personality, but also the integrated history of his race, nation, society, community and family. The fact of biological heredity in which the biological datum, the constitution of the body and the brain are integrated to its previous genetic history in multifold directions as regarding the emergence of a special type of intellectuality, emotiveness or conative character, is well-known, and I should not dilate on it in this lecture. But apart from this biological heredity where the history of the bodily constitution is an important determinant of the emergence of the character of the mental plane in the individual, there are other important considerations, to which I like to direct my attention. I refer to the fact that apart from body-relations a mind-complex has an implicit co-presence with other mind-complexes which gradually becomes more and more explicit and enlarges its horizon to more and more extensive limits and through its influence works an important change on the ethical structure of man. The mind-complex is not only related to other mind-complexes through the medium of his body, but a mind-complex as soon as it emerges forth as a separate entity from its body reveals its nature as one that exists in and for other mind-complexes. Even when the infant lisps forth the few words in its infancy, it shows in an implicit manner the consideration that it has for its parents, brothers and sisters whose language it picks up, and whose manner of denotation it imitates. The quickness with which a baby picks up his child-vocabulary, his manners, behaviours, terms of expression, and even wit and humour, which is absolutely non-biological, completely demonstrates the fact that as the mind is emerging in the baby, it is trying to associate itself to conceive other selves in himself and co-express himself to others. An intelligent child displays social habits to such an extent that he may easily be regarded as if he were already a member of the society, understanding his duties and responsibilities to other persons of the family, or visitors, and showing in a more or less marked manner many characteristics of the secondary social personality also. This shows that just as the mind emerges it manifests that it exists in co-presence with other minds of the family and with such members of the society with whom the family is in close contact, and the diverse personalities which were implicit in it, and on account of such co-presence gradually makes itself explicit. As the child goes to school he comes in association with his superiors, inferiors, and friends and thereby finds himself in contact with the miniature society for which he was already well-prepared in the first few years of his family life. The real social life begins at a much later stage when the family or the society wants him to look not only to his own interests but to serve their interests also both individually and in the collective manner. Society, from our point of view, is not merely an aggregation of individuals, nor an organism in which each member is a part of it, nor a mystical entity standing over and against the individuals, but an ever-enlarging whole in which both the society and the individuals exist as inter-dependent entities or beings in mutual co-presence, co-alliance, conflicts and annulment of conflicts. Society thus considered is not the physical compresence of individuals but the mental compresence of a number of striving ideas, ideals, traditions, economic and other instincts, of a large body of minds. It is thus a spiritual entity and though it may in a sense be regarded as made up of individual constituents, it has an emergent form by itself, and from a certain point of view may be regarded as an individual unit. The various departments of social activities, such as the political, the religious, the economic and the like may in a modern society have such a wide and deep scope, that each of these departments may separate itself out in relief, and the social minds co-operating in that department may behave as a separate whole showing their special characteristics as if they were a single individual. In older societies there was often an overlapping, and a mere custom appeared simultaneously as religious, economic and moral. Thus caste-consciousness in older societies of India functioned in religious, moral, economic, social and political ways. In modern societies the activities of each type are so wide and deep, that they operate together and act independently as it were by themselves. This fact often finds expression in such phrases as religious mind, social mind, political mind, economic mind. The ideas and tendencies and their relating activities in these different spheres stand out as separate from one another, following their own special characteristics and individualities. But still, they must have some community, some common field in a broader sphere in a greater social mind from which they had emanated as it were, and from which they must draw their nourishment, and which must be regarded as the ground of the continual changes which are being effected through the mutual jostling of the different social individualities and which remain as reserve-power as it were. In an ordinary individual, we have the different personalities—primary biological, secondary biological, primary social, and secondary social—which are jostling against one another and are yet deriving their nourishment and direction or restrictions ultimately from pure personality, which works or shows implicitly from the earliest stages of individual development.

It will thus be seen that though our personalities apparently seem to be individual entities, our life is not merely a resultant of the conflict or co-operation of these personalities. There is a common field of life in which they share a joint existence and which serves as the reserve tending towards the true norm of the more and more extending processes of self-affiliating realisation. Thus there is an eternal message of hope for all individuals and nations that even in times of an individual moral crisis or a national moral crisis the different personalities would not necessarily wreck themselves into destruction by mutual conflict. When these personalities weaken themselves by conflict or through want of nourishment, the reserve personality operates towards the good and rejuvenates the entire concrete life. This explains reformation in individual life and renaissance in national life. This is possibly on account of the fact that though the emergent personalities appear to be different from one another and to possess a separate independant existence of their own, they are ultimately nothing but modifications of the self-relating activity. And their mutual difference and unity are both partial abstractions of a nature which cannot be duly expressed without emphasising it, now on this side, now on the other. Both the unity and the multiplicity are but transitional stages through which alone the self-relating activity is intelligible to our intellect.

It thus appears that the parallel personalities participate in one another, both independently and also by sharing the life of a bigger whole with which they are all connected. A diminution or usurpation of the fund of life of this bigger whole is bound to prove disastrous to the life of the concrete composite personality as a whole. I have said above that the infant is born in a potential society of its family. As his ties with the family in various directions go on increasing, he forms a family personality by which he perceives within his own universe the different members of his family and the varied relations that he has formed with them. As he is gradually introduced to a bigger society, his social life extends into his adult stage and he perceives within his universe the diverse social tendencies and his place among the fellow-members of his society,—his duties and responsibilities, his expectations and ideals, and his ideas regarding the extent to which he can surrender himself to others and the extent to which others should surrender themselves to him. He thus feels the joys and sorrows associated with such apperceptions and gradually learns to form his social personality. This social personality is something different from the family personality. It is in some sense superior to the family personality, as it demands a larger and greater extent of the development of the self-affiliatory processes. But just as in an ordinary individual, there are secondary social personalities, so the social ego or mind behaving itself in the individual may have its own aberrations and degrading tendencies which baffle the way to its integration with other social egos or minds. It may be filled with arrogance, vanity, jealousy, just as any composite individual may be found to possess in his individual sphere. In the family personality also there may be similar aberrations as well as a tendency towards larger and more extensive self-affiliatory processes. In the case of a conflict of an individual between his family personality and his social ego, it does not necessarily follow that it is his clear duty that he should prefer the latter to the former. He has to think with proper deliberation whether he, by his action, is promoting the aberrating side of the social ego or the self-affiliatory side. A self-affiliation on the aberrative side is a mis-understanding of the whole situation. The demands of the social ego are to be preferred, as it is only on this side that it shows a greater and deeper scope for the development of the self-affiliatory processes. So also in a conflict between an individual family and society there are situations in which the rights of the individual for his self-satisfaction may be regarded as superior to the self-aberratory demands of either the family or the society or the two together.

A nation is a biological (or economic) and secondary biological (or political) unity of one or more social egos, which have the potentiality to grow and is always tending to grow into a more and more integrated social unit, both on the secondary social as well as on the primary social sides, generally under limitations of a geographical and a unified race-consciousness. Passing from individual, family, community and society, the growth of the nation-ego happens to be the latest development. Its primary and fundamental character is to stand for the economic and the political advantages of the society as a whole within specified geographical limits as for the furtherance of similar advantages of its constituents as also against other nation-egos appearing forth from under other geographical limits. The right of a nation as a separate entity as against the rights of its constituents such as individuals, families, communities and societies within it, consists in a demand of efforts and sacrifice that the latter must make and undergo for the attainment of the good in which the constituents as a whole or the majority of them may participate, howsoever the good may be defined. The good is not necessarily restricted to the economic and the political, but may also be extended to many other types of values which are possible in the case of individuals. The nation, thus, has a right to demand any economic or political sacrifice on the part of the constituent individuals or communities such that by it the majority of such constituents may reap the benefit. The individual has, on the other hand, the right to demand of its nation the fulfilment of its moral economic and political welfare. Thus every individual has a right to demand of its nation that it should be well-fed and well-clothed and kept above the ordinary biological wants ; but since values are heterogeneous, no nation has a right to demand the sacrifice of such values on the part of its individuals that may not lead to the participation in those values by the majority of the fellow-members of the society. The same principle applies to the conflict between the individual, family and society. For the principle is that in the case of values which are not commensurate with one another, it would be immoral to sacrifice the higher for the lower.

Modern times have seen the rise of a nation-consciousness in the manner as it was never witnessed in the past. The nation-consciousness is built upon a large sphere of consciousness in which the largest majority of a people living within a certain geographical area may participate. Since it is impossible that the largest majority of people should be able to enjoy the realisation of the highest developments of which human beings are capable, it cannot be expected that the highest notes of human aspiration should sound themselves in nation-consciousness. There is a tendency towards vulgarisation as we pass from individuals to groups or crowds, and from crowds to nations. A democratic government, in which the largest body of people may be allowed to shape their own destiny in the nation, can have largely their

O.P. 62/8

biological interests taken care of, in which alone they can all participate, and as such it is likely to be more animalistic unless there are positive safeguards. Pure autocratic governments also, where the sovereign ruler cannot stimulate the highest sentiments in his people, must also remain content only in rousing the biological instincts and aspire for the solidarity of his people by that means. The best form of government can only be where a leader who is filled with the highest moral sentiments enjoys the fullest confidence of his people and is able to open new points of view, ushering new outlooks of an enlightened interest in the higher destiny of man. It will thus be seen that, howsoever great a nation may be in opulence, pomp, glory, and prestige, the national mind remains largely in the economic and political stage, and it is always possible that there should be many individuals in it who have outgrown the national limits and have formed a mentality in which the biological and the secondary biological instincts and tendencies have shrunk to their minimum and the highest aspirations have bloomed forth in such a manner that they are one with the humanity of all times and faiths. Such a union is spiritual in the highest degree, for here one rises above the limitations of his body and unites himself with the highest interests of man, and in love and sympathy finds himself with his fellow-men, and in working out his own destiny works out the destiny of the spiritual man, and establishes the kingdom of Heaven on earth.

The national mind being largely in the biological stage shows only the economic and political needs and problems, and, through opposition and conflicts, forms its own integrity as a separate unit. The individuality of the biological mind shows best in its hunger, its efforts in hunting others, seeking conflicts, mistrusting everybody, fighting with others, snatching away others' due share of food and dislodging them from their position. All this is a sign of the growth of the animal mind. When we look from the national point of view, we see that they have on their banners lions, bears, eagles,—all rapacious birds and animals, which show the mentality of the national personality. One nation is trying to exploit others either through economic tariff or bayonets, roaring canons, poisoned gases or the like on the battle-field. Peoples, the individual members of which have contributed so much to the well-being of humanity physically, intellectually and spiritually, are not ashamed to behave as animals in the collective spheres. Though, on the one hand, the individual may be regarded as being only a part and constituent of the nation, yet, on the other hand, he may be regarded as largely transcending the lower limits of it, and has, therefore, a right to transcend it. He is within it, and yet transcends it. Instances are not rare when, like diamonds in the mine or pearls in the ocean, great minds have come forth when their nations were plunged in utter darkness (e.g., Mohammed, Jesus). But on the whole, the bulk of the people share the national mind in its outlook of morality. Thus when a nation spreads the poison of distrust and mistrust to other nations, when it is revengeful and self-seeking, it is but natural that whatsoever there may be in the teaching of the learned treatises of ethics, and whatsoever good instructions and exhortations may be given in the individual and the social sphere for becoming good, the influence of the national grossness and vulgarity is bound to affect the masses, both in the individual and in the social sphere. If the nation is not filled with high ideals and if it does not strive to effect them into practice, if it is filled with grossness and animality, it is bound to reflect its nature on large *masses of its constituent minds ;* and their vulgarity is bound to reflect itself on the national mind, and drag it down to still lower levels. There is, thus, a vicious circle from which there is no escape. In times of war, when the animality of the national mind rises to a high level, the animal instincts of large masses of the peoples are excited, and even those who are in ordinary times gentle and mild, become ferocious and wild through the infusion of the national *virus* of hatred. The only scope of regeneration and recovery from the poisoned atmosphere can only be through influence of great individuals who do not succumb. In the efforts of such men to eradicate the evils of their own nations there are conflicts again between the individuals and the nation in which the former have often to emolate themselves for the good of their country. The individual morality is thus very closely related with national morality. It is not enough for individuals if they are moral only in their private spheres of life, as members of their family or society, in their private dealings with their fellowmen ; but they have to infuse their spirits and bring their influence upon the nation such that they may contribute to higher national consciousness and thereby affect the dealings of the nations among themselves.

Just as it is a clear duty of individuals living in society to contribute to the economic and spiritual welfare of their fellow-members and find themselves in ties of sympathy and love—where no sacrifice is felt as sacrifice but as self-realisation, so nations ought also to strive to respect the integrity of other nations and never to treat them as means to an end. "Every nation is an end in itself" should be the motto of every nation in its behaviour and dealings with other nations. When the truth of this is lost sight of and a nation looks upon itself as the ultimate end of its actions and other nations as the means, such as *Deutschland uber alles* (Germany over all), the nation itself is turned into a common enemy to the existence and integrity of other nations and in no time becomes itself a prey to the rapacious instinct of other nations. Each nation ought, therefore, to make every effort to know the actual conditions of other nations and to profess, in words and deeds, its concern for the welfare of and friendship for them and to devote a part of its national funds to the furtherance of that end. "Grow all" should be the motto of each nation, rather than "grow I". No dogma of individual morality can be fruitful unless it is supplemented by the still higher truth of inter-national morality. It is regrettable that no writers on ethics have shown the close relationship that subsists between inter-national morality and the individual morality. If a nation is deliberately immoral in its dealings with other nations, it can hardly expect its individuals to be moral in the social spheres. Clouds of the national religion are bound to sweep in darkness the little cheery sun-shine that may prevail in the family and the social spheres.

The national weight will drag the individual down to the sway of its biological instincts.

When nations will realise the responsibility that they have in the growth and well-being of other nations, not in a spirit of furtherance of their own economic welfare, but through an inspired and enlightened feeling of sympathy and love in recognising other nations as their fellow-beings and should make every possible effort for securing this fellowship on a sound basis, that is, when the traditions of individual morality could be found operative in the national spheres, and nations should work together for their mutual well-being through spirit of love, the mission of the great Jesus will be fulfilled and the kingdom of Heaven will be established on earth.

APPROACH TO METAPHYSICS

It may not be considered very wrong to think that a search after Reality may in some sense be regarded as the fundamental task of metaphysics. There may be many who think that the attempts of metaphysics during the last two or three thousand years in this direction have been a series of failures ; judging from that, the presumption is that there is not much to hope from metaphysics, and that, therefore, it is now high time that we should leave it off. This, I think, is in one sense a misconception. To answer by way of comparison, we could say that because the moral endeavours of the whole humanity after perfection have been a record of failures, we should think of giving up our moral endeavours. I have no mind to enter into any detailed examination as to how far the failures of metaphysics have been greater than those of morality, for, I think it to be more or less useless. The failures of the moral endeavours of my past life may stare me in the face, but still so long as I have the moral instinct in me, I should be continuing the moral struggle. Hunger cannot be satisfied with the knowledge that food is not available. There is in us a thirst after Reality which justifies those intellectual attempts of ours which go by the name of metaphysics.

Whether these intellectual efforts are required ultimately to point to some kind of solid experience as the ultimate result or whether the efforts themselves are sufficient to satisfy the craving of the mind in this direction, is a matter in which the Western and the Indian minds are not in thorough agreement. I do not say that there is any history of open and positive disagreement and quarrel over this matter between them, but, it seems from the history of philosophy of the two countries, that European minds were always generally satisfied with the theoretical and rational enquiry whereas the Indian minds, though they enforced strictest rational enquiry, always demanded some real experience which could verify the net results of the intellectual enquiry. With the Indian thinkers mere theoretical accuracy of thought leading logically to a certain conclusion, was not considered to be sufficient. It is curious that there were certain metaphysical results which they considered as being strictly verifiable in experience, and in which all the conflicting systems of thought, which were in hopeless quarrel over the epistemological, ontological and logical parts of the theoretical enquiry, were practically in agreement.

I hold no brief for India, but I pause to think about the scope of metaphysics. There is always a way of conventionally putting a limit somewhere. But with this I am not satisfied. Of course you can always have your definition and you can always say that thus far and no farther should we go. But with me the ground and justification of all metaphysical enquiry lies in the innate craving of the mind to get at the Reality. And I ask myself whether this enquiry should merely be limited to certain theoretical deductions and constructions or whether it is incipiently an attitude of the mind to reach an experience which it was only imperfectly trying to grasp by the processes of logical thought. Does the notion of Reality mean merely a notion, or a consistent system of ideas giving satisfaction to the logical propensity of the mind just as a piece of poetry may in some external sense be regarded as a system of thoughts or imageries satisfying our æsthetic temperament? Or does the notion of Reality involve the suggestion that behind the search after the theoretical consistency of a construction of the nature of Reality, there is a deeper and more or less unanalysable tendency of the mind to come to a truth which will not only be logically unassailable, but should also be felt as an experience leaving in it the final justification of its search after Reality? Is a philosopher merely a caterer to the taste of the logical propensity of the intellect as a confectioner is to the palate? Is our notion of Reality, a system of ideas which will explain a certain class of facts and relations in which we as men are widely interested? Certainly in this sense metaphysics cannot be verifiable and is not, therefore, verifiable. Must it not then be an intellectual myth or fancy which is different with different individuals? We read Shelley, Browning and Keats and enjoy, and so do we read Kant, Hegel and Lotze. But there is this difference that there is no pretension on the part of the former for any exclusive privilege. Each philosopher, on the contrary, claims that his system is the only valid theory to the exclusion of those of others. What this claim for validity means is, however, again uncertain and vague; it generally takes two forms, namely, that one system is logically more consistent than the others and that it satisfies the demands of our nature better than the others do.

The precise meaning, however, of the latter claim is not so easily intelligible and many philosophers have often taken advantage of this vagueness (often unconsciously) and have uncritically given it some sort of a convenient interpretation and have tried to convince others in the same way. The fact that this satisfaction of the demands of our nature is offered as a criterion for the validity of any system or as a claim for its acceptance, again leads us to think that apart from the craving of the intellect for a logical consistency, there is some other craving which requires to be satisfied in our enquiry after metaphysics.

It seems to me that most branches of human enquiry, science, philosophy, æsthetics etc., require some sort of satisfaction obtainable by direct experience which it wants to supplement by intellectual consistency or vice versa. When one deals with æsthetics, he understands that whatever may be the consistency of the canons of criticism, their ultimate test must lie with the satisfaction of our æsthetic sense ; when one deals with physics, he understands that all its laws must stand the test of sense-experience. But in philosophy, we cannot point to any special kind of experience whose satisfaction we want ; the sort of satisfied experience that we want seems to me to be something like a focussed point where all our demands have somehow met. If I may apply an imagery, I should say that our different sorts of cravings as men were being projected forth in our own inner space like rays of light and that if they were not obstructed in the way by their individual satisfactions, they would all converge together at a spot, further than which, there is nothing more. It seems to me as if this projected point of focus is incipiently felt as the goal which all the satisfactions of our individual tendencies point to. Each experience gives us a touch of it only in the sense that it points to a region ever beyond, to a distant glimpse of a vanishing point transcending the series. But this is a digression, and we cannot anticipate the results of any metaphysical enquiry until it has been actually demonstrated. What I want to do in this paper is simply to discuss the method that ought to be adopted for the building up of any metaphysical hypothesis that can justify itself to us.

The subject matter of metaphysics is much wider than that of any other investigation, and it is said that it seeks to harmonise them all. But I do not know what we mean by this. Harmony is a word which has an intelligible sense in music, because there it corresponds to a particular kind of experience. In music the different notes are heard and their commingling in a certain manner producing the harmony is also a matter of direct experience. When this harmony is felt, our musical craving is satisfied and we do not expect anything more. The relations between the different tones before the harmony has formed were not one of logical inconsistency, but a defect in their æsthetic expression which made us expect that the proper place of the tones would be served if they could make themselves the means for the production of that experience which our musical sense was wanting for its satisfaction. The dissatisfaction produced by a single note is due to the fact that it gives the suggestion of a kind of experience which our æsthetic sense was longing to have, but at the same time fails to produce it. I do not say that the combining of the tones gives this sense by the process of addition, but I think that the experience of harmony is an experience totally of a different kind,—just as water is different from Hydrogen and Oxygen of which it is composed. The musical tones were all individually real in the sense that they were experienced, and in this sense they had as much reality as the harmony ; but the reality of the harmony is higher in quite another sense, namely, that it represents the ultimate satisfaction of the craving of the æsthetic sense. The experience of the harmony thus in a sense transcends the experience of the separate notes, but it is all the same felt to be the ultimate meaning of them all—in the sense that they were somehow implying or suggesting it imperfectly.

It is precisely in this experience of an implied imperfect satisfaction of the tones and the realised perfect satisfaction of the harmony that the higher reality of the latter is felt. If this finds any corroboration with the logical definition or deduction of harmony as the reality of music by any thinker, we should surely welcome it as an additional proof ; but our experience of the harmony must demonstrate to us its reality. It cannot be accepted simply by dictation. So, if our enquiry after the ultimate Reality in metaphysics should seek to find a Reality which would harmonise all our experiences, this could only be done on the basis of the test of a corresponding experience. Words would not be of much avail. I should require that such discovery of reason should also be testified by experience. When the notes commingle together and form the harmony, we can seldom detect their exact process; but when the harmony is produced, it is felt to be the Reality which the notes were implying. Similarly, even if the exact processes through which our individual experiences commingle together may not be detected at every stage, the final stage must be a matter of direct experience and there ought to be found sufficient links in the intermediate stages to justify the fact that the inner notion of ultimate Reality realised, was the thing to which other experiences of ours were pointing.

I must make it clear that I am not appealing to any kind of mysticism or emotionalism, though I think, these emotions and mystic experiences should always be regarded as relevant considerations for any one who proposes to investigate all our experiences. I am only arguing that no theory of epistemology or of metaphysics formed from outside could ever have the right to dictate to us. Logic is the language with which we interpret our diverse experiences to one another. It can work upon facts and give us the clue to many new relations of facts, but it does not create new facts, nor does it stand a guarantee for the validity of the result, if the validity of the facts supplied to it cannot be certified beforehand. Whatever Spinoza's opinion may have been, metaphysics, I think, is not geometry. You cannot take a maxim or a principle either as an axiom or as a postulate and then, sitting upon it, continue to spin and spin until you have got a web big enough for covering all experiences with an Absolute along with them. I do not deny that even in this procedure there may be found some results with which one could be in agreement, but I think that to depend only on such a process without any reference to experience, is hopelessly wrong in metaphysics. It is done nowhere. Even in geometry, when you start from certain principles and arrive at certain results, these are verified in experience though their validity may be claimed apart from those verifications. Geometry starts with certain axioms and postulates regarding the nature of space relations and from them, by a process of logical reasoning, proves other space-properties. This result is valid as a logical deduction, but this is verifiable too by actual experience in accordance with our other experiences of time-relations and space-relations. But if the deductions of geometry could not be verified otherwise, and if it would not have directly taken part in other experiences with which we are interested, they might still have remained valid for thought, but no one would have thought to relate these logical constructions with other parts of our experience. Physics makes abstractions from experience, but at each step these abstractions are verified in experience.

A metaphysician surely misses his vocation if he considers himself to be Moses, the law-giver. He cannot claim to dictate to us what Reality is ; but his business is to seek and find what people imply when they speak of Reality. He should seek to find out by an analysis of experience, as well as by the synthetic implications of experience, the validity of the range and scope of our craving after finding the Reality. He should examine the place of our metaphysical tendencies in our other groups of tendencies and the results of our diverse mental experiences.

Our logical faculty is the faculty with which we can leave off the details of any presentation in thought which are unessential for any particular purpose and link ourselves to other identical or similar traits with which we are interested at the moment. This is at once its advantage and defect. Without this faculty we should have been lost in the fleeting presentations and could not have pursued a definite line on the ground of any identity of relations. But its defect is that if we should trust ourselves merely to it, we might be brought to places which we had no inclinations to visit. When using abstract logical thought as vehicle of journey for finding out Reality in experience, we are always to get down at stations at convenient intervals and assure ourselves with the experience of the place that we are proceeding along the right route.

Logic with me means the process by which our thought may be led to get beyond the immediate experience of the present, either as sensuous percepts or as felt wholes, which are only realised as a continuum, but not analysed into constituent parts. No thought can be satisfied with what is merely immediately given, either through the senses or directly to the mind. The logical faculty of thought (if I may be allowed such an expression) always seeks to break up the immediacy of anything that is given, into differences, and then guided by any particular kind of interest to pick up any of these and unite them with other entities, similarly broken up and abstracted from other unities. When our experiences remain as mere immediacies, or felt wholes of the moment, they remain shut up within themselves; conceived as such, these are isolated facts which can seldom be connected up with one another. Each felt whole stands alone by itself. But the activity of the mind could not be content with such immediacies, for the essence of activity consists in the passage from one to the other and we notice two kinds of such movements in our mind, the one, automatic and random, and the other, necessary and connected. The first is represented by all that is given through the senses and through automatic suggestions and associations, and the other, by the logical process though voluntary, yet necessary, connecting elements of abstraction in a definite order.

Both these are essential for thought. The presentations of our thought come to us quite uncontrolled by us, but the activity of the mind is not satisfied by this involuntary movement, for it wants consciously to unite those presentations in some way or other, and when this is found impossible it detaches or abstracts certain features from the concrete felt wholes in diverse experiences, tacitly treats them as actually existing entities and unites them in a new unity. We may start with a certain abstracted feature and continue the process of establishing its relations with other abstracted features. But however we might do it in one single line, or multiply it in diverse lines, we cannot get at the truth of our experience. The automatic inrush of new experiences is the materials over which the logical activity of analysis and synthesis works. What is the exact nature of the relation between any two logical abstractions taken at random is more than we can say. It was Hegel's belief that they were so connected with one another that you could start from any logical abstraction, and if you had sufficient patience to continue the process of analysis and synthesis, you could arrive at any other abstraction. They were to him but moments or links in a self-contained evolving cycle of the dialectic process. But however good may be some aspects of the general results of his philosophy, all his attempts in this direction failed, and even if he had been successful in showing such an universal self-developing inter-connection between the categories, the question as regards the complete wholes of experience would have been left quite untouched. Hegel would probably have dismissed them as unimportant, but that would not improve matters.

However less we might know about it, there is probably an unconscious or subconscious bond which holds together the different isolated felt-wholes forming a totality of inter-connected experiences. The unity which the free play of our logical faculty gave us, was of a quite different type ; it was the conscious establishment of new unities, on the basis of the materials supplied by automatic presentative experience appearing either directly or through memory. Without the presentative wholes, there cannot be any realisation of the logical activity and without the latter, the former sinks below the threshold of thought. The inner demand of our nature craves to be satisfied in both ways. It seeks to arrive at new relations between the abstracted features with which discursive thought deals and it also wants to have the experience of the concrete presentative wholes. These two worlds, namely, that of logical thought, and that of a logical concrete experience, are neither completely different nor merely parallel, but are more like two sets of curves which are continually intersecting and separating ;

and they are so inter-woven that in adult life, the mind in its continual passage from one to the other, hardly notices the two as distinct and the passage from concrete experience to logical thought by analysis, and from logical thought to experience by synthesis, is felt to be so sure, so necessary and so orderly that the mind runs on through them, seldom suspecting that in its progress, it is always in touch with two different kinds of worlds. There is probably somewhere a knot which ties the two fabrics together in a universal and unalterable order. But what the nature of this knot is, is yet to be discovered. People who set out to discover the reason of this bond of unity have often ended in making an easy solution by dropping either of these altogether and resting contented with the one. Thus there have been mystics and philosophers who regarded all logical thought as untrue appearance, unwarranted construction and illusions, and based their ultimate enquiry into the nature of reality upon the immediate experience of such a concentrated nature as could completely get rid of the logical movement, or upon an intuitive grasp of the truth by pure sympathy alone. There also have been philosophers who considered logic as the only truth and regarded the method of the logical movement of thought as representing the method of movement of the Reality itself. The march of logic is as a rule linear, and these philosophers attempted to show that all experiences were evolving in a circular chain the method of which was in essence the same as was involved in logic. The success that they attained in this cannot certainly be regarded as indisputable. And when they had to face the problem of explaining the concrete wholes of experience they generally tried to avoid it as unimportant.

The main point which I want to emphasise is this: that the process of thought in logical abstraction and that of enjoying the experience of concrete wholes being complementary to each other, no attempt at finding out the nature of Reality could be justified which made an abstract principle, the sole criterion of Reality. In such specific notions of ours as the space-time notion, where the one unified notion is so ultimate and so unique, that it is hardly affected, complicated by other experiences, the logical deductions have the greatest chance of holding good, independent of verifications from experience; for all our mathematical judgments are hypothetical in the sense that provided there is this space-time notion, these deductions from it must hold good. But this cannot hold with reference to our enquiry after Reality, for it involves as its data the whole of our experience. As I have hinted above, our logical chain of reasoning holds good for our experiences within certain limits. We cannot put ourselves in a logical train of reasoning and proceed on and on without reference to experience and ultimately come to a point where we could be sure that there must be a Reality or an experience within which all other experiences have been enmeshed. When logical abstractions are made from the concrete wholes of experience, the extent to which these abstractions may stand as representatives of the concrete wholes from which they have been taken is always limited; and, therefore, there is always the chance that any unverified logical train should land us in a place where we had no intention to proceed. Cases are by no means rare where philosophers were driven to a conclusion by a logical course of reasoning and having come there tried to convince themselves that, that was exactly where they had intended to come.

The enquiry after Reality is an enquiry which proceeds from the totality of our being ; it is not a mere pastime of intellectual exercise ; it is, therefore, necessary that any result that is attained in this course must be such that it should not only be made somehow logically consistent, but should be felt in the experience as a whole in which we are really interested. The business of a metaphysician should be to interpret experience and not to hold forth a logical principle and then stifle all those experiences that would refuse to obey it. Our notion of Reality is not a mere logical principle, a rule or a maxim, but if it indicates anything, it indicates an imperfectly felt Reality which carries with it the actual suggestions of its perfecter form. So the search after Reality that metaphysics ought to adopt should always follow the indications to Reality that may be actually found in our experience and not imposed upon them from outside by excessive logical subtlety. A theory unfounded and untestified by experience in metaphysics may more or less be regarded as mythologies of metaphysics which may no doubt be attended with its own peculiar pleasure due to a robust intellectual exercise or a fine flight of fancy.

If I am asked to give an example of a metaphysical system where logic overdoes its part, I may just try to give an example after the manner of certain philosophers.

"Anything which requires something else for understanding it is self-contradictory and therefore appearance."

"I can call something self-contradictory and unreal only because I know the real."

"The Reality is that which is self-contained."

"Such a Reality must exist" and "It is of the nature of an experience in which all other experiences are welded up into the whole." The abstract logical principle which shows itself in all the above ramifications of thought is that, what is self-contained is Reality. By the very hypothesis, the Reality is to contain all. So the next attempt consists in declaring that it does contain all. There are many confusions and inconsistencies of such a system, but to these I do not refer, for I am not now engaged attempting any serious criticism of it. But what I want to point out is this, that no one has the right to ask me for any definition of Reality without previously testing it in the light of our experience. Another important point about it is that even if there was such a Reality as a super-experience in which all other experiences melted down, I do not think that I should be least interested about it unless I find it indicated in my experience. So long as it is a mere matter of logical deduction from a doubtful proposition, I do not see how it can satisfy either our earnest and sincere enquiry after truth or our search after Reality. In our search after truth or Reality, we try to satisfy the inherent demands of our nature in those directions. If there was any super-experience in which all our experiences melted down, without the whole affair being in any way felt or indicated in experience, it would have little interest for us. It could surely have a great value as a philosophical hypothesis, if such a hypothesis is in any way explained, at least a fairly large amount of our experience is involved in that tendency of our mind which demands satisfaction from metaphysics.

I do not want to bring in the discussion, whether any particular person's Absolute does so or not. But if that philosopher does not try to demonstrate that it does, apparently he does not think it necessary to do it. Once you assume unconsciously that all you are required in metaphysics is to start with an abstract principle and apply its litmus-paper test to all things, in order to determine if there is any such absolute acid which will dissolve all things, and accept uncritically that this test is the right one, you may find such kinds of Absolutism pretty satisfactory. Any piece of well-sustained subtle argument affords us a certain amount of intellectual satisfaction, but it will, I think, be wrong to think that a metaphysician's duty is finished if he can dazzle or outwit us by subtle arguments. We do not want a cosmology from a true metaphysician of our times. We want our metaphysician to take into consideration at least all the important cravings manifested in experience such as logical, æsthetic, moral, religious etc., and tell us what ultimate fact or facts of Reality may be assumed on their direct evidence. I admit that this will indeed be a difficult task, but I feel that even if our progress be slow, it will at least have a stronger and more hopeful basis.

I cannot help thinking that the philosophy which aims at giving us some sort of a cosmology without largely depending on experience, will on the whole resemble mythology only with this difference that it would use subtle logic on many unessential parts of the scheme. With a Jupiter or a God of the Old Testament, with his wrath and kindness, we could certainly explain many things in quite a smooth way. There are, so far as it appears to me, systems of philosophy which resemble these mythical explanations, or at least the task of building systems of metaphysics becomes in the hands of clever thinkers something like intellectual pastimes. There was a time when any one who occupied a Chair of Philosophy in Germany prepared a system of metaphysics which people were asked to believe.

But at this stage, I believe, I ought to modify some of the statements I have made, or else I may be misunderstood. I beg to point out that I do not wish to maintain that no philosophers ever attended to experience in framing their constructive scheme of philosophy. This would indeed be impossible, for they could never apply any logical principles, maxims or criterions without having before them some field of experience, in which they could discover them. It is also true that they had to apply to some extent these principles on experience in order to test their validity. But with most of them, the tendency had been to refer to experience, only so far as could yield them an abstract principle, and when this is once got, they forthwith proceeded to construct their work without further reference to experience. When they were challenged with experiences, which did not tally with their abstract principles, they tried to explain away the experiences, or twist them in such a way as to suit their principles. The satisfaction that these systems give, is limited to the extent to which their abstract principles are certified by experience. In this sense, I should think, that most systems contain some partial truth. It does not matter much, if we cannot agree with any system of philosophy, in its details, or even, so far as its general results are concerned, for it is enough, if after critically sifting their doctrines, we can find something true in their explanations of experience. We can fruitfully utilise the labours of the philosophers of the past, if we stick to these. At this point, I think, it is well to remember that the results of the labours of the philosophers of India of the past will be specially valuable, for, they, partly on account of their insular geographical position, and partly on account of distinctive national peculiarities and climatic conditions, interested themselves in some important aspects of experience which did not attract much attention in Europe. A careful study and appreciation of these is bound to stimulate us into new channels of thought.

The general results of this paper consist in this that, I consider the justification of all enquiry into the nature of Reality to be based upon a natural craving of the advanced human mind in this direction. Our enquiry in this direction can only satisfactorily proceed, if we search our experiences and try to find out from their direct evidences, implications and suggestions, if we can discover any notion of reality which will satisfy the craving after

Reality, manifested in a general manner in all our experiences. Any undue importance given to deductions and constructions from abstract principles are likely to be futile. A carefully conducted logical reasoning with a view to discovering what is given or implied through the wide field of our experience with regard to the notion of reality can only help us out of the difficulty. The labours of past workers can be of help to us mainly so far as they have penetrated into the evidence and implications of experience. No deductions from a hastily formulated abstract principle can hope to be successful, for, the search after Reality being essentially a tendency of the mind, the object of search has to be achieved in the field in which the mind moves, namely, the experiences. A neglect of these considerations has led some philosophers (Bosanquet—*Essentials of Logic*, p. 106) to think that philosophy can tell us no new facts and can make no discoveries and that all it can tell us, is the significant relation of what we already know. Many questions may be raised here as to the nature of the experiences, or their relations with logical thought and self, but these questions can only be discussed in the chapters that would follow.

SOME ASPECTS OF BUDDHIST PHILOSOPHY*

Sanskrit scholarship is under a deep debt of gratitude to the works of Western scholars. The many-sided activities of Sanskritic researchers of the present day would have been well-nigh impossible if occidental scholars had not opened so many new avenues and continued persistently their labour of love to unravel the mysteries of Indian civilisation and culture. By their researches in Vedic philology and literature, their editing of the Pali canons, their connecting Tibetan and Chinese studies with Sanskrit, their archeological discoveries in India, Central Asia, Turphan, Indo-China, Java and Bali and by their scholarly works in many other spheres of Sanskritic studies, they have opened up almost a new world of civilisation to the students of Ancient India. But in one sphere, namely, that of Indian philosophy their works have not, however, been as remarkable, though in this field also they have been opening new sources of study for Buddhistic researches by their translations from Tibetan and Chinese. The reason for their backwardness in Indian philosophy is primarily threefold. Firstly, the Sanskrit of the philosophical texts and commentaries is often too difficult for them; secondly, most of the European Orientalists lack proper sympathy for Indian philosophical and

*"*The Buddhist Conception of Nirvāṇa*" by Th. Stcherbatsky, Leningrad, 1927, and "*Nirvāṇa*" by L. de la Vallée Poussin, Paris, 1925.

religious thoughts; and, thirdly, there are probably no European Orientalists who are also *bona fide* students of philosophy. As a rule, the European Orientalist is seldom able to understand a difficult piece of philosophical Sanskrit and when he tries to understand it he can proceed only philologically and most often misses the true philosophical import. This is enhanced by the fact that he starts with a preconceived notion, implicit or explicit, that Indian philosophical or religious literature does not contain any such original or deep thoughts as might stimulate our present-day philosophical enquiries. His interest in Indian matters is almost wholly antiquarian and he is always satisfied with curious and antique aspects of Indian culture in his investigations. He seldom has proper respect for the thinkers whose thoughts he is trying to decipher and consequently great thoughts pass before his eyes while he is running after shadows. There are, however, a few notable exceptions, and Professor Stcherbatsky is one of them. He studied the old Nyāya at Darbhanga and Benares. He can speak in Sanskrit as fluently as a Benares Pandit can. He is an excellent scholar of Tibetan. He knows half a dozen European languages almost as well as his own mother tongue. And above all, he has a genuine sympathy and high respect for Indian thoughts and thinkers and when he approaches Indian philosophy, he does so with the deep reverence of a humble learner. He has long been devoting himself to the study of mediæval Buddhism, the Vaibhāṣikas, Sautrāntikas and the Mādhyamikas. His present work, *The Conception of Buddhist Nirvāṇa* has been published from the publishing office of The Academy of Sciences of the U.S.S.R., Leningrad, April, 1927. It may be considered as a sister volume to the author's *Central Conception of Buddhism* published by the Royal Asiatic Society, London 1924. The author was stimulated to write this work as a criticism of L. de la Vallée Poussin's *Nirvāṇa,* Paris, 1925. The book contains 246 pages, of which only 62 pages are devoted to the main work of the book ; 150 pages are devoted to the translation of Chapters I and XXV of Nāgārjuna's *Mādhyamikasūtra* and the *Prasannapadā* commentary by Candrakīrtti, as an appendix. The remaining 34 pages form various indices of the book.

One of the main theses of Professor L. de la Vallée Poussin, which Professor Stcherbatsky combats, is that at the beginning *nirvāṇa* meant a simple faith in the immortality of the soul, its blissful survival in a paradise, a faith emerging from practices of obscure magic. I may quote here one or two passages where Prof. la Vallée Poussin tries to emphasise the view that the original conception of *nirvāṇa* did not evolve in opposition to the Brahmanic view of a permanent state of liberation, but it itself meant an ever-living eternal deliverance as a positive state of supreme happiness. It is to be regarded as an invisible state of existence into which saints retired. Thus he says in his *Nirvāṇa* (Paris 1925, p. 57) "Surtout rien ne permet d' affirmer que le nirvāṇa des bouddhists fut concu en opposition aves quelque théorie brâhmanique que ce soit. Le Nirvāṇa, Immortal ou Délivrance, nous apparait comme une donnée rudimentaire, vierge de toute spéculation métaphysique, bien plutôt engagée dans le mythe que dans la métaphysique.

Le Nirvāṇa est un séjour invisible où le saint disparaît, souvent au milieu des flames et dans une sorte d' apothéose." In support of it he refers to a passage in the *Udāna* VIII. 10. where the Buddha is represented as saying "On ne reconnait pas où va le feu qui s'est peu à peu éteint: de même estil impossible de dire où ont les saints parfaitement délivrés qui ont traversé le torrent des désirs, qui ont atteint le bonheur inébranlable." He further holds that there has been a primitive Buddhism, very much different, even as it would seem, quite contrary to what later on finds its expression in the Pali Canon. Pessimism, Nihilism, Soul-denial, psychology without a soul, annihilation as ultimate end, all these features that mark out Buddhism among other religions, Indian as well as non-Indian, did not exist (*Nirvāṇa,* pp. 17, 27, 33-34, 46, 52, 115-116, 125, 129, 132 etc.). He further considers Buddhism as a branch of *yoga* or asceticism, but as to the meaning of this *yoga,* he thinks, one feels uneasy when such a question is asked (rien de plus malaisè. p. 11). But, yet on the next page, he informs us that this *yoga* was nothing but vulgar magic and thaumaturgy coupled with hypnotic practices (Nous pensons quc le yoga est, dans les temps pré-bouddhiques, ce qu'l restera au cours de l'histoire ; essentiellement un ensemble de pratiques en honneur dès les plus vieux âges de l'Inde âryenne ou autochtone, pratiques des orciers et des thaumaturges, et dont il semble que la recherche des états hypnotiques soit le motif dominant). He further thinks that this *yoga* was a technical routine in itself quite foreign to every moral, religious or philosophic view—C'est une technique étrangère en soi à toute morale comme à toute vue religieuse ou philosophique (p. 12). The *yoga* from which, according to Prof. la Vallée Poussin, Buddhism sprang forth was thus this kind of *yoga* without any speculative tendencies. And the Buddhism of the Hīnayāna remained in this condition beginning from the Mahāvagga up to Buddhaghosa as a *yoga*, almost without any alloy (p. 53).

The objections against the views expressed in Prof. la Vallée Poussin's *nirvāṇa* as raised by Prof. Stcherbatsky in the first part (pp. 1-68) of his book under review are thus directed to two principal points viz., la Vallée Poussin's theory that the early Buddhism was but a *yoga* of the thaumaturgical nature and that the conception of *nirvāṇa* in early Buddhism was but a simple faith in soul's immortality. Prof. Stcherbatsky urges that there is no vagueness in the meaning of the word *yoga*. The word *yoga* can be derived, in an objective sense (*yujyate etad iti yogaḥ*), meaning the concentrated thought itself as a psychical condition, or in the instrumental sense (*yujyate anena iti yogaḥ*), as the method through which this condition has been created, or in the locative sense (*yujyate tasmin iti yogaḥ*), as the place where this concentrated thought has been produced. In the third sense the word *yoga* or more exactly the term *samāpatti* is used as a designation of the mystic words in all the eight planes of mystic existence where the denizens are eternally merged in trance. In the second sense *yoga*, rather the word *samādhi* as the faculty of concentrated attention, denotes a mystical power which can transfer the meditator to higher worlds and change life altogether. *Yoga* is neither vulgar magic nor thaumaturgy but is in essence that concentrated meditation that induces a condition of quiescence. He then goes on explaining the method of *yoga* according to *Abhidharmakośa* of Vasubandhu (300 A. D.) and describes how in the incessantly changing elements, that produce delusion of a personality the struggle of moral progress between the good and bad inclinations takes place. Though the momentary elements of moral inclinations cannot really influence one another, yet in consequence of the predominance of the good elements the immoral elements are driven out. The immoral faculties or elements are of two kinds, one, that can be removed by insight or reason, (*dṛṣṭi-heya*) and the other that can be removed by concentrated attention only (*bhāvanā-heya*). The fully developed faculty or concentration becomes a mystic power which can transfer the inddividual into higher planes of existence or spheres of purified matter (*rūpa-dhātu*) or still higher regions of pure spirits (*arūpa-dhātu*) with ethereal (*bhāsvara*) bodies. The denizens of these spiritual realms are merged in contemplation of some unique idea, e.g., the infinity of space, the infinity of thought or of the void or in a dreamy semi-conscious state. Their condition is merely cataleptic. In this state since the meditator does not require any food, the sense-data of smell and taste do not exist for him. The feeling of hatred is totally absent. These beings have no need for clothes, they are provided with houses by their own *karma*. The phenomenon of sex is spiritualised and there are no organs of physical procreation ; gross sexual passion does not at all exist though there may be delicate feelings. The birth of a new being is quite free from all pain and filth.

The new-born child does not come out of a female, and those who happen to be nearest to the place of his birth are his parents. But it is also possible that sages who are living on this earth can develop such mystic powers, that though their bodies may belong to this earth, they may attain powers of vision and sense objects of other higher worlds of the superior mystical meditators, referred to above. This shows that given a certain change, in the nature of one's existence, where the necessity of food, clothing and homes have been eliminated, there will be newer and superior spiritual elements forming the structure of his personality which are akin to those of the mystic meditators of the higher worlds. According to some schools the highest cataleptic states of trance are eternal (*asaṃskṛta*), i.e., they do not differ from *nirvāṇa*. But, according to the majority of schools, *nirvāṇa* is beyond even that. It is the absolute limit of life, the extinction even of this kind of the thinnest vestige of consciousness which is still left in the highest of all imaginable worlds of cataleptic trance. Apart from the above described, general functions of *yoga,* the Hīnayāna Buddhism also believes in the possibility of a sudden illumination by which the saint directly views the universe as an infinite continuity of single moments in gradual evolution towards final extinction. Arguing in the above manner, Prof. Stcherbatsky holds that the doctrine of *yoga* is to be regarded as an "inseparable, inherent part of the pluralistic universe of separate elements (*dharma*) gradually evolving towards extinction," though the possibility is not excluded that the germ of the *yoga* doctrine is older than the Buddha himself. Continuing in the same strain Prof. Stcherbatsky demands—"In any case there is no historically authenticated Buddhism without this theory, without the mystic worlds and its inherent part, the philosophic explanation of *yoga*. All *yoga* practices which had not this philosophic and moral aim, all sorcery and thaumaturgy, the Brahmanical sacrifices not excepted, were strongly condemned by the Buddha. They were considered as one of the cardinal sins. The details of the conditions in the worlds of the mystic and the degrees of mystic concentration have always given opportunities to much scholastic controversy between the schools. We can safely assert that within the pale of Hīnayāna Buddhism there is no place for trivial sorcery." (pp. 18, 19.)

Before passing to the discussion of *nirvāṇa*, it may be considered desirable to review the views of the two great scholars of Buddhism, L de la Vallée Poussin and Stcherbatsky, on *yoga*. Both of them apply the word *yoga* to denote the earliest practices of concentration among the Buddhists. Prof. Stcherbatsky gives its threefold etymology in the accusative, instrumental, and locative senses. But is this application strictly correct? The word *yoga* can be derived from three different roots of different meanings, the intransitive verb *yuj* in the sense of concentration (*yuj samādhau*), the transitive verb *yuj*, to control (*yojayati*) and also from the transitive verb *yujir*, to connect (*yunakti*). the suffix *ghañ* for the formation of technical words in all case-senses except the nominative, and as such Prof. Stcherbatsky is right in deriving the word *yoga*. The word *yoga* is formed by the addition of the suffix *ghañ*. Paṇini's rule III. 3, 19 allows the addition of in three different senses. But *yoga* in the sense of *samādhi* or concentrated thought (*yuj samādhau*) cannot be formed in the accusative sense, as the root *yuj* of *yuj samādhau* is intransitive. It does not also seem proper that *yoga* can be formed in the locative sense to denote the higher worlds where the mystic meditation is performed, for the location of a meditative operation cannot be placed in a spatial world. Prof. Stcherbatsky has not indicated the source from which he has taken these derivations. But whatever may be the source, the objections pointed out seem to be strong. The word *yoga* in the sense of *samādhi* cannot probably be found in earlier literature. The root *yuj* with the suffix *ghañ* irregularly forms another word *yuja* to denote periods of time and also parts of a chariot, and in these senses the word *yoga* is pretty old as it is found in several places in the *Ṛgveda*. The word *yoga* is sometimes found in the *Ṛgveda* as in VII. 67. 8., but in the sense of journey or drive. In the *Śatapatha-brāhmaṇa* 14, 7, 1, 11 the word *yoga* is used in connection with the word *ratha ;* in the *Mahābhārata,* in various senses derived from "connecting" (evidently from *yujir yoge*). The word *yoga* is used also in the *Kaṭha Upaniṣad* (6, 11)) to denote controlling of senses. The word is used several times in the *Gītā,* but in howsoever diverse senses it may seem to have been used, they are all derived directly or indirectly from the sense of conecting (*yujir yoge*). Manu uses the word *yoga* in the sense of controlling, evidently from *yuj, saṃyamane* (*Manu* 7. 44). The *Mahābhārata* III. 2639 also uses the word *yoga* in the sense of controlling. But nowhere in any literature earlier than Patañjali do we find the *yoga* in the sense of *samādhi*. Any actual verbal use of the intransitive verb *yuj, samādhau* is hardly available. Turning to Pali use, the word *yoga* is found in the derivative senses of connection, control and effort as in *pubbayoge*, or in *cittassa niggānhane yogo karaṇīyo*. It seems, therefore, that the word *yoga* was not familiarly used in any literature earlier than Patañjali in the sense of *samādhi* and its accessory disciplines. The word *yogin* also, in the sense of a man who habitually practises the *samādhi* processes, is hardly available in any literature earlier than Patañjali. The *Gītā* which in my opinion is pre-Buddhistic, as I have shown in my second volume of the *History of Indian Philosophy*, has no doubt the word *yogin* in it, but the word *yoga* is almost always used in the *Gītā* in the sense of connecting or its other remote derivative meanings, but not in the sense of *samādhi*. It is probably Patañjali who first used the word *yoga* in the sense of *samādhi*. Vyāsa thus gives the meaning of the word *yoga* as *yogaḥ samādhiḥ*. Vācaspati definitely points out that the word *yoga* in Patañjali is derived from *yuj samādhau* and not from *yujir yoge* (*yuj samādhau ityasmāt vyutpannaḥ samādhyartho. na tu yujir yoge ityasmāt saṃyogārtha ityarthaḥ—Tattvaiśāradī*).

Prof. Stcherbatsky is, therefore, right in contending against the view of L de la Vallée Poussin that Buddhism is a branch of *yoga*. He is also right in holding that *yoga* in the sense of *samādhi* is not to be found in pre-Buddhistic literature. But I should like to go further than this and assert that in Buddha's time the word *yoga* meant only control or the effort of control and the different disciplines that constituted in later times the *yoga* processes were not brought under one systematic concept of *yoga*. The application of the term *yoga* in Vasubandhu's work ought not to lead us to believe that the word *yoga* meant in early Buddhism a comprehensive science holding within it the processes of *śīla, samādhi* and *prajñā*. It is possible that (*dhyāna*) meditations were practised by many people as isolated endeavours and it is also possible that beliefs about the mystical powers of those who perform these meditations, were current in certain circles. From the *Kaṭha*, we know that senses were felt like uncontrollable horses and sense control was very much praised and that cataleptic states of trance were also regarded as high achievements of perfection. It may thus be supposed that the Buddha collected all these floating traditions, interpreted them in terms of his own *dhyāna* experiences and assimilated them into his own system of thought. The way in which the Buddha systematised the different practices, associated them with high nobility and perfection of character and welded them together in a comprehensive whole, served as a model to Patañjali who adapted it in his own way with some very important modifications. Far from being a branch of *yoga*, it was Buddhism which made *yoga* what it was. It is needless to say that Prof. Stcherbatsky is perfectly right in saying that the Buddhism of the Buddha has nothing of sorcery and thaumaturgy in it. The mere fact that any one indulging in mystic experiences believed in certain mystic worlds in which mystic experiences could be continued without the impediments of bodily limitations of hunger, thirst and lust, cannot constitute sorcery. If it did, then even Christianity, which indulged in the belief in the kingdom of God, in resurrection, in the day of judgment and in the angels of God, would also be called sorcery. The fact that Buddhism firmly believed in the gradual advancement and elevation of our being through more and more moral purity, the gradual destruction of passions and antipathies and the gradual moral strife in which the higher and nobler states of the mind gained supremacy over the lower ones and with the dawn of the superior wisdom all desires and rebirth became finally extinct, makes Buddhism one of the highest religions of the world. In fact, it is difficult to believe that a scholar of la Vallée Poussin's attainments should indulge in such baseless and uncritical fancies. And one may well suppose that Prof. L de la Vallée Poussin did not actually mean it; and it is on account of the lack of precision and looseness of expression that it appears that he identifies Buddhism with sorcery, beggary, mendicancy and thaumaturgy; for, on page 25 he says that these saints were very much higher than sorcerers as they looked forward towards gadual elevation and saintliness—Mais si les Yogins ou ascètes prébouddhiques tiennent du "mendiant" qui jeûne contre les villages qui refusents, l' aumône, tiennent du sorcier et mettent à très haut-prix l'hypnose et la thaumaturgie, ils sont souvent mieux que des sorciers et des mendiants: ils visent à la sainteté; ils sont souvent, avec des idées philosophiques rudimentaires et inconsistantes, une conception arrêtée de la destinée de l'homme, une sagesse. Le yoga, vers l'époque que nous considérons, s'était ordonné ou s'ordonnait suivant trois ou quatre pensées maîtresses, les pensées qui dominent l'Inde post-védiqué, l'Inde brâhmanique bouddhique, hindoue, transmigration avec des enfers et des paradis ; mérite et démérite ; delivrance de la trans-paradis ; merite et démérite ; délivrance dc la transmigration, bonheur supreme et définitif ; chemin qui conduit á la délivrance, à savior le Yoga, l'effort, la discipline méditativc et ascétique.

On the subject of *nirvāṇa,* Prof. Stcherbatsky points out that Prof. la Vallée-Poussin holds that since in the Pali Canon the word 'immortal' is used as one of the epithets of *nirvāṇa* and since in the later literature *nirvāṇa* is described as a reality (*vastu*), it can well be supposed that the pre-canonic Buddhism believed in immortality of the soul. He further says that Prof. la Vallée Poussin explains Buddha's silence on the question of *nirvāṇa* as his incapacity in the philosophical field. But if this is so, how can Prof. la Vallée Poussin argue that early Buddhism believed in the doctrine of the immortality of the soul? If the Buddha denied an eternal soul against the eternalist, but maintained the doctrine of moral responsibility against the materialist, how can he be supposed to be believing in the doctrine of an immortal soul? Prof. la Vallée Poussin draws a historical outline to explain the growth of Buddhism in which he says that there was in the beginning a simple faith in soul and immortality and a primitive teaching of an indefinite character, mainly of obscure magic, after that a mixed period supervened, when this simple creed was contaminated with confused ideology and this allows us to ask whether Buddhism at that period was not a gnosis. At last Buddhism received a super-structure of inane scholasticism and we have scholastic period of Buddhism just as one we had in mediaeval Europe. Primitive faith, then a period of gnosticism, and then a period of scholasticism,—these are three stages of the development of Buddhism, just as we had in the development of the Western Church.

In criticising the above view, Prof. Stcherbatsky points out that early Buddhism never believed in the doctrine of the existence of the self or its immortality. If by later scholastic Buddhism, the Vaibhāṣikas are meant, then it is not true that they represented in their teaching anything substantially different from the views of the early canonical schools, for, the Vaibhāṣikas are only the continuators of one of the oldest schools, the Sarvāstivādins and their teachings are therefore quite different from the Sautrāntikas who may be regarded as initiating a new school of Buddhism. Hīnayāna, therefore, ought to include the Vaibhāṣikas, and the Sautrāntika school may be regarded as a new transitional school leading to the Mahāyāna school of pure idealism. Early Buddhism started from a sound philosophical idea of a pluralistic universe, it denied substance and established lists of ultimate realities (*dharmas*). Some of these elements are highly artificial constructions. The maxim which guided these assumptions was that corresponding to each difference of the connotative terms of language, there must be differences of things or entities. The Sautrāntikas differed from the Vaibhāṣikas in attributing on nominal existence to these felt differences in experience. They thus objected to the comprehensive list of elements or entities as the ultimate data of the Vaibhāṣikas and only believed in the sense data and the mind data. It is therefore wrong to take them in the same class with the Vaibhāṣikas under the sweeping term of scholasticism. The Sautrāntikas flourished for at least five hundred years from the first to the fifth century A.D., side by side with the Vaibhāṣikas and the Mahāyānists. Vasubandhu and his pupil Diṅnāga may be regarded as partly Sautrāntika and partly Vijñānavādin. Ultimately the Sautrāntikas merged into the Mahāyānists or the Vijñānavādins. When the Vaibhāṣikas declared *nirvāṇa* to be something real, they did not mean that *nirvāṇa* was a kind of paradise. They only regarded *nirvāṇa* as the annihilation of all life and as a materialistic lifeless reality (*nirodhasatya vastu*). Sautrāntikas, on the other hand, admitted the existence of the Buddha's cosmical body and adhered to the Mahāyāna conception of identifying *nirvāṇa* with the living world itself and denying its reality as a separate element transcending the living world. Thus both the Vaibhāṣika and the early Buddhist schools regard *saṃsāra* and *nirvāṇa* as real. But *nirvāṇa* is real only in the sense of a materialistic, lifeless reality (*yasmin sati cetaso vimokṣaḥ acetanaḥ*). The Sautrāntikas believed *saṃsāra* as real and *nirvāṇa* as unreal (i.e., separately unreal). The Vijñānavādins or the Yogācāras believed *saṃsāra* as unreal and the *nirvāṇa* as real. The Mādhyamikas regarded both the *saṃsāra* and the *nirvāṇa* as unreal (i.e., separately unreal).

According to the Vaibhāṣikas, existence is of two kinds as phenomenal and as eternal. Phenomenal existence of matter, mind and forces are but complexes of elements. Only space and *nirvāṇa* are eternal existences. The phenomenal elements are however all real in the present, past and future. This reality is thus conceived in two ways, firstly, as momentary flashings in actual life and, secondly, in their abiding and everlasting nature (*dharmalakṣaṇa* and *dharma-svabhāva*). They held, therefore, that when all flashings in actual life stopped in *nirvāṇa*, there remained that lifeless entity in which all flashings of passion and life became extinct. It is impersonal eternal death, but only as a separate element and as the ultimate reality of the elements, in their lifeless condition. The simile of the extinction of light is to be explained as meaning only this lifeless condition. The difference between this view and ordinary materialism is that in the latter every death would be *nirvāṇa* (*deha-cchedo mokṣaḥ*). And this view is therefore called *ucchedavāda*. In the Vaibhāṣika view, however, there is no *nirvāṇa* at every death, but the different worlds in which a saint may be born are produced by *karma* and the elements composing his personality are gradually one after the other reduced to a state of quiescence and extinction until in final *nirvāṇa* all are extinct. The moral law through a long process of evolution reduces the living world into a state of final quiescence, where there is no life, but something lifeless and inanimate. It is therefore wrong to think that the Vaibhāṣikas regarded *nirvāṇa* as a *vastu* or reality in the sense of spiritual immortality. The Sautrāntikas, however, denied this materialistic *nirvāṇa* and regarded it as being the ultimate extinction of the entire cyclic processes of life without any residue of any kind. There was, however, a class of Sautrāntikas who believed that there was a subtle consciousness which outlived the final extinction of *nirvāṇa* and that it was from this that the elements which manifested as life experiences (see Vasumitra's *Samayabheda-uparacanacakra* in *Asia Major* II. 1. pp. 1-78, Leipzig, 1925). It is possible to trace the germs of the *ālayavijñāna* of the Yogācāras in this doctrine. Later on, however, the Sautrāntikas objected to this doctrine as it leads to the denial of the external world in the Yogācāra school. It is also possible that this view was drawn from the Mahāsāṅghikas who did not wish to believe in the total disappearance of the Buddha in a materialistic *nirvāṇa*. The Yogācāra view consisted in the belief in one pure knowledge as being the ultimate reality which seemed through ignorance as being modified into the diverse modes of phenomenal experience. In the Mahāyānist view, therefore, there is no difference between the *nirvāṇa* and the *saṃsāra*. Prof. Stcherbatsky then compares the Vaibhāṣika view of *nirvāṇa* with the *Nyāya-Vaiśeṣika* view of salvation, and the Mahāyānist view of *nirvāṇa* with the Vedānta view of salvation. He also supplements this with a valuable general analysis of the principle of relativity of the Mādhyamika school.

The main argument of Prof. Stcherbatsky against Prof. la Vallée Poussin may be summed up in two propositions: firstly, that nowhere in early Buddhism has the doctrine of the existence of self been preached, and, secondly, it is said that this negative conclusion is strengthened by the fact that the Vaibhāṣikas, who are the continuators of early Buddhism, believed in a form of lifeless reality as being the *nirvāṇa*. I am in general sympathy with Prof. Stcherbatsky's conclusions, but I do not think that he has sufficiently proved them. Firstly, the assertion that in early Buddhism we do not come across any belief regarding the soul's immortality as *nirvāṇa,* however true it may be, should have been attested by exhaustive references from the Pali canons. Secondly, admitting that the Vaibhāṣikas were the continuators of early Buddhism, it still remains to be seen how far the Vaibhāṣikas made new additions to the views of early Buddhism or left off some of their doctrines or changed and modified them. This would mean an exhaustive comparison of the contents of the Pāli canons, their commentaries and the Vaibhāṣika works. And unless this is done, it may be dangerous to make assertions regarding the views of Pāli canons from assertions in Vaibhāṣika works.

Judging from the early Pāli texts it seems very probable that *nirvāṇa* was a ethico-religious state of the extinction of desires as a result of ethical practices, contemplation and insight. As such it need not be regarded as transcendental. Such a state, however, clearly belongs to transcendental, rather than normal psychology. It is, therefore, sometimes described as unspeakable, and as immeasurable, as in *Sutta Nipāta* 1076 (*atthaṃ gatassa na pamāṇamatthi*). It is also sometimes described as an eternal reality and as such it is described as *accutaṃ ṭhānaṃ, amataṃ padaṃ, amata nibbāṇa dhātu.* In the Abhidhamma period it is sometimes described, positively, as a sphere of existence, and, negatively, as a condition of utter annihilation. F. Heiler in his *Die Buddhistische Versenkung* very aptly says that "only by its concept *nirvāṇa* is something negative, but by its sentiment it is a positive term of the most pronounced form. In spite of all conceptual negativity, *nirvāṇa* is nothing but eternal salvation after which the heart of the religious yearns." It is by extinction (*nibbāṇa*) of the fire of passions (*rāga aggi*) that the ultimate freedom is attained and there is the final extinction (*parinibbāṇa*). The fire of passions and desires can only go out in consequence of the cessation of the causes that were producing them, they cannot be destroyed by force all on a sudden. It is, therefore, that in the earlier texts *nibbāṇa* is compared to a dying fire (*aggi anāhāro nibbuto—Majjhima* I. 487) and not to a fire blown out. Compare also *anāhāro nibbāyettha, Apadāna* 153. also *padīpassa eva nibbāṇaṃ vimokkho āhu cetaso.* The eternality of *nibbāṇa* in all probability refers to the undisturbed tranquillity and peace through the cessation of rebirth, and there is probably no text which can lead to the supposition that it is a state of the immortality of soul *ajaram amaraṃ khemaṃ pariyessāmi nibbutiṃ* (*Vimāna Vatthu* 514), *sabdasaṅkhārasamatho nibbāṇaṃ* (*Saṃyutta* I. 136). The same idea is repeated in *Majjhima* I. 508, *ārogga paramā lābhā nibbāṇaṃ paramaṃ sukhaṃ aṭṭhaṅgiko ca maggāṇaṃ khemam amata gāminaṃ. Nibbāṇa* is also often described as cessation of desire *tanhākkhaya* as in *Vimāna Vatthu* 73, also in *Saṃyutta* I. 39—*tanhāya vippahāṇena nibbāṇam iti vuccati,* also in *Vinaya* I. 5—*sabdasaṅkhārasamatho nibbāṇaṃ.* The idea of *nibbāṇa* as the ultimate extinction and the psychosis as a whole is to be found in *Saṃyutta* I. 136. *Aṅguttara* II. 118, IV. 423, V. 8, 110 etc. Again in *Sutta Nipāta* 1094 we find a similar passage—*akiñcanam anādānam etaṃ dīpamanāparaṃ nibbāṇam iti naṃ brumi*; so also in *Saṃyutta* II. 117, *bhavanirodho nibbāṇam iti*. In one of the earliest passages also *nibbāṇa* is described as cessation and as wisdom—*upasammāya abhiññāya sambodhāya nibbāṇāya samvaṭṭati*, again in *Vinaya* V. 86 *nibbāṇa* is definitely described as non-self—*aniccā sabbe saṇkhārā dukkhā ñattā ca saṅkhatā, nibbāṇaṃ ca evaṃ paññatti anatta iti nicchaya*. Coming to some of the most authoritative traditional interpretations of Pāli Buddhism, I shall for the sake of brevity only refer to some passages of Buddhaghoṣa's *Visuddhi Magga*, Buddhaghoṣa defines *nibbāṇa* as the substanceless cessation of desires (*tanhā*)—*yasmā......tanhāya nikkhanto nissato visaṃyutto tasmā nibbāṇaṃ ti vuccatī ti*. On page 295, *nibbāṇa* is described as the highest moral quality along with other moral qualities—*khanti paramaṃ tapo titikkhā nibbāṇaṃ paramaṃ vadanti buddhā*. On page 498 *nibbāṇa* is again described as the supportless liberation, the getting rid of, the forsaking and the entire and absolute cessation of desires through disinclination to them—*yo tassa yeva tanhāya asesavirāganirodho cāgo paṭinissaggo mutti anālayo ti evan nirodhaniddese atthato ekam eva nibbāṇaṃ*. On page 507 a subjective and objective distinction of the meaning of *nibbāṇa* is made. On the subjective ethico-religious plane *nibbāṇa* is described as in the passage as *asesavirāganirodho* and on the objective side it is called the noble truth of *dukkhanirodho*. It is said there that it is on this account that *nibbāṇa* is described as peace (*śānti lakkhaṇaṃ*) and as eternal (*accutirasaṃ*). It cannot be said that because ordinary men cannot perceive it, *nibbāṇa* is therefore non-existent like the hare's horn. For, had *nibbāṇa* been non-existent, the ennobling of character and contemplation and wisdom which are methods of the attainment of *nibbāṇa* would be futile. For, if *nibbāṇa* does not exist, then the processes of character-discipline etc. do not exist, and if they do not exist, then passions and afflictions which are destroyed by them do not exist also,—which is impossible. *Nibbāṇa* thus is not non-existent, it is not also mere destruction (*khaya*), but it is the destruction of passions (*rāgakkhayo*). *Nibbāṇa* is called deathless and eternal, because it is attained only through the right path and not produced by anything (*pattabbam eva h' etṃ māggeṇa, na uppādetabbaṃ : tasmā appabhavam eva, appabhavattā ajarāmaraṇaṃ, pabhavajarāmaraṇaṃ bhāvato niccam*). It does not seem that *nibbāṇa* can be described as an existent with positive characters, it can be called as a negation of non-existence only because it is attainable by special wisdom and steady efforts which are positive in their nature *cāsithilaparākkamasiddhena onnavisesena adhigamanīato sabbaññuvacanato ca parammatthena sabhavato nibbāṇaṃ nāvijjamanaṃ*, page 509. Again, on page 567, it is said that just as a crow when set free from a merchant's boat on sea flies to the shore if it is visible, whereas, if no shores are visible returns back to the mast of the boat, so if a man perceives *nibbāṇa* as the wisdom of disinclination to all *saṅkhāra* elements (elements forming one's individuality), he leaves the course of the out-flow of all *saṅkhāras* and springs forward to *nibbāṇa* ; if he has not the wisdom of disinclination to *saṅkhāras*, he falls again and again in the course of the flow of the *saṅkhāras*. It is also said there in a description of the nature of liberation as *nibbāṇa* that he who takes to *nibbāṇa* as mere void (*suññatā*) perceives it as such. Again on page 666, it is said that just as a man suffering from heat desires cold, so does one suffering from the fire of rebirth desire *nibbāṇa* as the cessation of that fire.

It is unnecessary to multiply examples. But it is clear from the above that the view of Prof. la Vallée Poussin that *nirvāṇa* in early Buddhism meant immortality of soul cannot be attested by textual references from Pāli cononical works or from the works of responsible commentators like Buddhaghosa. So the negative contention of Prof. Stcherbatsky may be regarded as absolutely correct. But it must also be said that there is no proof in favour of his view that the philosophy of *nirvāṇa* of the Vaibhāṣikas was identical with the view of *nirvāṇa* of early Buddhism, or that in early Buddhism *nibbāṇa* meant a lifeless reality as the elements of *dharmas* as Prof. Stcherbatsky holds. Space does not allow me to enter into any discussion regarding the view of *nirvāṇa* among the Vaibhāṣikas. I fear, I have to differ on some important points here also from Prof. Stcherbatsky. But I must reserve it for some future occasion.

Prof. Stcherbatsky's illuminating work *"Conception of Nirvāṇa"* throws a flood of light on many obscure points of the development of the history of Buddhist philosophy, and every scholar of Buddhist philosophy will feel grateful to him for his contribution. But yet it is only in his translation of the first and the twenty-fifth chapters of Nāgārjuna's

Mādhyamika Kārikā and its commentary by Candrakīrtti, that he shows his great scholarship of Buddhism, wonderful mastery over abstruse dialectical Sanskrit and over all, his superior philosophical acumen, a rare combination among scholars of any country. I shall not enter into any details, but I fear that the translation may not generally be regarded as very exact,[1] but it is exceedingly readable, and excellent on the whole. There are only a few scholars either in this country or in Europe who can read Candrakīrtti's commentary with such ease and insight as Prof. Stcherbatsky has done. Though he has translated only two chapters of the book, yet I feel confident that they will be a real help to most Buddhist scholars in being introduced to Candrakīrtti and his master.

I now propose to subjoin a running review of some of the most salient points of Nāgārjuna's

---

1. To give only one example, let us turn to the adoration verse with which Chandrakīrti starts his introduction to his commentary on the *kārikās* of Nāgārjuna. The verse runs as follows:—

yacchāsti vaḥ kleśaripūnaśeṣān, santrāyate durgatito bhavācca : tacchāsanāt trāṇaguṇācca śāstrametat dvayañcānyamateṣu nāsti Stcherbatsky's translation:—(indeed a philosophic treatise should contain a doctrine of Salvation, it then "rules and it saves)". "It rules over all our enemies, our passions. It saves us from the misery and from phenomenal experience (altogether). These two advantages are not to be found in other philosophic doctrines."

Suggested translation:—Because it checks all your enemies of passions and saves you from misfortunes and rebirth, therefore on account of this checking power and the quality of saving (two parts of the word *śāstra* from *śās* and *tra* yielding these two different meanings) it is (called) a śāstra. And these two do not exist in other systems (which therefore may be called a *mata* but not a *śāstra*).

philosophy as contained in Prof. Stcherbatsky's translation of the first and twentyfifth chapter of the *Mādhyamika-vṛtti* which form an appendix to his work under review.

Nāgārjuna's main thesis was that all things are relative and hence indefinable in themselves and hence there was no way of discovering their essence, and since their essence is not only indefinable and indescribable but incomprehensible as well, they cannot be said to possess any essences of their own. Nāgārjuna was followed by Āryadeva, a Ceylonese by birth, who wrote a separate work on the same subject in 400 aphorisms. For about two centuries after this, the doctrines of Nāgārjuna were in a sleepy condition as is evidenced by the fact that Buddhaghoṣa of the fourth century A.D. does not refer to them. During the Gupta empire Asaṅga and Vasubandhu flourished in the fifth century A.D. In the sixth century A.D. the relativistic philosophy of Nāgārjuna again flourished in the hands of Buddhapālita of Valabhi in Surat and Bhavya or Bhavyaviveka of Orissa. The school of Bhavya was called Mādhyamika-Sautrāntika on account of his supplementing Nāgārjuna's arguments with special arguments of his own. At this time the Yogācāra school of Mahāyāna monism had developed in the north and the aim of this school was to show that for the true knowledge of the one consciousness (*vijñāna*) all logical arguments were futile. All logical arguments showed only their own inconsistency. It seems very probable that Śrīharṣa was inspired by these Yogācāra authors and their relativistic allies from Nāgārjuna to Bhavya and Candrakīrtti, the master commentator of Nāgārjuna's *Mādhyamika Kārikā*. Buddhapālita sought to prove that the apprehension and realisation of the idealistic monism cannot be made by any logical argument, for all logic is futile and inconsistent, while Bhāvyaviveka sought to establish his idealistic monism by logical arguments. Candrakīrtti finally supported Buddhapālita's scheme as against the scheme of Bhāvyaviveka and tried to prove the futility of all logical arguments. It was this Mādhyamika scheme of Candrakīrtti that finally was utilised in Tibet and Mongolia for the realisation of idealistic monism.

In taking up his refutations of the various categories of being, Nāgārjuna first takes up the examination of causation. Causation in the non-Buddhistic systems of philosophy is regarded as being the production from some permanent or abiding stuff or through the conglomeration of several factors or through some factors operating over an abiding stuff. But Nāgārjuna not only denies that anything ever is produced but also that it is ever produced from any one of the above ways. Buddhapālita holds that things cannot arise of themselves, for if they are already existing, there is no meaning in their being produced; if things that are existing are regarded as capable of being produced again, then things would eternally continue to be produced. Bhāvaviveka criticising Buddhapālita says that the refutation of Buddhapālita should have been supplemented with reasons and examples and that such a refutation would imply an undesirable thesis that if things are not produced of themselves, they must be produced by other factors. But Candrakīrtti objects to this criticism of Bhāvaviveka and says that the burden of proof for establishing the identity of cause and effect lies with the opponents, the Sāṅkhyists who hold that view. There is no meaning in the production of what already exists and if that which is existent has to be produced again and that again, there will be an infinite regress. It is necessary to give any new argument to refute the Sāṅkhya *satkāryavāda* view for it is enough to point out the inconsistency of the Sāṅkhya view. Thus Āryadeva says that the Mādhyamika view has no thesis of its own which it seeks to establish for it does not believe in the reality or unreality of anything or in the combination of reality and unreality.[2] This was exactly the point of view that was taken by Śrīharṣa. Śrīharṣa says that the Vedāntists have no view of their own regarding the things of the world and the various categories involved in them. Therefore there was no way in which the Vedānta view could be attacked. The Vedānta however is free to find out faults with other views and when once this is done and the inconsistencies of other positions are pointed out its business is finished for it has no view of its own to establish. Nāgārjuna also thus says in *Vigraha-vyāvarttanī*:

> "When I have these (of my own to prove),
> I can commit mistakes just for the sake
> (of proving)
> But I have none. I cannot be accused
> (of being inconsistent).
> If I did (really) cognise some (separate) things,

2. *sadasatsadasacceti yasya pakṣo na vidyate / upālambhaścireṇāpi tasya vaktuṃ na śakyate // Mādhyamika-vṛtti* p. 16.

I could then make an affirmation or a denial
Upon the basis of these things perceived or (inferred)
But these (separate) things do not exist for me.
Therefore I cannot be assailed on such a basis."[3]

Candrakīrtti thus emphasises the fact that it is not possible for the Mādhyamikas to offer new arguments or new examples in criticising any view, for the Mādhyamikas have no view of their own to support. They cannot even prove their own affirmations and if their affirmations contain any thesis, they quarrel with it also themselves. So the Mādhyamika scheme of criticism consists only in finding fault with all theses whatever they may be, and in replying to the counter-charges so far as inconsistencies could be found in the opponents' theses and methods, but not by adducing any new arguments or any new counter-thesis, for the Mādhyamikas have no thesis of their own. In an argument if one can only follow the principles that are admitted by them no one can be defeated by arguments carried on the basis of principles admitted only by his opponents.

Things are not also produced by any conglomeration of foreign factors or causes, for had it been so then there would be no law of such production and anything might come from any other things, darkness from light. And if a thing cannot be produced out of itself or out of others, it cannot be produced by

3. *anyatpratītya yadi nāma paro'bhaviṣyat jāyeta tarhi bahulaḥ śikhino'ndhakāraḥ sarvasya janma ca bhavet khalu sarvataśca tulyaṃ paratvamakhile' janake'pi yasmāt*

Mādhyamika-vṛtti p. 36.

a combination of them both. Again, the world could not have sprung into being without any cause (*ahetutaḥ*).

The Buddhist logicians try to controvert this view by pointing out that whatever a view may be it must be established by proper proof. So in order to prove the thesis that all existents are unproduced, the Mādhyamikas must give some proofs and that would involve a further specification of the nature of such proofs and a specification of the number of valid proofs admitted by them. But if the thesis that "all existents are unproduced" is a mere assertion without any proof to support it, then any number of counter assertions may be made for which no proof need be shown ; and if proofs are not required in one case, they cannot be required in the other case as well. So one could with equal validity assert that all existents are real and are produced from causes. The Mādhyamika answer to such an objection as formulated by Candrakīrtti is that the Mādhyamika has no thesis of his own and so the question whether his thesis is supported by valid proofs or not is as meaningless as the question regarding the smallness or the greatness of a mule's horn. Since there is no thesis, the Mādhyamika has got nothing to say regarding the nature of valid proof (*pramāṇa*) or their number. But it may well be asked that if the Mādhyamika had no thesis of his own, why should he at all hold the proposition that all existents are unproduced (*sarve bhāvā anutpannāḥ*)? To this the Mādhyamika replies that such propositions appear as definite views only to the ordinary people, but not to the wise. The proper attitude for the wise is always to remain silent. They impart instructions to those who want to listen to them only from a popular point of view. Their arguments are not their own or which they believe as right, but only such as would appeal to their hearers.

It is not out of place here to mention that the Mādhyamika school wishes to keep the phenomenal and the real or the transcendental view wide apart. In the phenomenal view things are admitted to be as they are perceived and their relations are also conceived as real. It is interesting to refer to the discussion of Candrakīrtti with Diṅnāga regarding the nature of sense-perceptions. While Diṅnāga urges that a thing is what it is in itself (*svalakṣaṇa*) Candrakīrtti holds that since relations are also per ceived to be true, things are relational as well. Phenomenally substances exist as well as their qualities. The "thing in itself" of Diṅnāga was as much a relative concept as the relational things that are popularly perceived as true ; that being so, it is meaningless to define perception as being only the thing in itself. Candrakīrtti thus does not think that any good can be done by criticising the realistic logic of the Naiyāyikas, for so far as the popular perceptions or conceptions go, the Nyāya logic is quite competent to deal with them and give an account of them. There is a phenomenal reality and order which is true for the man in the street, on which all our linguistic and other usages are based. Diṅnāga in defining perception restricts it only to the unique thing in itself (*svalakṣaṇa*) and thinks that all associations of quality and relations are extraneous to perceptions and should be included under imagination or inference. This however does violence to our ordinary experience and yet serves no better purpose, for the definition of perception as given by Diṅnāga is not from the transcendental point of view and thus represents the lower point of view. If that is so, why not accept the realistic conceptions of the Nyāya school which fits in with the popular experience. This reminds us of the attitude of the Vedāntists who on one hand accepted the view point of popular experience and regarded all things as having a real objective existence, and yet on the other hand considered them all as false and unreal from the transcendental point of view of ultimate reality. The attitude of the Vedāntists on this point seems to have been directly inspired by that of the Mādhyamikas. The attempts of Śrīharṣa to refute the realistic definition of Nyāya were intended to show that the definitions of Nyāya could not be regarded as absolute and true as they used to think. But while the Mādhyamikas who had no view-points of their own to support could leave the field of experience absolutely undisturbed and allow the realistic definitions of Nyāya to explain the popular experience in any way it liked, thc Vedānta had a thesis of its own, namely, that the self-luminous Brahman was the only reality and that it was through it that everything else was manifested. The Vedānta, therefore, could agree with Nyāya interpretations of experience and their definitions. But as the Vedānta was unable to give the manifold world-appearance a footing in reality, it regarded it as somehow existing by itself and invented a theory of perception by which it could be considered as being manifested by coming in touch with Brahman and being illusorily imposed on it.

Continuing the discussion on the nature of causation, Nāgārjuna and Candrakīrtti hold that collocations of causal conditions which are different from the effect cannot produce the effect as is held by the Hīnayāna Buddhists, for since the effect is not perceived in those causal conditions, it cannot be produced out of them, and if it is already existent in them its production becomes useless. Production of anything out of some foreign or extraneous causes implies that it is related to them and this relation must mean that it was in some way existent in them. The main principle which Nāgārjuna employs in refuting the idea of causation or production in various ways is that if a thing exists it cannot be produced, and if it does not exist it cannot be produced at all. That which has no essence in itself cannot be caused by anything else, and having no essence in itself it cannot also be the cause of anything else.[4]

Nāgārjuna similarly examined the concepts of going and coming and says that as the action of going is not to be found in the space traversed over, nor is it to be found in that which is not traversed over and apart from the space traversed over and not traversed, there cannot be any action of going. If it is urged that going is neither in the space traversed nor in the space untraversed, but in the person who continues to go, for going is in him in whom there is the effort of going, then that also cannot be right. For if the action of going is to be associated with the

4. *Mādhyamika-vṛtti* p, 90. line 6.

person who goes, it cannot be associated with the space traversed. One action cannot be connected with both ; and unless some space is gone over there cannot be a goer. If going is in the goer alone then even without going, one could be called a goer which is impossible. If both the goer and the space traversed have to be associated with going, then there must be two actions and not one, and if there are two actions that implies that there are also two agents. It may be urged that the movement of going is associated with the goer and that therefore going belongs to the goer, but if there is no going without the goer and if there is no goer without going, how can going be at all associated with the goer. Again in the proposition "the goer goes" (*gantā gacchati*) there is only one action of going and that is satisfied by the verb "goes," but what separate "going" is there by virtue of the association with which a "goer" can be so-called and since there are no two actions of going there cannot be a goer. Again, the movement of going cannot even be begun, for, when there is no motion of going, there is no beginning and when there is no motion of going, there cannot be any beginning. Again, it cannot be urged that "going" must exist since its opposite "remaining at rest (*sthiti*)" exists, for who is at rest? The goer cannot be at rest for no one can be a goer unless he goes ; he who is not a goer being already at rest cannot again be the agent of another action of being at rest. If the goer and going be regarded as identical then there would be neither verb nor agent. So there is no reality in going. "Going" stands here for any kind of passage or becoming and the refutation of "going" implies the refutation of all kinds of passage (*niṣkarṣaṇa*) as well. If seeds passed into the state of shoots (*aṅkura*), then they would be seeds and not shoots ; the shoots are neither seeds nor are different from them ; yet the seeds being there, there are shoots. A pea is from another pea, but yet no pea becomes another pea. A pea is neither in another pea nor different from it. Again one may see the beautiful face of a woman in a mirror and feel attracted by it and run after her, though the face never passed into the mirror and there was no human face in the reflected image. Just as the essenceless reflected image of a woman's face may rouse attachment in fools, so are appearances of the world, the causes of our delusion and attachment.

It is needless to multiply examples and describe elaborately Nāgārjuna's method of the application of his dialectic for the refutation of the various Buddhistic and other categories. But from what has been said, it may be possible to compare or contrast Nāgārjuna's dialectic with that of Śrīharṣa. Neither Nāgārjuna nor Śrīharṣa are interested to give any rational explanation of the world-process, nor are they interested to give a scientific reconstruction of our world-experience. They are agreed in discarding the validity of world-experience as such. But while Nāgārjuna had no thesis of his own to uphold, Śrīharṣa sought to establish the validity and ultimate reality of Brahman. But it does not appear that he ever properly tried to apply his own dialectic to his thesis and tried to show that the definition of Brahman could stand the test of the criticism of his own dialectic. Both Nāgārjuna and Śrīharṣa were however agreed in the view that there was no theory of the reconstruction of world-appearance which could be supported as valid. But while Śrīharṣa attacked only the definitions of the Nyāya, Nāgārjuna mainly attacked the accepted Buddhistic categories and also some other relevant categories, which were directly connected with them. But the entire efforts of Śrīharṣa were directed in showing that the definitions of Nyāya were faulty and that there was no way in which Nyāya could define its categories properly. From the fact that Nyāya could not define its categories, he rushes to the conclusion that they were intrinsically indefinable and that therefore the world-appearance which was measured and scanned in terms of those categories were also false. Nāgārjuna's methods are largely different from that of Śrīharṣa in this that the concepts which he criticised were shown by him to have been intrinsically based and constructed on actions or qualities which had no essential nature of their own, but which were only understood in relation to others. No concept revealed any intrinsic nature of its own and one could understand a concept only through another and that again by the former or by another and so on. The entire world-appearance is thus based on relative conceptions and is false. Nāgārjuna's criticisms are however largely of an *a priori* nature which do not treat the concepts in a concrete manner and which are not also based on the testimony of our psychological experience. The opposition shown therefore is very often of an abstract nature and occasionally degenerates into verbalism. But as a rule they are based on the fundamentally-relative nature of our experience. They are never half so elaborate as the criticisms of Śrīharṣa, but at the same time they are fundamentally more convincing and more direct than the elaborate round-about logical subtleties of Śrīharṣa's dialectical criticisms. It cannot be denied that based on the dialectical methods of Nāgārjuna, Buddhapālita and Candrakīrtti, Śrīharṣa's criticisms following an altogether different plan of approach, show wonderful powers of logical subtleties and fineness, though the total effects can hardly be regarded as an advancement from the strictly philosophical point of view, while the frequent verbalism of many of his criticisms is a discredit to his whole venture.

CROCE & BUDDHISM*

PREFACE

Schopenhauer expressed the hope that the discovery of Sanskrit would bring a new epoch in the development of European thought, just as the introduction of Greek studies had done in the Renaissance period. But obviously enough that hope has not been yet so well fulfilled. The discovery of Sanskrit gave of course a very great impetus to the studies of comparative philology and also to a certain extent to those of comparative mythology and religion, but it does not seem to have touched the inner vein of European culture and civilisation. Apart from the differences that exist between the intrinsic value and purpose of Greek literature and Sanskrit literature, one fact may be pointed out with little fear of contradiction, that as compared with the knowledge of Greek literature in Europe, Sanskrit is known more by name than by actual acquaintance —exception being made only in the case of a few orientalists or Sanskritists who are working in this or that country. This may be due to various reasons. But one fact seems to be almost certain that European thought was in a state of whirlpool, when Greek studies were introduced during the Renaissance, and Greek culture shone forth like a light-house at a

*Read at the International Congress of Philosophy at Naples by the writer as the representative of the Calcutta University, Senatore Croce being in the chair.

distance, when Europe was groping its way in the dark in the black waters of the middle ages. But when Sanskrit was discovered in Europe, she was at day-break near in sight of the promised land and she cared little for the discovery of old light-houses.

Another reason why Sanskritic studies suffered in Europe is the vastness of the literature as compared with Greek. India is a country almost as big as the whole of Europe excluding Russia and in almost every part of it works were being composed for the last two thousand years or so and in some parts where there was early penetration of Aryan culture for more than 5000 years. Even when allowance is made for the want of printing machines in early days and other modern facilities for publication, it is easy to imagine what a huge literature India must have produced on a large variety of subjects. It is well worth pointing out here that during this very long period of Indian civilisation, in spite of foreign invasions and dominations, there is such a strange continuity of culture and thought, that the literature and thoughts of any period explain and interpret the others. The whole thing appears as immense and deep as the vast ocean that partly surrounds India and one is simply overawed by the sight of it. Foreign civilisations, that encroached upon India, have but left probably just as much permanent impression on her as the furrows that a ship makes, when she makes her way through the sea. Political dependence also often discredits the value of a culture and makes it difficult for it to attract the attention that it deserves, for attention is often drawn more easily by a hard blow than by passive self-contained look such as that which India can give. Misrepresentations, sometimes deliberate, and sometimes due to ignorance, had their share in discrediting Sanskritic culture and its value.

Of all the different branches of investigation and study that are comprised within Sanskritic culture, Philosophy is the most important. In Indian culture it is like the nucleus from which everything else has grown. It is therefore natural that the philosophic and religious literature (Philosophy sometimes gets mixed up with religion) are by far the most extensive. The language of remarkable philosophical works of great depth, penetration and subtlety is indeed very precise, definite and clear in their own way, but is very technical, and European works on Indian philosophy, which show a thorough grasp and mastery of this language, are indeed very few. The Sanskritist has indeed another difficulty; he is also a linguist or an archæologist and these interests even with most of the very best Sanskrit scholars in Europe outweigh the cultural or the real philosophical interest. The result is that with most of the old type of Sanskrit scholars, there is a strong tendency not to rejuvenate what appears to be dead but to mummify what is living and pulsating with thought. For the Sanskritist generally starts with the postulate that he is before a dead culture: he has around him nothing but the dead bones: and if anything appear to be living, it must be made to die by the axe of his interpretation, before he can feel himself at ease to work on it. A celebrated Russian Sanskritist once remarked to me that when we had succeeded in making a thing unintelligent, mysterious and dead, then only we say—"Look, now it is true and genuine Indian ; it looks antique." Happily however there are some in the generation of scholars who have perceived this defect and it is hoped that they will do better than their teachers in interpreting Indian thought and culture.

But I do not know of any European philosopher (i.e., who has studied European philosophy thoroughly and whose chief interest is philosophy) who commands an adequate knowledge of Sanskrit to make a deep study of Indian philosophy in the original.

My contention is that most of the elements of contemporary European thought are found anticipated in Indian philosophy. I do not maintain for a moment that Indian systems of thought are identical with modern ones or *vice versa,* but I wish to maintain that the important elements are all there in more or less varying modifications. Much of what passes as modern philosophical discoveries are like old wines in new bottles. I also wish to maintain that a study of modern thoughts in their old garbs as they appear in Indian philosophy is likely to have highly suggestive value for the health and vigour of new philosophical achievements. It may open new channels for the progress of philosophy and the extension of world-culture. I could not within the limited space of a short paper expect to prove my contention in its details. I have therefore taken as an example the most important Italian thinker Croce, whose doctrines, may, at all ordinary appearance, seem to be far removed from any known systems of Indian thought, and have tried to compare him with some schools of Buddhism and have tried to show that in spite of differences, some of the fundamental positions of Croce are the same as those of Buddhism. The same similarity with other schools of Indian thought could very easily be shown of Gentile, Varisco etc., of modern times, or to Rosmini, Gioberty, Galuppi, Thomas Aquinas, Campanalla, Bruno and many others, as well as of other German, French, English and American thinkers.

I wish humbly to point out to the learned philosophers of this great assembly that time has come when we can strengthen and rejuvenate philosophical investigation by initiating a new branch of studies called "Comparative Philosophy." I do not ask my kind audience to accept any of my conclusions, but I shall consider myself very happy and my tedious and long journey to this remote country successful if even one of those whose chief interest is philosophy should take to the study of Indian philosophy in original and try to form his own conclusions from the first-hand data that he finds after a systematic and thorough study of the original texts.

I
Croce and Buddhism

One central fact that emerges from a careful study of different systems of Indian Philosophy is that most of these are filled with a deep conviction of the spirituality of man and the universe. The maturer philosophical documents of early India may be said to have begun at least as early as 700 B.C.

and tracing its history up to the beginning of the 18th century, there has never been a period when the philosophical talent of India has been unproductive. Systems of thought running through so many centuries and passing through changing fields of social and religious developments, would naturally have something in their modes of conception and expression which might be considered as merely contingent and local ; there are also many points in which they so often differ, and try to refute each other ; but there is at least one principle which most of them materially accept, viz., that the highest truth is the spirituality of the self and the universe has either the same essence as the self or resembles it in a remarkable degree or is dependent on it in such a way that all its changes are motives by an inherent purpose of gradually bringing about, through different stages of success and failure, the ultimate self-realisation of the freedom and spirituality of man. The conception of this spirituality, however, varies more or less in one or other of these systems. Thus according to the Jains the self in its pure state is possessed of infinite perception (*ananta-darśana*), infinite bliss (*ananta-sukha*) and infinite power (*ananta-vīrya*) ; according to the Vedānta the pure soul as the highest reality is the identity of pure consciousness (*cit*), being (*sat*) and bliss (*ānanda*); according to the Ṣāṃkhya and the Yoga, the self is nothing but the self-shining entity of pure intelligence. Even those, who deny the existence of a permanent self such as the idealistic Buddhists, do not deny the spirituality of man and the universe as they are both in some sense considered mental products. But though these Buddhists did not believe in a self as a permanent entity, yet there were the thoughts, emotions, and acts of will and these were fused together in a way which gave the illusory impression of an unchangeable indivisible entity, a person, and his whole worldly career had but one supreme ideal before him, viz. the realisation of the true nature of this person as the point of unity of thoughts, emotions and acts of will.[1] But the central conception of Buddhism does not consist in its abstract denial of a permanent metaphysical entity either in the inner or in the outer world, but in its conception of all phenomena as streams (*santāna*) of appearances (*dharma*). What we call inner or outer was but a result of abstraction, as it is based upon a false bias in the existence of a metaphysical entity "the soul" with which the phenomena generally regarded as "internal" are conceived to have an intimate relation. But no such distinction of inner and outer is possible. Whether it be a sensuous colour such as a green or a red patch, a rectangular, triangular or curved space which limits it or thoughts, ideas, emotions, an act of will or whatever else it might be, it is nothing but

1. The Vātsīputrīya and the Sammitīya schools of Buddhism however believed that there was a *pudgala* (individual) which existed more or less as a permanent entity undergoing rebirth though its existence at any particular moment in relation to the elements of the inner psychosis was conceived as being of the same kind as fire to the logs of wood which produced it. Compare Th. Stcherbatsky's *The Central Conception of Buddhism*, p. 71 and his *Soul Theory*, p. 830. Also L de la Vallée Poussin's article on the Sammitīyas in the *Encyclopædia of Religion and Ethics*.

a phenomenon—an appearance. Buddhism never discusses properly the ultimate nature of these appearances. They are what they appear, they are but the appearances of certain characteristics or *dharmas*. Beyond them there were nothing else as entities in which these characteristics inhered. The distinction of Buddhism from other phases of Hindu thought consists in this its anti-metaphysical character. It does not like Kant consider that there is a permanent datum which abides as an unknowable reality which we cannot reach, but the existence of which we believe to be the ground of all that appears to us. All discussion as to what may be the ultimate nature of reality beyond the appearances, Buddha considers to be irrelevant (*avyākatā*). There is therefore no distinction here between a world of reality and a world of appearance, as a noumenal and phenomenal world. There is in Buddhism therefore no Absolute or God as the ground of all existence. It did not also like Bradley, consider the reality to be the totality. A careful reader may, indeed, find much similarity in the application of the dialectic of the great Buddhist philosopher Nāgārjuna and that of Bradley in showing the contradictions in all the phenomena or the appearances when they were taken in a detached manner from off the entire setting in which they appear. But their purposes and ultimate conclusions seem to be entirely different. What Bradley wanted to achieve by the application of his dialectic was to prove that the appearances in themselves were self-contradictory and therefore false and from that to deduce that all these contradictions vanished in an unaccountable manner in the totality

—the Absolute—which alone is reality. Thus he says:

> "Reality is above thought and above every partial aspect of being, but it includes them all. Each of these completes itself by uniting with the rest, and so makes the perfection of the whole. Now anything that in any sense "is" qualifies the absolute reality and so is real. But on the other hand, because everything, to complete itself and satisfy its own claims must pass beyond itself, nothing in the end is real except the absolute."[2]

Nāgārjuna however employs his severe philosophical dialectic which is even sharper and more acute than that of Bradley to destroy all useless metaphysical enquiries into the ultimate nature of the appearances, to undermine the popular faith in the existence of ultimate metaphysical entity or entities underlying the stream of appearances. The appearances are as he said *niḥsvabhāva,* i.e., devoid of any further intrinsic nature which is truer and more real. Buddhism, thus, though in one sense anti-metaphysical, is not anti-philosophical. Its philosophy consists in formulating a concept or a view which would explain the passing changes and cycles of phenomena. Its theory of the twelve links of causation, the theory of the *dharmas,* the theory of *pratītya-samutpāda* as causation in which one group is seen to follow another in a series, are not attempts to go beneath the changing series of appearances in search of an abiding reality, but to conceive the entire process of all phenomena in one sweep of rationalisation from experience. The doctrine of *pratītya-samutpāda* or dependent origination is like a formula which summarises the facts of experience

2. Bradley's *Appearance and Reality* (1908) p. 555.

and not an attempt at a deduction of the phenomena from a fixed principle. There is a changing series of phenomena around us, and Buddhism accepts it as such, and seeks to hold them all in a dynamical concept of change. It does not seek to explain this change by a reference to the unchangeable but by history. At any particular moment there are numerous sets of appearances called internal and external which for that moment form the entire phenomenal appearance of the world. These are followed at each successive moment by numerous other sets of appearances. The phenomena at any particular moment are determined by their previous history and their position in their own series. Buddhism does not try to discover what each phenomenon is in itself, but to hold it before our view as an appearance, the essential feature of which consists in having a "before" and an "after". Its philosophy is identical with its history. The phenomena are happening and passing, and the main point of interest with Buddhism was to find out "what being, what else is", "what happening, what else is". The phenomena are happening in a series and we see that there being certain phenomena there become some others. Each phenomenon is what it is in consequence of its previous history, i.e., its place in relation to the series of other phenomena which preceded it. What are called *skandhas* are but the psychical states such as the sense data, feelings, conceptual knowledge, volitions and synthetic mental states and consciousness. All these states rise depending one upon the other and determine the history of a man's personality. When a man says that he perceives the self, he only deludes himself, for he only perceives one or more of these. There is no abiding person, but only a history of the successively changing appearances of mental states. The Buddhists in common with other Hindus believed in rebirth, though they did not believe in any permanent entity which remained constant from birth to birth. What we have from birth to birth is just a projection of what we have in this life, a history of the successive appearances of mental states. Death is only a moment in the series. But it is not a break, for even after it the history of the series which had come up to the moment of death continues and new psychical states arise determining new states of existence. At most, death is only a moment which is followed by considerable change in the nature of the history; each birth is like the beginning of a new epoch of history, but the beginning of an epoch is not the beginning of history. The history continues from beginningless time and each birth and death brings a new page of it. The individual himself is identical with history. What is called *bhava-cakra* (wheel of life) or the twelve *nidānas* are but more or less remarkable consecutive stages in this history in a triad of three lives. The individual appearances are, when taken by themselves, unconnected, their connection is in their history which is the same as the law of causation. The interconnected life of these appearances is but another name for the "laws of causation" (*pratītya-samutpāda*) —the connected origination of some appearances in relation to other appearances. It is this combined (*saṃskṛtatva*) and interconnected mode of existence of all appearances, i.e., their truth as history that is understood by *pratītya-samutpāda*.[3] The earlier Buddhist literature, the *suttas* almost exclusively use this term *pratītya-samutpāda* to the "wheel of life" spoken above, probably because the "wheel of life" was an epitome of all other appearances and their history. It is therefore that the *abhidhammas* deal with *pratītya-samutpāda* as being equivalent to *saṃskṛta-dharma* and apply it to all interconnected phenomena that reveal their truth in history.[4] According to Buddhism, the being of an event or an appearance has no further concept to define it than that it has been determined by something else or it is determining something else.[5] The concept of truth or philosophy is, therefore, identical with the concept of history, namely that of determining and that of being determined. It is these two important characteristics—its anti-metaphysical character and its conception of history as the true concept of philosophy—that differentiate Buddhism from all other systems of Indian thought.

But it is these important features of Buddhism that lead us to think of its similarity with some modern systems of thought and notably with the system of thought associated with the eminent name of Benedetto Croce, as distinguished from the anti-metaphysical lines of thought of the Comtian school according to which thought has to pass from mythology and theology to the positivistic stage. The positivist method is empirical but neither

3. Yaśomitra on *Abhidharmakośa*, II, 46.
4. *Abhidharmakośa*, III, 25.
5. *Nyāyamañjarī*, p. 447.

immanent nor transcendent. Croce's method as well as that of Buddhism differ from that of positivism in this that it is not empirical, and differ from many systems of Absolutistic philosophy in this, that it is not transcendent. Croce's method and that of Buddhism agree in being immanent. It is this immanence that distinguishes it from the empirical methods of science. Both Croce and Buddhism seem to agree in taking the history of reality as it appears in and through the interconnected phenomena. But how far this seeming agreement is correct and if it is so, in what sense it is so, deserves careful elucidation.

Before enquiring into Croce's treatment of the point in question it is necessary to remember that he did not present so much a final philosophy as a well-conceived view of philosophy. As a matter of fact there cannot be according to Croce any final philosophy, for philosophy according to him is the concept, which uniting with it universality, expressiveness and concreteness, is also ever changing. There is no philosophy which can be called as the philosophy or the philosophy par excellence. It is merely the universalising in a concrete manner the materials created by intuition, that is called philosophy and as such with every new epoch, with every new man or rather with every new moment there is a *concept*, a philosophy which has its special uniqueness. A philosophic idea dawns in the mind of a man at a particular point of time and space and under certain definite circumstances and conditions without which it could not have been what it was. The philosophy of Kant could not have been what it was at the time of Julius Cæsar or Pericles, for it presupposes

O.P. 62/17

the knowledge of various branches of natural science such as could not have been attained at that time or of various branches of philosophy which had an important bearing on his own philosophy such as that of David Hume, and these again presupposed many other things which happened before David Hume and these others and so on. Thus Croce says:

> "Kant truly lives again in our own day in a different name. He is the philosopher of our own time in whom is continued philosophic thought which once took among others, the Scoto-German name of Kant. And the philosopher of our day, whether he will it or no, cannot abandon the historical conditions in which he lives or so acts as to make that not to have happened which happened before his time. Those events are in his bones, in his flesh and blood and it is impossible to drive them out"[6]

The problem of philosophy with any person depends largely on the history of philosophical problems and their solutions before his time. Philosophy changes with the change of history, and since history changes at every moment, philosophy at every moment is new. Even in communication or translation philosophy changes, as it involves the solving of new problems that presented themselves to us. The new philosophic proposition is made possible only by the old; the old lives eternally in the new that follows it and in the new that will follow that again and make old that other which is new.

The idea of history according to Croce is the concept and its character of unity in distinction that determines the representative or intuitive material that enters into it. We cannot think of history as a whole without distinguishing it at the same time

6. *Logic*, p. 312.

into the history of doing, the history of knowing, the history of aesthetic production, philosophic thought and so on. Again, none of these distinctions can be thought of except by placing it in relation with the others or with the whole and thinking it in complete history. The intimate logical unity and distinction which is the soul of Croce's "true concept" is as much the soul of history as of philosophy. Every historical proposition qualifies the real in one of its aspects and distinguishes it from the point of view of others. Philosophy and history are the one single form of the spirit, not mutually conditioning each other but identical. Thus Croce says:

> The *a priori* synthesis, which is the reality of the individual judgment and of the definition, is also the reality of philosophy and of history. It is the formula of thought which by constituting itself qualifies intution and constitutes history. History does not precede philosophy nor philosophy history ; both are born at one birth"[7]

One may try to distinguish philosophy from history by asserting that in the former a special emphasis is accorded to the concept or system whereas in the latter narrative is specially prominent. But every narrative includes the concept and every concept throws light on the facts. So though history and philosophy may ordinarily be differentiated, yet if the meaning of a historical and a philosophical proposition is fathomed to the bottom their intrinsic unity is indubitable.

What all this comes to is that according to Croce the true functions and modes of operation of philosophy and history consist in the conceptualisation or

7. *Ibid*, p. 325.

the establishing of a relation of distinction in unity among the materials of intuition and hence they are identical. But when I spoke of history and philosophy being identical in Buddhism it was apparently in an altogether different sense, yet they may not be so different. In it, I first traced the conception of history of any particular event or thought or action as its determination by all that has gone before. The event or thought in question is in one sense distinct from all that has gone before and all that is to come after in this that it has been determined by the "before" series and it will in its turn determine the "after" series. This is its *kārakatva* and its essence. Apart from its concept it has no further conceivable meaning. The idea of universality or unity in distinction in the form in which it appears in Croce is an European product and no one would venture to say that exactly this idea occurred in India about two thousand years ago in Buddhism. But if we examine the situation critically, we may almost unhesitatingly say that there is as much material agreement as could be expected. At each particular moment there are all sorts of appearances, elements, or entities, sensuous and mental, and it is depending on this that other groups of sensuous and mental entities make their appearance at the second moment. None of the sensuous appearance can be conceived without a reference to a review of them as being united with and dependent upon other preceding sensuous mental appearances ; yet these entities are all distinct from one another. These sensuous-mental materials are unique and inexpressible (*nirvikalpa*) in themselves and so far as their givenness is concerned, they have in some sense an independent character, but if they are to be interpreted they must be conceptualised. This conceptualisation (*savikalpa*) is derived from the mind and as such does not belong to them in their character as the merely "given". Conceptualisation unites the intuition of the moment with what had gone before and this according to Buddhism did not form any part of the intuition.[8] On this point there seems to be a difference between Croce's intuition and this intuition of *nirvikalpa pratyakṣa* of Buddhism ; for, Croce's intuition is a concrete something standing independently by itself though in some cases it may be in the case of civilised men impregnated with concepts. It certainly includes perception but it is not limited to it, as imagination has an equal right to be treated as intuition. The perception of pen or paper before me is certainly intuition ; but the image that I may now have of a different pen or paper I had when I was in England is also intuition. Intuition can happen not only of the so-called sensations spatially and temporally arranged, but also of mental things, such as an emotion of pain, an effort of will. Its another characteristic is that it naturally objectifies itself in expression. Thus Croce says:

"How can we have an intuition of the contour of a region, for example, of the island of Sicily if we are not able to draw it as it is in all its meanderings? Every one can experience the internal illumination which follows upon his success in formulating to himself his impressions and sentiments, but only so far as he is able to formulate them. Sentiments or impressions then, pass, by means of words from the obscure region of the soul into the clarity of the contemplative spirit."

8. *Nyāyabinduṭīkā*, p. 11.

"Intuitive knowledge is expressivc knowledge independent and autonomous in respect to intellectual function ; indifferent to discrimination posterior and empirical to reality and unreality, to formations and perceptions of space and time, even when posterior ; intuition of representation is distinguished as form from what is felt and suffered from the flux or wave of sensation, or from psychic material."

Concept according to Croce is knowledge of relations of things and those things are intuitions ; and concepts would not be possible without intuitions just as intuitions would not be possible without the material of impressions. This river, this lake, this brook would be examples of intuition, but what they are in general (not this or that particular water) would be one single constant concept.

In Buddhism the datum of intuition has indeed an unique form but this is indeterminate and inexpressible. It assumes an expressible form only when it is conceptualised. Yet the datum of intuition is not mere sensations in the European acceptance of the term, it has an unique form corresponding to the object (*svalakṣaṇa*) and it is this that constitutes the sensuous datum of the reality in intuition.[9] It is true no doubt that this primary intuitive material when fused with concept may also be considered as being intuited as if it were, yet it cannot be considered as the cognitive object (*dṛśya iva avasīyate tathā'pi na dṛśya eva*). It is the primary part of unique intuition that forms the determinant of the conceptual and though inexpressible in itself, it becomes expressible by the conceptual process that it induces. The unique intuition is always individual whereas the

---

9. *Nyāyabinduṭīkā*, p. 16.

concept is general and universal. It applies to the pen and paper now before me as well as to those that are in a different time and place. It has no unique and individual character.[10] So long as we limit ourselves to the unique character of the individual we are in intuition, when we are in the general we are in the concept. So far as the simple result is concerned, Croce seems to be at one with Buddhism; what constitutes the difference is this that Croce does not only include the intuitive material but also the form, but yet he refers the "general" to the concept. Buddhism also admits that the intuition of the individual has its own unique objectve form. It is the same individual intuitive form which on one hand appears as the "determined" (*vyāyasthāpya*)—the mental, and on the other hand the determinant, the physical. But Buddhism in considering the character of the intuition of the individual can describe it only as unique (*svalakṣaṇa*) whereas Croce regards it as expressive. Here it seems to me that Croce is at a disadvantage, for how can an intuitive datum be expressive without reference to the "general" which according to him is the province of the concept. This in a way he admits, for he says:

> "But, think what one may of these instances, and admitting further that one may maintain that the greater part of the intuitions of civilised man are impregnated with concepts, there yet remains to be observed something more important and conclusive".[11]

---

10. *Nyāyabinduṭīkā*, p. 7.
11. *Aesthetic* I.

But the answer that he gives is that those concepts which have become mingled and fused with unique intuitions have lost all their autonomy and independence and have now become simple elements of intuition. Thus Croce says:—

"Those concepts which are found mingled and fused with intuitions are no longer concepts, in so far as they are really mingled and fused, for they have lost all independence and autonomy. They have been concepts but they have now become simple elements of intuition".[12]

But the fact that the concepts have been fused with intuitions does not according to Buddhism make them lose their conceptual character; Buddhism appreciates however the difference of these concepts from other ordinary concepts by calling them "induced concepts" (*balotpanna*).[13] Without the operation of these "induced concepts" the individual intuition in spite of its unique character, is for want of expressibility, definition and determination non-existent as if it were (*asatkalpam*).[14] The dependent character of the concepts in such cases is also plainly admitted by Buddhism, for it says that here the concepts themselves are in the background and bring out the proper and unique character of the intuition *svavyāpāraṃ tiraskṛtya pratyakṣa-vyāpāram adarśayati.*[15] In all this, Buddhism seems to me to be in the right. This "putting themselves in the background" of the concepts seems also to be plainly admitted by Croce. Thus he says:

12. *Ibid.*
13. *Nyāyabinduṭīkā*, p. 19.
14. *Ibid.*
15. *Ibid*, p. 20.

"The philosophical maxims placed in the mouth of a personage of tragedy or of comedy, perform there the functions not of concepts but of characteristics of such a personage ; in the same way as the red in a painted figure does not there represent the red colour of the physicist but the characteristic element of the portrait."[16]

From this point I must pass on to Croce's distinction of concepts and pseudo-concepts or fictions. Concepts according to Croce have a truly universal character and they therefore apply even to the smallest fragment of representable life. The fictional concepts are different from these for their content is furnished by a group of representations or by single representations which are not ultra-representative. Taking examples of the fictional concepts of the first type as house, can we see that they are but convenient symbols of certain individuals however great their number may be. But a true concept having a perfectly universal character, say, for example, *quality, development* or *beauty* are such that we cannot conceive of any reality given representation which exhausts in itself any of these, *quality, development* or *beauty*. True concepts are indentical with logical thinking and pseudo-concepts are only made as fictions. True concepts being the outcome of logical activity are not only universal and expressive, but they are concrete also, for though a concept transcends all and every intuition which it concerns, it is also immanent in the intuition. Concept thus is a form of knowledge as distinct from the intuition which is always singular and individual. Just as the works

16. *Aesthetic* I.

of great artists and poets are intuitions as much as the poorest intuitions of the humblest human being, so the discoveries of great philosophers are as much concepts as the simplest reasonings or the exercise of logical activity of ordinary men. Pseudo-concepts, however, are mere fictions invented for the practical need of classification or of enumeration and calculation and are dependent on the logical activity as resulting in pure concepts. Human knowledge has a two-fold form, as intuition and as concept; they may be distinguished as two distinct elements not in the relation of before and after but as inseparable in the unity of synthetic mental activity. The conception of the concept is not a lifeless doctrine but is the result of the continuous activity of the mind striving for grasping significance. The unity of intuitions and concepts is the synthesis *a priori* which is the fundametal logic of all philosophy. The logical activity of synthesis *a priori,* though it is dependent on intuition for its material, without which it will be barren and empty, is in itself autonomous and independent which is not derived from experience but is the condition of all experiences. Thus Croce says:

"The concept is a logical *a priori* synthesis, and therefore a unity of subject and predicate, unity in distinction, a distinction in unity, an affirmation of the concept and a judgment of the fact, philosophy and history together. In pure and actual thinking, the two elements constitute an indivisible organism. We cannot affirm a fact without thinking it, we cannot think without affirming a fact. In logical thinking, the presentation without the concept is blind, it is a pure presentation unfurnished with logical light, it is not the subject of a judgment; the concept without the presentation is void."[17]

17. *Logica,* p. 293 (Carr's translated quotation).

Subject to the reservation already referred to, the similarity of the Buddhist doctrine with that of Croce, naturally strikes as deserving an enquiry. The difference between the *svalakṣaṇa* and *sāmānya-lakṣaṇa*, which are in some sense the equivalents of Croce's intuition and concepts, the individual and the universal, has already been noticed. These two also represent two distinct moments, but not of time as 'before' and 'after' but in the same synthetic unity of thought. Thus Kīrtti says:—Right knowledge consists in the similarity of the object with its knowledge. It is supposed that a knowledge must have the same characteristic as the object from which it arises; that which arises from blue is like blue. But it may be contended that the similarity of characteristics is identical with the knowledge itself, and if this is so then the objectification (*pramāṇa-phala*) and the awareness as right knowledge (*pramāṇa*) becomes identical and how can one thing be both the producer (*sādhanā*) and the produced (*sādhya*)? How would not this go against the view which defines right knowledge as consisting of similarity of characteristics (*sādṛśya*). The answer to such a question is that the knowledge of objects arises out of similarity. If there is an awareness as blue (*nīlanirbhāsaṃ vijñānaṃ*), we say a blue object has been perceived. But the affirmation that "blue" has been perceived cannot be made by the visual organ through which knowledge is said to have arisen. When there is an intuition like the blue, the affirmation is determined that there has been the perception of the blue. There is nothing like the relation of the producer and the produced (*janya-janaka-bhāva*) that aforesaid objection can be made that it could not take place in the very same thing. The relation could certainly be of the type of the determined and the determiner (*avasthāpyā-vasthāpaka-bhāvena*). So the same entity could both be the awareness and the object pointed out by it (*pramāṇaphala*). The cause of determination is similarity of characteristics. It is the intuition as "blue awareness" which is the determiner of the affirmation of knowledge "blue has been perceived, by virtue of the affirmative element preceeding out of it." This affirmation being of the nature of negation of opposites conforms to the positive "blue awareness" as definite knowledge. This affirmative element however belongs to the 'induced concepts'.[18] The above observations, though expressed in a quaint antiquated style, show that the 'intuition' involving the primary object-characteristic, the object which is referred to by it, and the affirmatory concept involving a negative and a positive aspect are all fused together in one moment as one identical entity or synthetic unity. The division of moments is one of abstraction and analysis. Reserving our remarks for the present regarding the relation of the "awareness" and the "object" pointed out by it, it may be said that what is given in one moment as one identical entity (*ekasmin vastuni*) is the affirmed awareness, involving rudimentary intuition and the induced concept arising out of it. Kīrtti disapproves the idea that conceptual affirmation and objectification may proceed as the natural evolution and development of the intuitive element alone. Though the intuitive element represents the unique object-characteristic,

18. *Nyāyabinduṭīkā*, p. 19.

yet it is devoid of the affirmatory character without which it remains unaffirmed, non-existent as it were. It is only by virtue of the concept integrated with it that the awareness is affirmed as intuition-concept and objectified. Thus without the intuition the concept is barren and void and without the concept the intuition is meaningless. The distinction of intuition and concept as appertaining to two different moments is one of abstraction, for the two are integrated together in one *a priori* synthesis. This synthesis, it must be observed, is not derived from posterior experience, but it is induced by virtue of the intuition out of its own law which is independent yet concordant with the intuition with which it is concerned.

But does Buddhism observe the distinction of concepts and pseudo-concepts or fictional concepts as Croce does, and if so in what way? For this I must turn to *Sāmānyadūṣaṇadikprasāritā* of Pandita Aśoka.. The distinction that Croce points out that true concepts are omni-universal, whereas pseudo-concepts refer either to groups of representations or single representations (e.g., triangle, free motion) is not suggested by Buddhism. But Buddhism in its own way denies reality to the pseudo-concepts. The main point of Pandita Aśoka's argument is that no such eternal class concepts can be intuited as standing apart from the momentary appearances. Among the distinct momentary entities unity is no doubt revealed but such an unity is always realised within the progressive series, but it never stands out abstractly isolated from it as an eternal class-concept. Universals certainly are manifested but there are no innumerable class-concepts having a dual or multiple existence side by side with the concrete individuals. As an individual in a series points itself through the affirmative process involving an oscillation as it were negating the opposites and affiliating itself with the likes, the universal with which such a position is concerned is expressed or revealed. That an unity is felt in the distincts in their manifestation or appearance, no one denies, but the point is, that there is no justification for the view that this is felt on account of the induced influence of corresponding universals existing by themselves. Pandita Aśoka in a long series of arguments refutes the reasons that may be adduced in favour of such a view. His own view is, as I have just mentioned, that the affirmation of each individual involves, by that very fact, a negation of the opposites and the sense of an unification along with it ; this is integral to the process of each and every affirmation, and the result of this is manifested as universals or concepts which have therefore no separate existence apart from the positing process of the concrete individuals.[19] Pandit Aśoka thus does not make any distinction between concepts and the pseudo-concepts but considers all universal as proceeding out of the synthetic activity involved in the positing of an individual.

Croce rightly claims to have modified Hegel's theory of opposites by his theory of distincts in the conception of the dialectic and, in spite of outstanding similarities of his views with that of Hegel, Croce should more properly be called a Vichian rather than

19. *Six Buddhist Nyāya Tracts*, p. 99.

a Hegelian.[20] In the doctrine concerning the organism of the pure concept, it accepts the *dialectic* view or the unity of opposites, but denies its immediate validity for the distinctions of the concept, the unity of which is organized as the unity of distinctions in the theory of degrees of reality. The Buddhist dialectic as *a priori* synthesis of opposites and distincts is however somewhat different from the Hegelian dialectic. What we learn about it from the acute and able discussion of Ratnakīrtti in his *Apohasiddhi* is that each individual appearance implicitly involves by virtue of its own manifestations a world of negations of itself, what are opposed or distinct from it (*anyabhāvaviśiṣṭo vijātivyāvṛtto'rthovidhiḥ*).[21] It acknowledges the difference between opposites (*vijāti*) and distinct (*anya*) but it neither, like Croce, indulges in a quadruple division of the forms of the spirit, nor lays any stress on the theory of distincts as having a special significance. Any particular appearance is identical with the negations involved in it which differentiate it from all other intuitions, but only implicitly; and it is the particular concept that works in a concerted way with it that reveals one or other of these negations as occasion arises. The intuition is something different from the concept *vikalpa*. But there is such a concordance between the two that what is implicit in the intuition is made explicit by the concept, such that in all our ordinary perceptions the intuition and the concept become fused together in such a way that,

20. See Croce's *What Is Living And What Is Dead Of the Philosophy Of Hegel.*

21. *Apohasiddhi*, p. 18.

though all our ordinary perceptions are complexes of intuitions and concept, they appear as indivisible intuitions, and hardly lead us to suspect their mixed nature. But without the explicating movement of the concept the intuitions held in their own implicitude could hardly have any expressible form. The negation involved in any particular intuition is reflected or manifested by the concept which always appears in an *a priori* synthesis with the intuition. Thus Jayanta in the course of stating the Buddhist position says that the elements of negation are reflected in the conceptual movement (*vikalpapratibimbaka*), and that they are all but forms of knowledge (*jñānākārakameva*). They as well as the universals, opposites and distincts which the conceptual activity manifests arise as the result of the previous history of the preceding members of the series of appearances which in that peculiar form of *vāsanā* (involving memory, reminiscences, mental history, cultural and historical situation of the mind) determine the intuition and the nature of the conceptual activity concerned with it (*vicitravāsanābhedopahitarūpabhedaṃ*).[22] But as the perceiver, perception, intuition, co-operative concerted action of the concept take place at one moment of time in one act of synthetic activity, all these stages abstracted by analysis become all fused together in one intuitive appearance.

Such a view in philosophy naturally leads to a non-formalist logic and this is recognised by Croce who came to know of the distinctions of *sārthānumāna*

---

22. *Nyāyamañjarī*, p. 308.

and *parārthānumāna* from H. Jacobi's paper *"Die Indische Logic"* in the Nachrichten v. d. Konigl Gesellschaft. d. Wissenschaft zu Gottingen, though he had hardly any opportunity of knowing the acuteness, subtlety and depth of thought found in most systems of Indian logic which explains his uninformed belief that Indian logic was much inferior to that of Greece as regards the wealth and depth of concepts. He speaks of the antiverbalist character of Buddhist logic. Thus says Croce:

"Indian Logic (by which he can only mean the non-Hindu Logic—Buddhist Logic in particular—excepting the treatise of Bhāsarvajña) studies the naturalistic syllogism *in itself*, as internal thought, distinguishing it from the syllogism *from others* that is to say, from the more or less usual but always extrinsic and accidental forms of communication and dispute. It has not even a suspicion of the extravagant idea (which still vitiates our treaties) of a truth which is merely syllogistic and formalist and which may be false in fact. It takes no account of the judgment or rather it considers what is called judgment, and what is really proposition, as a verbal clothing of knowledge: it dees not make the verbal distinctions of subject, copula and predicate ; it does not admit classes of categorical and hypothetical of affirmative and negative judgments. All these are extraneous to logic, whose object is the constant knowledge considered in itself".[23]

Syllogism in Buddhism consists of the rise of cognitions of some reality comparable to intuitions, proceeding out of identity, causal relation or a perception of absence. A mere formal syllogism without having any reference to any particular intuition has no place in Buddhism. The final reference is always to the concrete individual. The difference between perception and inference consists only in the mode

23. *Logic* IV, 4.

of the application of the concept of *a priori* synthesis. Thus when the concrete individual is suggested merely by virtue of the application of the concept of identity and causality, we call it inference (***anumāna***), and when the concrete individual is presented by the fusion of an immediate and implicit datum of perception with the concepts we call it *pratyakṣa*. It is on account of this non-formalist view of Logic that the Buddhists preferred to accept the *antarvyāpti* doctrine (i.e., the view that the relation of concomittance holds directly in a general way between two concepts) to the ordinary *bahirvyāpti* view of other schools of Indian logic (involving enumeration of a specific instance where such concomittance has been observed).

I shall now pass on to the last and most important aspect of the general agreement of Croce's philosophy with that of the Yogācāra school of Buddhism—the absolute spirituality of everything. According to Croce, there are two ultimate types of spiritual creation—as knowledge and as will or activity. The first has two forms relating to individual intuitions and concepts which are universal in their character and which though independent and autonomous in themselves have the intuitions as their materials. The other type, the activity, has also two forms, that relating to the individual good or economical and that relating to the universal good or utilitarian, and here also, as in intuition and concept, the two are interrelated. But these two ultimate types are not parallel but one is bound always with the other. Thus Croce says in his *Philosophy Of The Practical*:

"From the aesthetic apprehension of reality, from philosophical reflection upon it, from historical reconstruction, which is its result, is obtained that knowledge of the actual situation, on which alone is formed and can be formed the volitional and practical synthesis, the new action. And this new action is in its turn the material of the new aesthetic figuration of the new philosophical reflection of the new historical reconstruction. In short, knowledge and will, theory and practice are not two parallels, but two lines such that the head of the one is joined to the tail of the other . . . . . . They constitute therefore the circle of reality and of life . . . . ."[24]

Every form which reality assumes or can assume for us has its ground within mind. There cannot be a reality which is not mind. Reality being thus identical with mind, it is only its forms that we may distinguish. Thus Croce says:

"If being is conceived as external to the human spirit, and knowledge as separable from its object, so much so that the object could be without being known, it is evident that the existence of the object becomes a position or something placed for the spirit, given to the spirit, extraneous to it, which the spirit would never appropriate to itself unless it were courageously to swallow the bitter mouthful with an irrational act of faith. But all the philosophy which we are now developing demonstrates that there is nothing external to the spirit, and therefore there are no positions opposed to it. These very conceptions of something external, mechanical, natural, have shown themselves to be conceptions not of external positions but of positions of the spirit itself, which creates the so-called external, because it suits it to do so, as it suits it to annul this creation, when it is no longer of use. On the other hand it has never been possible to discover in the circle of the spirit that mysterious and unqualifiable faculty called faith, which is said to be an intuition that intuites the universals or a thinking of the universal without the logical process of thought."[25]

Nature thus is not a concept of something real but it is the hypostasis of a manner of elaborating

24. *Philosophy Of The Practical* II. 3

25. *Logic*, pp. 127, 173.

reality not philosophical but practical. Its concept thus is only a function of the spirit.

All reality, whether it be intuitions, concepts or activity are therefore but creations of the spirit which follows its own law in all its theoretic and practical activity. But apart from these creations there is nothing in the spirit which one may be trying to get at. The spirit is identical with its endless process of unfolding—the *a priori* synthesis. Thus Croce says in one place—"The *a priori* synthesis belongs to all the forms of the spirit; indeed the spirit considered universally is nothing but *a priori synthesis.*" The view of Yogācāra Buddhism is largley akin to the general position of Croce as indicated by his above views though its divisions of the modes of operations of the spirit are different. It holds that two different modes of operation are found in our understanding, one is called the *pravicayabuddhi* or the conceptual mode and the other is called the *vikalpalakṣaṇa-grahābhiniveśa-pratiṣṭhāpikā-buddhi,* or the function of the spirit by which intuitive materials are supplied for the application of the conceptual activity. The first mode always seeks to take things in either of the following four ways that they are either this or the other, either both or not both, either are or are not, either eternal or non-eternal. The second mode consists of that habit of the mind by virtue of which it constructs diversities and arranges them (created in their turn by its own constructive activity—*parikalpa*) in a logical order of diverse relations of subject and predicate, causal and other relations. He who knows the nature of these two categories of the mind knows that there is no external world of matter, and that they are all experienced only in the mind. There is no water, but it is the sense-construction of smoothness that constructs the water as an external substance ; it is the sense-construction of activity or energy that constructs the external substance of fire ; it is the sense-construction of movement that constructs the so-called external substance of air. In reality there is nothing which is produced or destroyed. It is only our constructive imagination that builds up things as perceived with all their relations, and ourselves as perceivers.[26] Though all these forms are but creations of the mind there is no further entity of mind which is to be sought beyond these creations. Nor will it pay any research to enquire into the intrinsic substance of these creations apart from their appearance in a series. All creations are thus spiritual without there being anything abiding as the permanent spirit, which may be known beyond their creations. This view of Buddhism must be distinguished from the Vedāntic idealism particularly in such works as *Vedāntasiddhāntamuktāvalī* of Prakāśānanda or the like, where though all perceptible reality is said to be of the nature of concept yet there is one truth the spirit of which remains as the unchangeable ground of all.[27] For in Buddhism there was no way of ascertaining the nature of the spirit, for it did not exist as an abiding reality apart from these passing creations. The conditions which led to the rise of any appearance are determined by the result or the

26. *Laṅkāvatārasūtra*, p. 85 and also Dasgupta's *A History Of Indian Philosophy*, Vol. I, p. 148.

27. *Pundit*. Benares, 1889.

history of the preceding series. This view of Buddhism which has already been mentioned must however be distinguished from somewhat similar views of Yoga as elaborated by Vyāsa and Bhikṣu. There the past and the future exist in the present as the latent and true potential. There history is present existence, and universal history is to reality what to each individual his own particular history is. For according to Yoga though every existence is momentary, nothing is lost, but everything that is past is conserved in the present and abides in it. Philosophy of any particular event or state is its history. But in Buddhism, as I have already explained, this is true in a somewhat different sense. There is nothing here that abides, but the cause of the rise of any appearance is its place in the history of true series, and there is no other philosophy of its own except the reference to the history of its rise.

The main points where I have compared or contrasted Croce with Buddhism are all fundamental with both of them. These are: —(1) anti-metaphysical character, (2) ideality of philosophy and history, (3) intuition and concept, (4) anti-verbalist character of logic, (5) spiritual nature of all phenomena.

GENERAL INTRODUCTION TO TANTRA PHILOSOPHY

The word "Tantra" has been derived in the *Kāśikā-vṛtti* in connection with the rule *titutra-tathasisusarakaseṣu ca* (7. 2. 9.) from the root *tan* to spread, by the *auṇādika* rule *sarvadhātubhyaḥ ṣṭran* with the addition of the suffix *ṣṭran*. Vācaspati Ānandagiri and Govindānanda, however, derive the word from the root *tatri* or *tantri* in the sense of (*vyutpādana*) origination, or knowledge. In *Gaṇa-pāṭha* however *tantri* has the same meaning as *tan* (to spread) and it is probable that the former root is a modification of the latter. The meaning *vyutpādana* is also probable derived by narrowing the general sense of *vistāra* which is the meaning of the root *tan*. It is natural therefore to expect that the word "Tantra" should be used to denote any kind of elaboration generally, and in conformity with such an expectation we find that the word is used in diverse meanings such as ceremonies, rites, rituals, doctrine, theory, science, or any scientific work and the like. The works on Sāṅkhya Philosophy were known as *Saṣti-Tantra-Śāstra,* and Śaṅkara also in explaining the *Brahma Sūtra, Smṛtyanavakāśa-doṣa-prasaṅga iti cet nānya-smṛtya-anavakāśa-doṣa-prasaṅgāt* speaks of Sāṅkhya as a Tantra written by a great sage (*smṛtiśca tantrākhyā paramarṣi-praṇītā*). Similarly in the *Mahābhārata* 12/7663 we read *nyāya-tantrāṇyanekāni taistai ruktāni vādibhiḥ*. So also we hear of a *Dharmatantra* as in *sasarja dharmatantrāṇi pūrvot-*

pannaḥ prajāpatiḥ, of a *Brahmatantra* as in *Brahmatantraṃ niṣebibhiḥ* (Harivaṃśa 12019), of a *Yogatantra* as in *yatayo Yogatantreṣu yān stuvanti dvijātayḥ*, of the *Āyurvedatantra* as in *aṣṭāsvāyurvedatantreṣu* (Suśruta 1. 3. 13) and also in a general way as in *vede ca tantre ca te eva kovidāḥ* (Bhāgabat) or as in *tena ca śiṣyopaśiṣyadvāreṇa loke vahulīkṛtaṃ tantraṃ*.

It is indeed needless to multiply examples of this kind to show that the word Tantra had a very wide latitude of meaning and was used loosely to denote any kind of Scientific or Philosophical literature which was more modern than the Vedic literature. Later on however the term Tantra was generally used in an exclusive sense to denote a body of writings comprehending the whole culture of a certain epoch in diverse directions such as religion, ritual, domestic rites, law, medicine, magic and so forth.

The special characteristic of the last mentioned literature which goes by the name of Tantra is this that it has preserved within itself all the important results of Indian culture which preceded it from the time of the Vedas and has attempted to reconcile them all in its own way. The *Karmakāṇḍa* of the Vedas, the Mīmāṃsā, the Vedānta, the Sāṅkhya, the Yoga, the Vaiṣṇava, the medical systems of Caraka and Suśruta, and the Purāṇas can all be traced in the Tantras as forming the different limbs of the body of its doctrines. But these have all been recast in a way which instilled a new life and vigour into it for many generations. Some of the peculiarities of its dogmas and doctrines may indeed appear very strange to many but those who have grasped the philosophy of this movement cannot but be struck with its bold and original method. In these days of scepticism and rationalism there is no doubt it often becomes difficult for us to appreciate the value of many of its dogmas (some of which would often appear so shocking to us) or to concede to some of its philosophical theories, or methods of religious practice, but to a student who can rise above his own individual likings and dislikings, it is bound to throw new lights and reveal many missing links in the history of the development of the religious practices of India.

The monistic philosophy of the Vedānta forms its backbone and we see that Brahman is regarded as the only true Principle of the world. Thus we read in the *Mahānirvāṇa Tantra* 3. 6-9.

sattāmātraṃ nirviśeṣam avāṅmānasagocaram
asattrilokīsadbhānaṃ svarūpaṃ brahmaṇaḥ smṛtam.
samādhiyogaistadvedyaṃ sarvatra samadṛṣṭibhiḥ
dvandātītair nirvikalpair dehātmādhyāsa-varjitaiḥ.
yato viśvaṃ samudbhūtaṃ yena jātañ ca tiṣṭhati.
yasmin sarvāṇi līyante jñeyaṃ tad brahma-lakṣaṇaiḥ.
svarūpabudhyā yad vedyaṃ tad eva lakṣaṇaiḥ śive.
lakṣaṇair āptumicchūnāṃ vihitaṃ tatra sādhanam.

"That which is changeless, existent only, and beyond both mind and speech, which shines as the Truth amidst the illusion of the three worlds, is the Brahman according to its real nature. That Brahman is known in *samādhi-yoga* by those who look upon all things alike, who are above all contraries, devoid of doubt, free of all illusions regarding body and soul. That same Brahman is known from his external signs, from whom the whole universe has sprung, in whom when so sprung, it exists, and unto whom all things return. That which is known by intuition may also be perceived from these external signs. For those who would know him through these external signs, *sādhana* is enjoined."

With Śaṅkara Vedānta however all *upāsanā* means knowledge or intuition. The value of *sādhana* is purificatory and lies in cleansing the mind of its impurities, so that the mind when once purged of its dross can at once feel its unity with Brahman in one act of intuition. All emphasis therefore is laid there on this intuitive side, whereas here, though the claims of the unity is fully recognised, the Brahman appears like the *Parameśvara* of the Vaiṣṇavas in its adorable aspect as *Īśvara* or *Īśvarī*. Thus we find that there is a form of *Brahma upāsanā* such as we do not get in the Śaṅkara Vedānta.

But it does not stop here, but presupposing the great importance of subjective experiences and convictions in religion goes on to say that for suiting the limitations of the worshipper the formless Brahman may be conceived as being possessed of form. The intellectual or spiritual incapacity of the worshipper may lead him on one side to think of an imaginary form of the formless and may also on the other hand quicken the lifeless form of an image with life simply by his faith. Thus the *Kulārṇava* says:

cinmayasyā'prameyasya
nirguṇasyā'śarīriṇaḥ.
sādhakānāṃ hitārthāya
brahmaṇaḥ rūpakalpanā.
* * * *
sattānāṃ nirviśeṣaṃ ca
avāṃ-mānasa-gocaram
sādhakasya ca viśvāsāt
sātvikī devatā bhavet.

It is for the benefit of the worshipper that the bodyless, qualityless, unfathomable Brahman of the nature of thought is imagined to be endowed with form. * * * * By the faith of his worshipper the *devatā* becomes spiritualised (*sāttvikī*). It is the fetishistic mind which makes its God a fetish and realises itself through it. Here we see that the Tantra has tried to reconcile the plurality of Gods and Goddesses of the Purāṇas with the Unity of the Vedāntists. It must, however, be said that this attempt had already been begun in the Purāṇas themselves and in other philosophical literatures.

Turning to the Tāntric metaphysics we find that the world is in one sense unreal and illusory as with the Vedāntists, for it owes its existence to the connection of *māyā* with Brahman; but the *māyā* is here not *tattvānyatvābhyām anirvacanīyam* (an unspeakable entity whose truth or falsehood cannot be affirmed) as in Vedānta, but possesses as much reality as the Brahman or rather is identical with him. Looked at from this point of view, the unreality of the world with the Tāntrikas is not of the same order as that of the Vedāntists, for it has been produced out of the Śakti which has the same integral reality as that of the Brahman. The change and "many" of the world are unreal so far as they are but the assumed modifications and forms of the same indentity of *māyā* in Brahman, and the Brahman in *māyā*, Śiva in Śakti and Śakti in Śiva. But they are real so far as they are the modifications of the real. The conceptual and other difficulties of such a philosophic position, the Tantra had not to face, for it was not a system of philosophy. It was essentially a religious form of worship the Tantra had to teach and the philosophic conception was only in the background.

In the material order of things, therefore, they could easily connect themselves with the Sāṅkhya or the Yoga metaphysics. There have been principally three orders of materialists in India, the Sāṅkhya, the Vaiśeṣika and the Buddhists, but we find that every system of thought in later days which conceded any reality to the external world borrowed from the Sāṅkhya their *prakṛti*, *buddhi*, *ahaṅkāra*, the *tanmātras*, and *aṇus* with such modifications as suited them. Thus the categories of the Sāṅkhya were admitted by the Tantra partly after the Sāṅkhya fashion and partly also after the Yoga fashion as it did not leave the movement in the hand of a blind destiny but had the *Īśvara* as the director of the movement. But it differed from them both in the most vital point, for with it, the *prakṛti*, *puruṣa*, and the *Īśvara* had the same identical reality and all that which appears as external, real *pariṇāma* (change), is really but the *sadṛśa-pariṇāma* taking place in the body of the *Īśvara*. Looked at from an external point of view, it appears as emanations in time, whereas it is all subsumed in one and the same movement in the body of the Lord. The same movement which appears as *pariṇāma* from one point of view appears as *vivarta* from another point of view.

The duality of the Tantra is thus, we see, not that of the Sāṅkhya or the Yoga. It is not also that of the Nyāya or the Vaiśeṣika inasmuch as the world as the atomic constitution has no existence or reality separate from God as with them. It is not the duality of Rāmānuja, as this world and the *jīvas* were not regarded to form a real composite body of *Īśvara* in the Tantra ; for here what appeared as the change and many outside was really but the self-identical change in the Lord. The Lord could not be differentiated as distinct from his own *Śakti* or the power of change even. So there could be no question here of thinking that the material world as such and the individual souls as such formed the body of the Lord.

It is, therefore, also clear that such a position cannot be the dualism of Madhva, who denied the *Īśvara* to be the material cause of the world and held that the individual souls and the inanimate world were entirely different from him. It is significant, however, to note that his conception of *Lakṣmī* reminds one of the relation of *Śiva* and *Śakti,* though here also it may be pointed out that *Śakti* is not like *Lakṣmī* regarded as distinct from the supreme Soul or *Śiva* in the Tantra.

It differs from that of Nimbārka in this that there it was held that Brahman had some qualities or capacities in Him which were of the nature of animate and inanimate worlds. There is a subtle form constituted of its natural condition. When Brahman realises His capacities and develops the subtle rudiment existent in Him in a gross form the visible material world is produced. We can easily contrast it with the Tantra view for we know that the qualities of *Īśvara* had never been attempted to be decomposed in this manner here. There was no such differentiation of parts of *Īśvara* as with Nimbārka, so that some of them constituted the universe and others did not. *Īśvara* is *sakala* and *niṣkala, saguṇa* and *nirguṇa,* both. When His *śakti* was regarded as different from Him with which He was united for the production of the creation, we call Him *saguṇa ;* but when we look at Him as being one with *śakti* or in other words when we do not look upon *śakti* as having a different reality from Him, He is *nirguṇa.*

Thus the Tantra system of thought can neither be called dualistic nor monistic. When we find the stress or emphasis to the monistic side as in the *Mahānirvāṇa Tantra* or the *Gandharva Tantra,* we may be disposed to call it monistic, but if we look at the dualism on the *sādhana* side we may be tempted to call it dualistic or pluralistic just as we please. Thus *Kulārṇava* says:

advaitaṃ kecidicchanti dvaitamicchanti cā'pare
mama tattvaṃ vijānanto dvaitā-dvaita-vivarjitam.

(Some conceive my reality as being one, others conceive it as dual, whereas the wise know it to be neither dual nor one).

The difficulty of this apparently dualistic position was removed in a real philosophic way. Thus first we find that *Śiva* is *prakāśa,* pure illumination, or abstract self-shining thought and *Śakti* is *vimarśa* or the inherent activity of thought. Thought and its inherent activity cannot be viewed as distinct from one another as one is involved in the notion of the other. The conception of the nature of thought involves its own activity. That which appears in its abstractions as pure *prakāśa* in one aspect or moment appears in its other aspect as *vimarśa* in the other moment. The conception of this notion may, therefore, be explained after the Sāṅkhya attempt of the identification of *mahat* or *buddhi* with *puruṣa.* There we read that the *buddhi* or *mahat* as it resembles the pure character of the *puruṣa* can stand in such a relation to it that the *puruṣa* is pure and *mahat* also being *sattva-guṇa-maya* is also pure, and, as such, they mutually reflect each other and are identified. The two are, however, different and this illusory identification is the cause of the production of the world order. But here we find that *prakāśa* is imaged in *vimarśa* which stands as a reflector which reflects the real nature of the *prakāśa. Prakāśa* comes to know of its own true nature only when it perceives itself as reflected through its *kriyā-śakti* or *vimarśa.* Abstract thought as such cannot posit its true nature. It is only when it returns back to itself through its own movement (*kriyā* or *vimarśa*) that it can posit itself and manifest itself as the Egohood. First point is the point of Pure Illumination, second point is the point of *vimarśa* and the third point is the unity of them both, the return of the *prakāśa* through *vimarśa* as the Egohood. The first point in Tantra is called the white *vindu,* the second red and the third black. The conception of this action of unification is only that of differentiation in the integrated. The One unperturbed whole holds within itself the point of *prakāśa, vimarśa* and their unification as the Egohood. This unperturbed whole is called in the Tantra the *mahāvindu.* In the Vedānta also the Ego (*aham*) springs out of the unification of Brahman with *māyā.* But there *māyā* is conceived as unreal and so the unity is also unreal ; but here the *vimarśa* is conceived as being involved in the reality of the *prakāśa,* through which the *prakāśa* reflects itself or returns back to itself and realises itself as the Ego. In analogy with the *vikṣepa-śakti* of *māyā* here also we find the *āvaraṇa-devatās,* but these are conceived here as the real transformations of the *śakti* in its process of self development. It is, therefore, a synthesis of the dualistic and the monistic and the essence of this synthesis is the subsumption of the conceptual system of thought in the "Elan", *śakti* or *spanda.* As the phenomena of *suṣupti* (dreamless sleep), *svapna,* (dream) and *jāgrata* (awakened state of consciousness) all three form together an important illustration round which the Vedāntic conceptions, such as the resolution of the colourless Brahman into the manifold without and the like, have collected themselves so it is that we find that the phenomena of the production of the sound occupy an extremely important position in the development of the Tāntric ideals. How the formless is endowed with millions of names and forms, how the colourless one could be resolved into the "many" is indeed the vital question in all philosophy. The conceptual or the philosophical difficulty of the position is enhanced by the fact that in our ordinary sphere of concrete life we do not generally find any such thing with which we can associate or compare it in order to visualise the philosophic position for common comprehension. This was also so necessary in India, where philosophy was not regarded as a matter for study only but the highest reality of life, the goal of realisation for each and every individual from the lowest peasant to the highest monarch. The Vedānta, therefore, pointed out the analogy of *suṣupti* (dreamless sleep) resolving itself into the *jāgrata* and other illustrations such as the reflection of the Sun in water etc., to explain the identification of the Brahman and the *māyā*. The Sāṅkhya offered the illustration of the reflection of the *jabā* flower on crystal, of a prince brought up in the house of a *caṇḍāla* and the like to give a practical help for an easy comprehension of the difficult points of the theory.

But there was another analogy which had hitherto been imperfectly utilised and which was developed and elaborated in all its details for the first time in the Tantra and served to symbolise the philosophical position of the Tantra. I refer to the production of sound.

We know that at the very dawn of philosophic speculation in India in the Mīmāṃsā school of thought *śabda* or sound was regarded as eternal. To take a brief review of the Mīmāṃsā doctrine of sound we see first that sound with them was always in the form of alphabet which being perceived by the ear goes by the name of sound. All sounds must be in the shape of some alphabet or other. There is nothing like indistinct or confused sound or mere *dhvani*. The word is also not in any way different from the letters which compose it. In the perception of a word the diverse perceptions of the letters owing to their close proximity coalesce and give us the notion of one perception though it is really but the combination of the many sounds. The idea of the word, however, should be regarded as One, as it admits of the denotation of one thing only. The word is nothing apart from the letters. The order of sequence belongs not to the letters but to the sounds and through these sounds it is imposed upon the letters that are manifested by the sounds. It is, therefore, that the letters alone can be held as being expressive.

The *artha* of the word is that which is denoted or expressed by it. The denotativeness of words is absolutely independent of human agency and belongs to the words by their very nature. When we do not understand the meaning of a word we cannot assume that the word is not denotative. On the other hand it is to be supposed that there is some peculiar power which is absent in us on account of which the denotation of the meaning has not been revealed to us. The word denotes a meaning, but in order to understand it, it is presupposed that we should have a knowledge of it. So the power of the hearer lies in this that he should have the knowledge of the fact that the word is expressive of such and such a meaning. Thus the expressiveness of the word is something that belongs to it by its very nature independent of any human agency.

Again, the denotative potency of a word has no

beginning in time and is, therefore, as eternal as the word itself. The word itself has no beginning for the simple reason that the thing it denotes has also no beginning, for the world itself with them had no beginning. All men have been applying the same names to the same things from time immemorial. So the denotations of common words must be eternal and not conventional.

The words themselves are also eternal, but the reason of their not being present to our consciousness is this that it requires some auxiliary agent to make them cognisable to our consciousness. This agent is the effort of the man in pronouncing a word. This effort produces an effect through intermediate stages on the auditory organ of the hearer and manifests or reveals the word already in existence. The several moments or stages in the physiological processes of speech may thus be shown. (1) The speaker puts forth an effort. (2) This effort brings the soul in contact with the air enclosed in the lungs. (3) In obedience to the impulse imported by the effort the air rises upwards. (4) In its upward progress it comes into contact with the vocal chords lying about the various regions of the body. (5) These contacts change the character of the air to a certain extent. (6) On issuing from the mouth the air passes onwards and reaches the ear of the persons. (7) On reaching the ear it produces a certain change which conduces to make it audible or manifest it. Though there are so many different stages in the process of the manifestations of the sound, the word has no cause bringing it into existence and thus it has the same eternality that belongs to *ākāśa*.

If we remember these main views of the Mimāṃsakas on sound it will be easier for us to comprehend how and with what modifications the Tantra grafted this on their composite of Sāṅkhya-Vedānta doctrine and the elaborate method of their religious practices. The Tantra assumes that the movement which has produced the world shows itself or is represented in us in miniature in the production of the sound. The process of the production of the sound is the epitome of the notion as it were of the cosmic process of creation. The same process which underlies the cosmic creation manifests itself in us in every case of the productions of sounds, so that the genesis of sounds is not to be taken as imaginary but a real symbol of the creative process. The Mīmāṃśakas regarded *śabda* and *artha* as mere inanimate or *acetana*. So the eternality there, was without any notion ; but the Tantra asserted that it is the spirit or intelligence which realises itself as the *śabda* and *artha,* mind and matter. Thus *Sāradā* says:

bhidyamānāt parād vindor
avyaktā-tma-ravo' bhavat,
śabda-brahmeti taṃ prāhuḥ
sarvāgama-viśāradāḥ.
śabda-brahmeti śabdā-rthaṃ
śabdam ity apare jaguḥ
na hi teṣāṃ tayoḥ siddhiḥ jaḍatvād ubhayor api.
caitanyaṃ sarva-bhūtānāṃ
śabda-brahmeti me matiḥ
tatprāpya kuṇḍalī-rūpaṃ
prāṇiṇāṃ deha-madhyagaṃ
varṇā-tmanā'virbhavati
gadya-padya-vibhedataḥ.

When the ultimate *vindu* splits itself there was an unmanifested sound of the Ego. It is this that is called *śabda-brahma* by those that are versed in all the *Āgamas.* Others would also call it *śabda-brahma, śabdā-rtha* or *śabda* but with them such a position is not tenable as with them both *śabda* and *artha* are inanimate. It is the underlying consciousness of all being that I would call *śabda-brahma.* It is this which reveals itself as the alphabets in diverse order as prose and verse at that centre of the living bodies known as *kuṇḍalī.*

Śabda here is not a mere *vyāpāra* or movement, a *śakti,* but its concept is as mystic as the concept of *Īśvara.* It contains within itself three moments of *jñāna* (thought) *ichhā* (will) and *kriyā* or movement in one concept. It is *Śiva* and *Śakti* as One. There is the *śabda-sṛṣṭi,* the creation of the exterior order of the world and the constitution of the human body with its nerves, nerve centres. No one of them is the cause of the other. But all the three are the manifestations of the same movement of the One. So it is that we find that the word *śabdā-rtha-sṛṣṭi* is used to denote the cosmic creation from the formless One as the movement in both the cases is one and the same.

In the Tantra phraseology the *nirguṇa* (formless) Brahman is called *niṣkala-śiva* and in its aspect as combined with *śakti* it is called as *sakala-śiva.* Now *Śakti* in its aspect as one with the formless *Śiva* is called the *para-vindu* or the *kāraṇa-vindu.* From this *kāraṇa-vindu* comes the *kārya-vindu* which represents the *kārya-śiva* and *kārya-śakti.* Their Unity, the *Śiva-Śakti-mithuna-piṇḍa,* is the *aham.* To these three moments may be traced, Will, Thought, and

Movement. The *Śiva* and *Śakti* however should not be taken in reality as representing the male and the female as is generally supposed. For they are styled male and female only to please the popular imagination as a mere linguistic expression. Thus the *Gandharva Tantra* says:

> *śaktir maheśvaro brahma*
> *trayas tulyā-rtha-vācakāḥ*
> *strī-puṃ-napuṃsako bhedaḥ*
> *śabdato na paramārthataḥ.*

Śakti, Maheśvara and Brahman all three signify the same meaning. Their distinction as male, female or neuter is merely due to linguistic usage. These three are also called, *raudrī, jyeṣṭhā* and *vāmā,* the fire, the moon, and the sun. The *vindu* and *bīja* are also characterised as the *sita-vindu* and the *śoṇa-vindu* probably to suggest the comparison of the seed and the ovum. That the *sakala-śiva* springs from the *niṣkala-śiva* who is the form of pure *caitanya* as undistinguished from its other aspect as *Śakti* or the principle of movement, shows that it is Thought with its inherent movement which posits itself as the *sakala-śiva* as the Unity of the three moments of *Jñāna, icchā* and *kriyā.* This movement on one side produces the exterior world-order as composed of the different modifications of the five *bhūtas* and on the other hand the mental order of thought as symbolised by *śabda,* and the body with its net of nerves and nerve centres. This unity of the three *vindus*—the interpenetration of *prakāśa* and *vimarśa* is spoken as the *Kāma-kalā,* the great *Tripurasundarī.* The meaning of the word *kāma-kalā* is described in the *Kāma-kalā-vilāsa* as:

kāmyate, abhilaṣyate svātmatvena paramārtha-mahadbhiḥ yogibhiḥ iti kāmaḥ, tatra hetuḥ kamanīyatayā iti. kamanīyatvaṃ spṛhanīyatvaṃ tena kalā vimarśa-śaktiḥ, dahano vahniḥ, induś candraḥ tāveva ākārau yayor vindor dahane-ndu-vigrahau vindū. ayam arthaḥ—agni-ṣoma-rūpiṇī vimarśa-śaktiḥ tad-ubhaya-bhūta-kāmeśvarā-vinābhūtā mahā-tripura-sundarī vindu-samaṣṭi-rūpā kāma-kalā ity ucyate, saiva upāsyatayā sarvā-gameṣu udghoṣyate.

Desired as the self by the *yogis* and, therefore, called *kāma* because He alone is desirable. *Kalā* means thought-movement of the form of the unity of the two *vindus,* fire and moon, i.e., the thought-movement of the form of fire and moon and identical with the *kāmeśvara.* It is also called the *mahā-tripura-sundarī,* the unity of the *vindus* called the *kāma-kalā* and it is She who is spoken of as the object of worship in all the Āgamas. Or, as in another place as:

kāmaḥ prakāśaika-svabhāvaḥ parama-śivaḥ. kalā tu akhila-vāṇī-rūpā paramā-haṅkāramayī vimarśa-vigrahā. etad ubhayā-tmakatvaṃ nāma svābhāvika-paripūrṇā-hambhāvaśālitvam.

Kāma means the homogeneous nature of our illumination, the *parama śiva.* *Kalā* means the thought activity as the Egohood or the *śabda.* The unity of these two is the realisation of the Ego in its fullness ; *kāma-kalā-vilāsa,* therefore, denotes the *vilāsa* or the manifestation of this *tattva* of *kāma-kalā,* the unity of *Śiva* and *Śakti.*

Now the *śabda* here is taken in the fashion of the Mīmāṃsakas as being made up of *varṇas.* The four stages of this *śabda* are (1) *parā,* (2) *paśyantī,* (3) *madhyamā* and (4) *vaikharī.* These four stages of the genesis of sounds which correspond with the four stages of the development of the formless thought into the concrete idea also represent the four stages in the process of receiving a sound. The materialisation of the formless thought into the sound and the spiritualisation of the sound into the idea both pass through the same identical stages. These four stages of the production of sounds, the abstract and the formless moment and the moments of will, ideation, and delivery may well be compared with the Mīmāṃsā genesis of sound which we have stated before.

Now we have seen that the *śabdā-rtha* symbolises the notion of the cosmic development. In connection with this we may notice that the Tantra view regarded that the human body and mind, the microcosm, was an exact parallel or counterpart of the macrocosm or the exterior world. It may not be out of place here to notice that the medical schools had also emphasised the same idea. Thus we see that *Caraka* says that the evolution and the nature of man resembles the evolution of the universe. All kinds of concrete existences in the universe find their exact parallels, and counterparts in the human system. *Caraka* further says that the courses of production, growth, decay and destruction of the universe and of man are exactly the same. Thus the universe is made up of the six *dhātus* and so is with man ; the process of generation, evolution, or production of the universe and of man is also the same. The same law of *pariṇāma* which guides the universe guides also the evolution of man. The law of decay and destruction are also the same. For as all evolution is the product of liberation of energy and redintegration of the atoms of the five elements followed by more and more differentiated and determinate character of the whole, so all destruction is the product of liberation of *rajas* or energy or disintegration of parts followed by more and more undifferentiated and indeterminate character of the whole.

But the main interest of Tantra not being of such a purely scientific character as this, it went much further to establish the parallelism into elaborate details in order to help the *yogi* to narrow the field of his concentration to himself alone so that during his practice or *sādhanā* he may find that he is a complete solar system in himself, a perfect and finished universe. This was naturally calculated to help him to concentrate his attention on himself, for when he has known himself he has known the universe.

They symbolised different parts of the body as sun, moon, stars, mountain, rivers etc. and mapped the whole body according to the world outside. But the most important point in this connection is that the creative force of the universe, which, as we have already found, was identified with the *varṇas* or letters, was placed in diverse parts of the body. This creative power, the mother of the universe, in its aspect as being identified with the *varṇas* or letters was called *mātṛkā*. Her self was formed of the fifty letters from *a* to *ha*. Thus we read in the *Phetkāriṇī Tantra* : *pañcāśad-varṇa-rūpā-tmā mātṛkā-parameśvarī*— From the *brahmarandhra* or the hole of Brahma fontaneille to the *mūlādhāra* runs the *brahma-daṇḍa* (spinal chord). Between these two extremities of the rod of *brahman* there are several stations called *pīṭhas* in *Śiva Sūtra*—but more usually *cakras*. Each of these *cakras* is presided over by a goddess *śakti* in the form of some *varṇas* who have to be mastered to escape being deceived by her. There are other goddesses presiding over other principles also. *Mātṛkā* is the queen of all these. These different *śaktis* serve to bind men to ignorance. If there should be an interval without objective cognitions, experienced or remembered, the pure consciousness without the limitation of the objective world will rise ; but the *śaktis* determine the man so steadily towards the world outside, that it is not possible for such an interval to exist and for the *caitanya* (intelligence) to shine in its true light. The *Jñāna-saṅkalinī Tantra* also associated these *cakras* with diverse emotions.

Thus at the lower extremity we have the *ādhāra-cakra,* the Sacro-Coccygeal plexus, with the four branches, nine *angulis* below the solar plexus, the source of a massive pleasurable aesthesia, voluminous organic sensation of repose. An inch and a half above it, and the same below the *mehana* is a minor centre called the *agniśikhā.* The *varṇas,* associated with the *mūlādhāra* are *vaṃ, śaṃ, ṣaṃ* and *saṃ.* The *svādhiṣṭhāna cakra,* the sacral plexus with six branches, is concerned in the excitation of sexual feelings with the accompaniments of lassitude, stupor, cruelty, suspicion, contempt. The *varṇas* associated here are *vaṃ, bhaṃ, maṃ, yaṃ, raṃ, laṃ.* The *nābhi-kuṇḍa* forms the junction of the right and left chains, *piṅgalā* and *iḍā* with the cerebro-spinal axis. Here is the *maṇipūraka,* the ten branches of which are concerned in the production of sleep, and thirst and passions like, jealousy, shame, fear, stupefaction.

It is associated with the *varṇas ḍaṃ, ḍhaṃ, ṇaṃ, taṃ, thaṃ, daṃ, dhaṃ, naṃ, paṃ,* and *phaṃ.* The *anāhata-cakra,* with twelve *branches* connected with the heart, the seat of the egoistic sentiments, hope, anxiety, doubt, remorse, conceit, egoism etc. The *varṇas* associated are *kaṃ, khaṃ, gaṃ, ghaṃ, ṅaṃ, caṃ, chaṃ, jaṃ, jhaṃ, ñaṃ, ṭaṃ, ṭhaṃ.* The *bhāratī-sthāna,* probably the junction of the spinal cord with the medulla oblongata, regulates the larynx and other organs of articulations.

The *lālana-cakra* is opposite the Uvula, which has twelve leaves,—the tract affected in the production of ego-ultruistic sentiments and affections like self-regard, pride, affection, grief, regret, respect, reverence, contentment etc. The sensory motor tract comprises two *cakras, ājñā-cakra* the circle of command (over movements) with its two lobes (the cerebellum) and the *mānasa-cakra* the sensorium with its six lobes (five special sensory for peripherally initiated sensations and common sensory for centrally initiated sensations as in dreams and hallucinations).

The *soma-cakra* is the seat of altruistic sentiments and volitional control, e.g., compassion, gentleness, patience, renunciation, meditativeness, gravity, earnestness, resolution, determination, magnanimity etc.

The *sahasrāra-cakra* (thousand lobed), the upper cerebrum with its lobes and convolutions, is the special and the highest seat of the *jīva* (soul).

To recapitulate, therefore, we find that the Tantra agreed with the Mīmāṃsakas that the *śabda* as well as its denotation was eternal. But this eternality with them was due to the fact, that the process of the genesis of sound, was regarded by them as being in miniature the same process which produced the cosmic creation. The creative power of the universe in all its diverse functions played exactly the same part, and existed in the same relations to one another in the *śabda* as in the universe.

Now again, the Tantra agreed with Mīmāṃsā in holding the *śabda* to be of the nature of *varṇas*. They, therefore, naturally thought that the creative force presiding over the *śabda* must be held to be the totality of the fifty *varṇas* from *a* to *ha*. The different *varṇas* represented and symbolised therefore the different parts or functions of the *mātṛkā* or the force as forming the essence and spirit of the totality of the *varṇas* or alphabets. These *varṇas* therefore being parts of the creative power were associated with particular conative, cognitive and feeling tendencies and were naturally also connected with corresponding physiological centres which formed the physiological data of these psychological functions. It is by virtue of these tendencies that all the phenomena of our psychosis could run on and keep us in a state of bondage. It is this phenomenal knowledge which binds us, as we find in the *Śiva Sūtra : jñānaṃ vandhaḥ*—knowledge is bondage. Now we know that the creative force is conceived as the unity of *śiva* and *śakti*. The force symbolised in each of the *varṇas* being a part and parcel of the great creative mother is but in miniature the same creative force and as such must be considered as being the unity of *Śiva* and *Śakti*—*śiva-śaktimayān prāhus tasmād varṇān manīṣiṇaḥ*. The *varṇas* therefore severally and jointly are to be conceived as *mātṛkā*—*Śiva-Śakti-mithuṇa-piṇḍa* and *sakala śiva,* for here the whole and the part have no existence as such but have the same identical reality. This is what is called the identity of *devatā* and the *mantra*.

We have seen before that the creative force forming the reality of the *varṇas* is the same as the creative force forming the reality of the world order. This reality, however, is perceived here in a very external way. Thus we find that the dependence of consonants and vowels is spoken of as the dependence of *Śiva* and *Śakti*. The consonants from *ka* to *ha* are spoken of as the twenty five *tattvas* of Sāṇkhya and *a*, *i*, and *u*, as the *icchā*, *jñāna* and *kriyā-śakti*. The fifteen *guṇas* of the five *bhūtas* (*ākāśa* + *vāyu* 2 + *tejas* 3 + *ap* 4 + *kṣiti* 5 = 15) and also the 15 phases of the moon, beginning from *pratipat* is spoken of as being represented in the *mantra* of 15 letters called the *Śrī Vidyā Pañchadaśākṣarī*. These are again resolved into the corresponding *śiva* and *śakti*, an elaboration of which from diverse aspects is found in many of the *tantras*, such as *Sāradā-tilaka* and the like. Such an identification reminds one of the determination of the world in terms of numbers in the Pythagorean School.

It must, however, have to be confessed that the Tantra is not the originator of symbolising in terms of *varṇas*, for this was first attempted in the Āraṇyaka period of culture as exemplified in the *hiṃkāro-pāsanā* or *oṃkāro-pāsanā* and the like into the details of which it will be unnecessary to enter. These of course have been largely elaborated into a complicated system of network in the Tantra, but in this the Tantra drew all the suggestions from the *pratīko-pāsanā* of the Upaniṣads and the Āraṇyakas.

Once we understand the *varṇas* or *mantras* as centres of force forming the reality of the exterior world or *mantramaya jagat* and the inner microcosm of man, it will be easy for us to comprehend the mystic *mantra-sādhanā* which is to a great extent a synthesis of the Yoga method of *samādhi* with the *pratīka* of the Āraṇyaka, on the lines of the Neo-Vedāntic Metaphysics of the Tantra. In the Yoga we find that the mind, when concentrated on any *tattva* in such a way that the *yogīn* becomes one with that, naturally passes through its inner dynamic or *rajas* into the subtler and subtler *tattvas* until it goes to *buddhi* and is finally liberated, for here the *yogin* perceives that he is pure *puruṣa* and is essentially different from the *prakṛti*.

In the Tantra, *yoga* is defined as the union of the *jīvātmā* and the *paramātmā* or *parama-śiva*. Now the *varṇas* being of the nature of *parama-śiva*, *śiva-śaktimaya* or *Tripura-sundarī*, the creative force of the universe, a concentration of the mind in such a way as to unify the *sādhaka* with it naturally helps him to pass gradually to the supreme force, the *Tripura-sundarī* or the *paramātmā* and to identify him with Her, and thus to effect the goal of *yoga*, the union of *jīvātmā* and the *paramātmā*. The doctrine of *ṣaṭ-cakra-bheda* is also the same process ; for here the *jīva* in the *kuṇḍalinī* is roused up and as it gradually identifies itself with different *cakras* it gradually passes on and on to the *sahasrāra*. We have seen above that the different *cakras* are the seats of the different forces of the *mātṛkā-śakti* and are associated with diverse passions etc. Now as the *sādhaka* identifies with each of these centres of force, the influence of these forces in binding him ceases and he passes from one centre of force to another until he identifies himself with the *paramātman* and is liberated. This identification of the *sādhaka* with the *mantra* is the triple identification of the *vedaka, vedya* and the *vidyā*; the *sādhaka*, the *devatā* and the *mantra*.

Mantra is not only the Force of *śakti* as external to the *sādhaka* but is also the mind or *citta* of the *sādhaka* which unites with it. For it is the one reality —the subject and the object. So we find that *mantra* is defined in *Śiva Sūtra* as *cittaṃ mantraḥ*. Kṣemarāja in annotating upon the *Śiva Sūtra* says that *mantra* is not merely an aggregation of sounds but the special *cittam*, the attainment of the unity with the divinity behind a *mantra* by means of meditation.

It is said in *Vijñānottara*, "The sounds that are uttered are not in themselves *mantras*. The proud Gods and Gandharvas were deceived by the false notion." It is said in *Mantra-sādhana*, "The indestructible *śakti* is regarded as the life of the *mantras*. Devoid of it, O fair-hipped one, they are as fruitless as an autumn cloud." The natural effort to fix permanently the energy that first rises from the desire to meditate on a *mantra* defined as above, is the means that brings about the union of the practiser of the *mantra* and the *deity* of the *mantra*, *vidyā* is the consciousness of identity with the supreme. The *vidyā*-bodied or *vidyā-śarīra* is one, whose form is *vidyā*, the lord, who is the totality of sounds. His nature is the manifestation of the consciousness of being the Ego of, and being identical with the whole universe. It is said in *Mantra-sādhana*, "*Mantras* are all made of letters, these are the same as *Śakti*; *Śakti* is the same as *mātṛkā* and she is the same as *Śiva*."

Apart from this *śākto-pāya* of *sādhana* through the *mantras* and the *āsana, prāṇāyāma, dhyāna, dhāraṇā, samādhi* in the yoga fashion, there is another means of attaining salvation spoken of as being the *sambhavo-pāya*. This means consists in steadily practising introspective meditation, by the effect of which there suddenly arises a flash of consciousness during the interval between the conceptual cognitive states, and the *ātmā* shines in its own light. Each individual has to experience it for himself and thus to become his own *guru*. Once the *sādhaka* has got it, he has to stick to it. The main object of this process of *sādhana* consists in making a dive into the flowing reality of *śakti* and to intuit it apart from the passing concepts, which, as they cannot show the reality, only serve to hide it all the more from our view and must therefore be called bondage. It is this intuitive grasp of the reality by introspection and a steady fixedness in it by effort which is the secret of this *sādhana*. It is very important to note to what an important measure it anticipates the philosophy of Bergson.

So far we have inquired only how, with what effort of will, the *sādhaka* united with the *tattva* of *Śiva-Śakti* in knowledge. But the Tantra was more a practical form of worship than a system of philosophy and as such there is here an important manifestation of emotion or *bhakti* which is the essence of every mode of practical religious worship. The development of this emotion of *bhakti* and its position with regard to the development of *bhakti* among the Vaiṣṇavas is a subject into which we cannot enter in a short introduction like this. I shall therefore only notice it in a cursory manner by two or three random quotations from Utpala just to show the profundity of this emotion among the Tāntrikas.

antarbhakti-camatkāra-carvaṇā-mīlitekṣaṇaḥ,
namo mahyaṃ śivāyeti pūjayan
syāṃ tṛṇāny api.

With the eyes half closing with the emotion of *bhakti* filling the inmost recesses, I shall be adoring myself as the *Śiva* though I may be worshipping but straws.

api labdha-bhavad-bhāvaḥ
svātmo-llāsamayaṃ jagat,
paśyan bhakti-rasābhogair
bhaveyaviyojitaḥ.

Realising my unity with yourself and realising my manifestation in the world as *Śiva* I shall enjoy eternally the bliss of *bhakti*.

rāgādimaya-bhavā-ṇḍake
luṭhitaṃ tvad-bhakti-bhāvanāṃ vinā taistaiḥ,
āpyāyatu rasair māṃ
pravṛddha-pakṣo yathā bhavāmi khagaḥ.

In this world, full of passions, I have fallen. Oh mother, feed and nourish me with your emotions, so that I may be fledged with winds like a bird.

bhakti-mada-janita-vibhrama-vaśena
paśyeyam aviphalaṃ karaṇaiḥ,
śivamayam akhilaṃ lokaṃ
kriyāś ca pūjāmayīḥ sakalāḥ.

Intoxicated with devotion, I perceive full with all my senses that all the world is full of *śiva* and all actions are but His adorations.

It will thus be seen that this worship was not only a synthesis of willing and knowing in the identification of the self with *śiva* but it was also essentially an identification of emotion or *bhakti.* Rather it was a thrill of joy which enlivened and overflowed the unity through the will and the knowledge. The reality is not the unity of *icchā, jñāna* and *kriyā* only, but also of bliss. It is therefore that she is spoken of as *nija-sukhamaya-nitya-nirupamā-kārā.*

YOGA PSYCHOLOGY

The word 'Yoga' occurs in the earliest sacred literature of the Hindus in the Ṛgveda (about 3000 B.C.) with the meaning of effecting a connection. Later on, in about 700 or 800 B.C., the same word is used in the sense of yoking a horse. In still later literature (about 500 or 600 B.C.) it is found with the meaning of controlling the senses, and the senses themselves are compared with uncontrolled spirited horses. The word probably represents a very old original of the Aryan stock, which can be traced also in the German *joch*. O. E. *geoc*, Latin *jugum*, Greek *zugon*.

The technical sense of the term in the system of philosophy which I am to discuss, is not only that of restraining the senses but of restraining the mental states as well, so as to bring the mind into absolute quiescence. Yoga in this sense is used only as a substantive and never as a verb. It probably, therefore, came into use as a technical expression to denote the quiescence of the mind, when people came to be familiar with the existence of such mystical states. Analogically and etymologically, however, it is related to the older sense of 'yoking.'

In the *Maitrāyaṇa Upaniṣat*, dating about 500 B.C. or so, we find a curious passage, a part of which I quote from Max Müller's version as follows:

"All that we call desire, imagination, doubt, belief, unbelief, certainty, uncertainty, shame, thought, fear,—all these make up the mind. Carried along by the waves of qualities thickening into imaginations, unstable, fickle, crippled, full of desires, vacillating, he enters into belief, believing 'I am he,' 'this is he,' he binds himself by his self, as a bird with a net. Therefore a man being possessed of will, imagination and belief is a slave ; but he who is the opposite is free. For this reason let a man stand free from will, imagination and belief ; this is the sign of liberty, this is the path that leads to Brahman, this is the opening of the door, and through it he will go to the other shore of darkness. All desires are there fulfilled. And for this the sages quote a verse : 'When the five instruments of knowledge stand still together with the mind and when the intellect does not move, that is called the highest state.' "

The testimony of early Hindu and Buddhist writings goes to show that probably about five or six hundred years B.C. the sages, who were engaged in asceticism and the acquirement of the highest virtue of self-control, had discovered that by intense concentration the mind could be reduced to an absolutely quiescent or unmoved state, and that at this stage the highest metaphysical truths flashed forth intuitively in a way quite different from what was ordinarily the case from inferential processes of thought. This state was thus regarded by them as leading to the highest that man could aspire to achieve. When this experience had been testified to by many sages, its place in the system of human knowledge and its value began to be discussed. The quotation given above represents one of the earliest specimens of such speculations. Later on, about 150 B.C. or so, Patañjali collected some of these floating arguments and speculations and gave them the form of a system of thought, which closely resembled the Sāṅkhya system of philosophy which was said to have been promulgated by Kapila. The resemblance of the Yoga way of thought with that of the Sāṅkhya is so great that they are regarded as representing two schools of the same system. The Yoga-system has undergone much elaboration and improvement at the hands of Vyāsa (200-300 A.D.), Vācaspati (900 A.D.) and Vijñāna Bhikṣu (1500 A.D.). It has associated with it its own metaphysics, cosmology, physics, ethics, theology and mystical practice. I propose to discuss in this paper mainly some aspects of its psychology. But as its psychology is very intimately connected with its metaphysics, I am afraid it may be impossible to avoid brief reference to some of its metaphysical doctrines also.

The Yoga system admits the existence of separate individual souls, of individual minds, of an objective world of matter and of God. It holds that both matter and mind are developed by the combination of an infinite number of ultimate reals (*guṇas*). These reals are of three different classes: forming the intelligence-stuff (*sattva*), the energy-stuff (*rajas*) and the mass-stuff (*tamas*). As space does not allow of entering into any detailed account of them, it may briefly be noted that the combination of these three different types of reals in different proportions and different modes is said to produce both mind and senses on the one hand and the objective world of matter on the other. Minds are said to differ from matter only in that they contain a very large proportion of the reals of the type of intelligence-stuff and energy-stuff, whereas the world of matter is formed by a large preponderance of the reals of mass-stuff and energy-stuff. The souls are distinguished from the minds and matter as being principles of pure consciousness ; they are said to be absolutely passive and inactive and devoid of any other characteristics. There is an inherent 'blind' purposiveness in the reals such that they tend to relate themselves to the principles of pure intelligence or consciousness and allow themselves to be interpreted as experience. This is rendered possible by the hypothesis that one of the classes of reals, the intelligence-stuff, is largely akin to the souls or principles of pure intelligence. The reals classed as the intelligence-stuff cannot, however, of themselves, give us conscious experience, for being always associated with the energy-stuff they are constantly changing. Conscious experience cannot be produced without reference to a fixed or steady purposiveness which should run through all the reals and unite them into a system referring to a person. What we perceive when we analyse mind is but a fleeting series of mental states. These are passing in quick succession. They will not stop for a moment, but are rapidly consuming themselves like a burning flame ; percepts, images, concepts, are all continually appearing and passing away. When, however, we notice carefully our conscious experience, we find that, though these are present in all our mental states, they imply a unity, a distinct purposiveness, without which they themselves become as blind as any physical phenomenon of inanimate nature can be. To take an example: I know that I have experienced a world of events during the last thirty years. These are all in me or in my memory ; but if I am asked of how many of these I am now conscious, I can hardly mention any except what are directly uppermost. If, however, I should try to think how many of Browning's love-poems I can remember, I find that I can recall a number of them. Only then can I say that I am directly conscious of these. There can be no doubt they were existing in the mind ; but we say that they were existing in a sub-conscious state (*saṃskāra*). During deep sleep I cannot say that my waking experiences are destroyed ; I can only say that I was then unconscious of them. This shows that our mind-states can exist in a condition in which they cannot be called awarenesses. Consciousness does not belong to them as their innate and intrinsic property ; but they come to consciousness somehow under certain circumstances. The condition under which our mental states are rendered conscious is due to their association with our self (*puruṣa*).

It must, however, be noted that this real self is never objective to us in our psychological experience. When in accordance with ordinary perceptual experience I say I see my book on my table, there is indeed in me a notion of self which connects itself with this experience. But this self forms a part of the act of cognition, and it associates itself differently with different experiences, and as such it is but a part of our thought. Each and every definite mental state shows itself to be associated with some notion of ego or 'I'. This notion is an indispensable stage through which the mental states must pass in order to get themselves fully expressed. But this notion of an 'I' is not a direct experience of pure self. It is simply a necessary stage in the process of the completing of the cognitive act, and as such its nature is not different from the nature of the cognitive experience. When I see my book on the table and think 'this is my book', there are at least three elements involved in the judgment: there is the sense-object; there is the definite apprehension of the book as such; and there is also the association of the book with the notion of 'I' to which it appears to belong. This interpretation of the experience as my experience in connection with the notion of an ego, varies with each different experience; for the nature of this association of the sense-objects with this ego has a different character in accordance with the change of the sense-objects. My experience of a part of my body as being mine is obviously more intimately mine than my experience of a book as my book. When I speak of my pen and my book, I am disposed to think that the notion of 'mine' is more or less of a homogeneous nature, and the only difference here is the difference of the object of cognition. But when I compare the notions of my honour, my son, and my stick, I see that the association of the three objects of cognition with the sense of 'mine' is very different on these three occasions. It may be objected that there is an ambiguity in the use of the word 'mine' on these three occasions. I agree, and this is precisely what I was trying to show. The main point is that our notion of 'mine' is no simple homogeneous and fixed element, but varies largely with the variety of experiences with which we have to deal. The notion 'mine' thus does not point to the experience of a permanent self in consciousness, but to the existence of a separate category of egohood which represents a confused mass of feelings, having its root far into the depths of the sub-conscious elements of our nature.

The self (*puruṣa*) in Yoga is thus not directly demonstrated in experience and cannot be found by an analysis of introspection. The existence of the self (*puruṣa*) is a matter of implication and not an object of direct apprehension in consciousness. The existence of the self is held to be implied on teleological grounds, and on grounds of moral responsibility and moral endeavour. If there be not a separate self for each of us behind all our experience, what would give the unity to our experiences? This unity is not given by any notion of 'mine', for we have already seen that the notion 'mine' is a variable element, and hence is as much of a changeable nature as are the mental states. On the other hand, we cannot say that our experiences have no unity and system in them. This unity thus presupposes a permanent subject with reference to which, or in unison with which, our experiences become systematized into a whole. There is an order and a purpose running through all our experiences, though the full meaning and value of them are not indeed clear to us. This much, however, we can understand, that probably our experiences are connected in such a way that something like a blind destiny runs through them, and that this blind destiny refers to some entity which is beyond them and with which they are somehow mysteriously associated. There is a difference between our sub-conscious and conscious mental states, and this is inexplicable except on the supposition that our conscious experiences are made conscious by some entity other than themselves. There is in us a sense of moral responsibility and a sense of striving after the good, and this also would be inexplicable except on the supposition of a self. The only psychological ground on which the self can be inferred is the necessity of accounting for the peculiar trait of consciousness, viz., of its illuminating, which cannot be said to belong to the mental states themselves.

The existence of the mental states in potential forms in the sub-conscious is the root-idea of Yoga-psychology. The sub-conscious mental states resemble the conscious mental states so far as the substance, stuff or constituents of which they are made up, is concerned, but still there is an essential difference between the two: viz., that the one are unconscious, while the other are conscious. Why, if their substance be the same, should the mental states at one time be conscious and at other times be unconscious? This seems to imply the association with some other element different from the mental states. So in Yoga the self has to be admitted, and its association with the mental states has also to be somehow admitted. This is, however, the obscurest part of Yoga-psychology.

But we here tend to digress from the field of Yoga-psychology to Yoga-metaphysics. Leaving aside the question of the transcendent influence of a pure intelligence by which the mental states are somehow electrified into consciousness, let us come to the consideration of these states.

Mind (*buddhi*) according to the Yoga system is a product of certain super-sensuous and super-subtle reals which are in essence characterized as feeling-substances. It is indeed difficult to understand what the Yoga thinkers understood by calling them feeling-substances. But since feelings are not treated separately from cognitive acts, it appears that the whole of the mind-stuff was regarded more or less in the light of a melted mass of feeling-stuff. We are generally accustomed in these days to think that feelings are mental experiences, whereas substances are things which have a non-mental or physical existence. There is therefore for us some confusion when we are told that the mind in Yoga is regarded as a product of the combination of three types of reals which are in essence but feeling-substances. But we should remember that, according to the Yoga-theory, with the exception of a transcendental element of pure consciousness or pure intelligence, all forms of cognition, volition and feelings are regarded as super-subtle, substantive entities or reals. Feelings are regarded as the ultimate forms into which both the cognitive and volitional modes return and out of which they differentiate themselves under certain conditions. If we should think of the mind-substance as apart from cognitive or volitional states, we should call it according to Yoga an indeterminate stuff of feeling-complexes. The cognitive form of the mental states no doubt constituted the only stage in which the feelings or the volitions could find themselves interpreted and expressed, for it was with this form alone that the light of the transcendent self in a person could become associated. The substances of these cognitive states, however, are but the stuff of feeling-complexes, and so each cognitive state has a feeling-tone inseparably connected with it, as pleasurable, painful or dull. A cognitive state in fact in Yoga means nothing but that state of the combination of the feeling-essences in which these could copy the objects of cognition and get the light of the self reflected on it. The energy which characterizes volition is already presupposed in the feeling-reals, and hence the volitional element is also present in every state of mind. We shall see below that a well-regulated volitional control was the chief thing in which the Yoga system was interested.

It is thus I hope clear that the special nature of the hypothesis of the mind-stuff is such that there is no room for considering feeling, willing and knowing as three distinctly separate mental functions. These, according to Yoga, are as the three aspects of the particular states of the same substances.

But it may be asked: If the mind-stuff is made up of so many diverse reals, how is any unity of action possible? We have already observed that there is postulated an inherent teleology in the mind-stuff such as to serve the purposes of the self. Blindly guided by this teleology the reals conglomerate in such a manner as to render the experiences of the self possible. It is said that as fire, wick and oil, though altogether different, combine together to form the flame, so the different types of reals combine together for the formation of the stuff of the experiences of the self. The three different kinds of reals which form the mind-stuff can by no means remain uncombined, or separated from one another. Moreover, these combinations are continually changing form like the flame of a lamp. During our waking state our senses are continually coming into contact with all sorts of objects, and as an effect of this contact these objects are automatically being copied or photographed in the mind, and at every moment a phase is formed in the mind which duly represents them. Moreover, as any perception passes away from the field of operation of the senses and another new perception comes in, the phase of the mind which represented the old perception passes away and a new one comes in its place. But the old phase is not wholly destroyed; it is only shifted into the region of the sub-conscious and may be revived partially or completely later on. Disappearance from the field of direct consciousness should on no account be regarded as destruction, any more than external things should be regarded as having ceased to exist when there is no perceiver to perceive them. And just as the physical objects, though to all appearance they may sometimes seem to have remained the same, may yet undergo considerable changes in the shape of atomic displacements unperceived by us, so is it the case with the mental states which pass into the sub-conscious. All physical objects are wasting away every moment, some rapidly and others slowly. The changes of those which waste away slowly can be marked only after a long time; nevertheless it has to be admitted that they have been wasting all the while. This wasting does not mean that they have been completely destroyed, but only that there has been disintegration in one form and re-formation into another. There is nothing which comes into being from nothing, and there is nothing which is absolutely destroyed. So the mental states also as they exist in the sub-conscious are continually wasting; nevertheless the waste in some mental states takes place so slowly that they may be said to exist more or less the same even after long intervals of time. There are other mental states, however, which waste away so quickly that even after a short interval they cannot be revived except in distorted forms. According to Yoga, some of these mental states reduced to mere impressions or modes of mind continue to exist even through the lapse of many births. They cannot be directly recalled into consciousness, but they still exist and mould or influence the nature of our thought. These semi-effaced mental states often determine the mode and nature of our choice. In most cases, when we think that we are acting freely, we are in reality being determined by these hidden experiences of the past operating unseen. These semi-effaced mental states which reveal themselves as unaccountable tendencies of the mind, are technically called *vāsanā*. It is said that the mind is netted with innumerable knots of these *vāsanās*. They represent the result of a host of experiences, the detailed features of which are often lost, but which have produced such deep impressions that they can largely determine the course of our choice and the nature of our enjoyments. The perceptual and other forms of our conscious mental states, including all the volitional and feeling aspects, when they are continually active and repeated, constitute potencies in the sub-conscious state of the mind. These potencies are in a large measure the determinants of the modes and the habits of our thoughts and volitions. These unseen potencies are, according to Yoga, of a twofold character: (1) those which are the results of the experiences of past lives and operate as innate tendencies or instincts of this life ; and (2) those which are the results of repeated experiences of this life.

Ordinary mental processes are said to be of five kinds: *pramāṇa, viparyaya, vikalpa, nidrā* and *smṛti*. *Pramāṇa* includes valid states, the states of perception, inference and belief in valid testimony. *Viparyaya* means illusory knowledge, which is produced by the operation of the defects of the senses, the rousing of wrong memories, causing non-observation of the distinction between the right and the wrong thing. *Vikalpa* means the processes of abstraction and contraction employed by us in following an argument or sometimes in using language. Thus when I say 'consciousness of the self' I make an unreal abstraction, for the self, according to Yoga, is identical with consciousness ; but for the convenience of language I separate them as though they were different from each other and then unite them. This state of the mind is of a distinctly different type, and without it thought and language are not possible. *Nidrā* (sleep) is also regarded as a separate type of mental process, when the volitional control of a man is absent and as a result thereof, by the loose play of the suppressed mental states of the sub-conscious, dreams are produced. In the state of deep sleep there is not a cessation of mental states ; the state represented therein is one of negation of all positive appearances, but, though a negation, it is considered as a mental process (*vṛtti*). *Smṛti* (memory) is also regarded as a separate mental process. Memory is produced by the recalling of the old *saṃskāras* or impressions in the sub-conscious by similarity, contrast, contiguity of time or place, ètc. It is said that memory may also be produced by the random working of the *saṃskāras*, in which case it is said to be determined by time.

But if in the perceptual state of our consciousness we are determined by the influx of sensations, and in our thought-processes, choice and volition by the accumulated experiences of the past acting as tendencies, we seem in no way to be our own masters and to have no power for moral endeavour at our disposal at all. Such a view, however, Yoga cannot admit ; for the whole theory of its psychology aims at explaining the fact that we can by the exercise of our will and concentration attain final emancipation from the bonds of all worldly experience. It therefore holds that there is a power (*śakti*) inherent in the mind by virtue of which it can endeavour (*ceṣṭā*) in any particular direction. It can react against the forces of the past tendencies, repress them and concentrate upon the states which may appear desirable to it. Undoubtedly the force of the tendencies of the accumulated experiences of the past in the sub-conscious cannot easily be overcome. Whenever there is any slacking of the will, these will try to have their own way and distract us into paths hostile to our best wishes. If we are with full consciousness exerting our will, there will be a constant fight between the sort of conscious states which we are trying to have, and the sub-conscious tendencies pulling us the other way. But if, as said above, none of our experienced states can be destroyed, it would seem that we can never hope to succeed in having our own way entirely.

Here, however, comes in the theme of the law of contrary mental states (*pratipakṣa-bhāvanā*).

Ordinarily no mental states are destroyed ; even when they seem to be destroyed, they work in a cumulative manner as tendencies of particular kinds. But the law of contrary mental states holds that any sub-conscious mental state or tendency can be ultimately destroyed by generating opposite mental states. Thus if I am jealous of a man, I shall naturally be led to think of his evil deeds ; but I can fight against this tendency and try to think of some of his good traits. In the first stages it will hardly appear pleasant to shake off my ill-will against the man ; but I may try it again and again and each attempt will make the task easier for me. For each good thought that I may be having at different times is being stored and accumulated in the sub-conscious. Here another law comes into operation, viz., the law that the repetition of any mental state will strengthen the corresponding impression of it in the sub-conscious. Thus in accordance with this law the power of the sub-conscious impression of good thoughts will gradually gain in strength. The evil thoughts come now only at random moments, and, hence, however strong originally, they may be destroyed eventually by continually thinking of the opposite good thoughts. When any particular evil thought ceases for a time to present itself before us, we are not to suppose that the evil tendency has been removed. In reality it is still existing, and if it is to be completely uprooted, the root of the impression of the opposite thought in the deepest parts of the sub-conscious has to be strengthened. There are different levels of the sub-conscious, and even when an impression has been destroyed in the shallower ones, it may still have roots

O.P. 62/25

in the deeper and may in time grow up again. So there is no permanent safety from any impression of an evil thought unless the roots of the opposite good thought are made to run as deep as the roots of the impression of evil thought. As a good impression in the sub-conscious grows stronger and stronger, its roots go deeper and deeper into the utmost levels of the sub-conscious, and as it spreads there it destroys the roots of the opposite evil thought which have been already enfeebled by its growth. The significance of the Yoga theory of psychology with regard to ethical conduct is that it is possible to control not only our external conduct but also our inner thought. Though the working of the sub-conscious is apparently unknown to us, we may be directing the working of the conscious to determine the growth of the sub-conscious in a way helpful to our purposes. We may cease to be disturbed by any evil thought or propensity, not by simply negating it, but by the acquirement of positive good thoughts and ideals. Thus we may so develop the habit of thinking of universal love and compassion and the tendency to overlook others' defects and of feeling happiness at the happiness of others, that it will become impossible for us to have a single evil thought against any fellow being.

It should be noted, however, that the Yoga ideal is not satisfied by a man's becoming solely moral. A Yogin seeks deliverance from every bondage, even from the bondage of his mind. The attainment of perfect morality and self-control by acquiring the virtues of universal non-injury, truthfulness, celibacy, purity, contentment, fortitude, etc. (technically called *yama* and *niyama*) is of course indispensable for him. But this is not all. This cannot give him full liberation. He would be a pure and free 'spirit' untrammelled even by his 'mind.' Thus when his mind has been sufficiently purified and is no longer disturbed by ordinary moral strivings, he endeavours to engage himself in a higher work, viz., that of staying the movement of the mind-states.

We have already said that the mind is always changing as the flame of a lamp. So long as this change of mind, this continual succession of mental states, continues, a man is as it were for ever being tossed upon the crests of the waves of thought. He is not master of himself. The Yogin, therefore, in order to suppress the ever-changing nature of the mind, tries to restrain his mind from the many different objects of thought and to hold one object only continually in his attention. The former process is called *dhāraṇā* and the latter *dhyāna*. In the first stages it is difficult to fix the mind on one object, and the object has to be continually replaced before the mind. By this process of continually presenting the same object to the mind, a habit is generated and a potency of fixation is acquired in the sub-conscious, and gradually the changeful character of the mind ceases and the mind becomes one with the object. At this stage there are no fluctuations of mental states ; the mind becomes one with the object of thought, absolutely still and motionless. This state is called *samādhi*. When the mind becomes thus fixed on one object, it is said that immediate cognitions of the real nature of the object dawn before the mind. This is called *prajñā*-knowledge. In its character as immediate and direct it resembles perception, but it does not fluctuate and so the nature of the reality of the object appears in one undisturbed flash. The mind is at this state one with this reality. It is this knowledge alone which the Yogin considers to be supremely real. As the Yogin advances in his path of meditation the impressions of this tendency to meditation grow stronger, so that to get into meditation becomes an easy thing for him ; and as at each stage of meditation he meets with new flashes of true wisdom, the potencies and impressions of his old phenomenal knowledge are gradually destroyed, and there comes a time when he is able to perceive the true nature of the self as distinguished from the mind. As this stage is persisted in, the ignorance through which the mind was being falsely identified with the self is ultimately destroyed, and as a result of this the connection of the mind with the self ceases and the soul (*puruṣa*) remains in itself in its own absolute pure intelligence.

In this part of the Yoga theory there seem to be three things which may appear to us as assumptions, but which the Yogins affirm to be undeniable facts of experience. These are: firstly, that the changeful processes of the mind can at a certain state be brought to a standstill ; secondly, that such a state can give us a new grade or dimension of knowledge ; and thirdly, that, as a culmination and highest advancement of this knowledge, the pure individual self as pure intelligence can be known. This kind of knowledge will not of course be knowledge in the familiar sense ; for all *samādhi*-knowledge is said to be non-conceptual knowledge and so of a different order. This difference in kind refers not only to the fact that *prajñā*-knowledge gives us a knowledge of reality, whereas perception gave us phenomenal knowledge only, but also to a difference in their essential nature or character. The *prajñā*-impressions tend to loosen the mind from the self. They represent a different dimension of knowledge completely foreign to phenomenal knowledge. We can never recall the knowledge gained by *prajñā* in our normal consciousness, for it is opposed to the latter, and the former can never be translated in terms of the latter ; the memory we recall is a phenomenal state of consciousness. This new dimension of knowledge is thus said to supersede scientific knowledge and not to supplement it. We should also remember that this *prajñā*-knowledge has nothing to do with telepathy, dual or multiple personality or the like, which are all but varieties of phenomenal knowledge.

If we do not believe the testimony of the Yogin, there is probably no way for us either to prove or disprove its reality.[1]

1. Read at an Open Meeting of the Quest Society, June 2, 1921.

PHILOSOPHY OF VASUBANDHU IN VIMŚIKĀ AND TRIMŚIKĀ

The scheme of Vedānta philosophy is surprisingly similar to the idealism of Vasubandhu (280-360 A.D.) as taught in his *Vimśikā* with a short commentary of his own and *Trimśikā* with a commentary of Sthiramati on it.[1] According to this Vijñānavāda (idealism) of Vasubandhu all appearances are but transformations of the principle of consciousness by its inherent movement and none of our cognitions are produced by any external objects which to us seem to be existing outside of us and generating our ideas. Just as in dream one experiences different objects in different places and countries without there being any objective existence of them, or as in dream many people may come together and perform various actions, so what seems to be a real world of facts and external objects may well be explained as mere creations of the principle of intelligence without any objective basis at all. All that we know as subjective or objective are mere ideation (*vijñapti*) and there is no substantive reality or entities corresponding to them, but that does not mean that pure non-conceptual (*anabhilāpyenā'tmanā*) thought which the saints realise is also false.[2] It is possible that the awareness

1. *Vijñapti-mātratā-siddhi* containing two treatises of *Vimśikā* and *Trimśikā*. Paris, 1925.

2. *yo bālair dharmāṇāṃ svabhāvo grāhya-grāhakā-diḥ parikalpitas tena kalpitenā'tmanā teṣāṃ nairātmyaṃ na tv anabhilāpyenā'tmanā yo buddhānāṃ viṣaya iti.* Commentary on *Vimśikā*, p. 6.

of anything may become the object of a further awareness, and that of another, but in all such cases where the awareness is significant (*arthavatī*) there are no entities or reality as represented by them ; but this should not be interpreted as a denial of the principle of intelligence or pure knowledge as such. Vasubandhu then undertakes to show that the perceptual evidence of the existence of the objective world cannot be trusted. He says that taking visual perception as an example we may ask ourselves if the objects of the visual perception are one as a whole or many as atoms. They cannot be mere wholes, for wholes would imply parts ; they cannot be of the nature of atoms for such atoms are not separately perceived ; they cannot be of the nature of the combination of atoms, for the existence of atoms cannot be proved.[3] For if six atoms combine from six sides, that implies that the atoms have parts, for if six atoms combine with one another at one identical point, it would mean that the combined group would not have its size bigger than that of an atom and would therefore be invisible. Again, if the objects of awareness and perception were only wholes, then succession and sequence would be unexplainable and our perception of separate and distinct things would remain unaccountable. So, though they have no real objective existence, yet perception leads us to believe that they have. People are dreaming the world of objects in the sleep of the instinctive roots of the habit of false imaginative construction (*vitatha-vikalpā-bhyāsa-*

3. *nā'pi te saṃhatā viṣayībhavanti, yasmāt paramāṇur ekaṃ dravyaṃ na sidhyati. Ibid,* p. 7.

vāsanā-nidrayā) and in their dreams they construct the objective world and it is only when they would become awake with the transcendent indeterminate knowledge (*loko-ttara-nirvikalpa-jñāna-lābhāt prabuddho bhavati*) that they would find the world-construction to be as false as the dream-construction of diverse appearances. In such a view there is no objective material world and our cognitions are not influenced by outside objects ; how then are our minds influenced by good instructions and associations, and since none of us have any real physical bodies, how can one kill another? Vasubandhu explains this by the theory that the thought-currents of one person can sometimes determine the thought-currents of another. Thus the idea of killing of a certain type may produce such a disturbance of the vital powers of another as to produce a cessation of the continuity of one's thought-processes which is called death.[4] So also the good ideas of one may influence the ideas of another for good.

In the *Triṃśikā* of Vasubandhu and its commentary by Sthiramati, this idealism is more clearly explained. It is said that both the soul (or the knower) and all that it knows as subjective ideas or as external objects existing outside of us are but transformations of pure intelligence (*vijñāna-pariṇāma*). The transformation (*pariṇāma*) of pure intelligence means the production of an effect different from that of the causal moment simultaneously at

4. *para-vijñapti-viśeṣā-dhipatyāt pareṣāṃ jīvite-ndriya-virodhinī kācit vikriyā utpadyate yayā sabhāga-santati-vicchedā-khyaṃ maraṇaṃ bhavati. Viṃśikā*, p. 10.

the time of the cessation of the casual moment.[5] There is neither externality nor subjectivity in pure intelligence, but still these are imposed on it (*vijñāna-svarūpe parikalpita eva ātmā dharmaś ca*). All erroneous impositions imply that there must be some entity which is mistaken as something else. There cannot be erroneous impositions on mere vacuity ; so these erroneous impositions of various kinds of external characteristics, self etc. have to be admitted to have been made on the transformations of pure intelligence.[6] Both Vasubandhu and Sthiramati repudiate the suggestion of those extreme idealists who deny also the reality[7] of pure intelligence on grounds of interpendence or relativity (*saṃvṛti*). Vasubandhu holds that pure consciousness (*vijñapti-mātratā*) is the ultimate reality. This ultimate consciousness is a permanent entity which by its inherent power (*śakti*) undergoes threefold transformation as the inherent indeterminate inner changes (*vipāka*) which again produce the two other kinds of transformation as the inner psychoses of mental operations (*manana*) and as the perception of the so-called external sensibles (*viṣaya-vijñapti*). The apprehen-

---

5. *kāraṇa-kṣaṇa-nirodha-sama-kālaḥ kāraṇa-kṣaṇa-vilakṣaṇa-kāryasya ātma-lābhaḥ pariṇāmaḥ*. Sthiramati's Commentary on *Triṃśikā*, p. 16.

6. *upacārasya ca nirādhārasyā' sambhavād avaśyaṃ vijñāna-pariṇāmo vastuto'stuupagantavyo yatra ātma-dharmo-pacāraḥ pravartate. na hi nirāspadā mṛga-tṛṣṇikā-dayaḥ. Ibid.* Compare Saṅkara's Commentary on Gauḍapāda's *Kārikā*.

7. Thus *Laṅkāvatāra*, one of the most important works on Buddhist idealism, denies the real transformation of the pure intelligence or *ālaya-vijñāna*. See *Laṅkāvatāra*, p. 46.

sion of all appearances or characterised entities (*dharma*) as the cognised objects and that of selves and cognisers, the duality of perceivers and the perceived is due to the threefold transformation of *vipāka, manana* and *viṣaya-vijñapti*. The ultimate consciousness (*vijñapti-mātra*) which suffers all these modifications is called *ālaya-vijñāna* in its modified transformations, because it is the repository of all experiences. The ultimate principle of consciousness is regarded as absolutely permanent in itself and is consequently also of the nature of pure happiness (*sukha*), for what is not eternal is painful and this being eternal is happy[8]. When a saint's mind becomes fixed (*pratiṣṭhita*) in this pure consciousness (*vijñapti-mātra*), the tendency of dual thought of the subjective and the objective (*grāhya-grāhakā-nuśaya*) ceases and there dawns the pure indeterminate (*nirvikalpa*) and transcendent (*loko-ttara*) consciousness. It is a state in which the ultimate pure consciousness runs back from its transformations and rests in itself. It is divested of all afflictions (*kleśa*) or touch of vicious tendencies and is, therefore, called *anāsrava*. It is unthinkable and undemonstrable because it is on one hand pure self-consciousness (*pratyātma-vedya*) and omniscience (*sarvajñatā*) as it is divested of all limitations (*āvaraṇa*) and on the other hand it is unique in itself.[9] This pure consciousness is called the

8. *dhruvo nityatvāt akṣayatayā ; sukho nityatvād eva yad anityaṃ tad duḥkhaṃ ayaṃ ca nitya iti asmāt sukhaḥ.* Sthiramati's commentary on *Triṃśikā*, p. 44.

9. *Ālaya-vijñāna* in this ultimate state of pure consciousness (*vijñapti-mātratā*) is called the cause (*dhātu*) of all virtues, and being the ultimate state in which all the *dharmas*, or characterised

container of the seed of all (*sarva-bīja*) and when its first indeterminate and indefinable transformations rouse the psychosis-transformations and also the transformations as sense-perceptions, these mutually act and react against one another and thus the different series rise again and again and mutually determine one another. These transformations are like waves and ripples on the ocean where each is as much as the product of others as the generator of others.[10]

In this view thought (*vijñāna*) is regarded as a real substance and its transformations are also regarded as real and it is these transformations that are manifested as the selves and the characterised appearances.[11] The first type of transformations called *vipāka* is in a way the ground of the other two transformations which contain the indeterminate materials out of which the manifestations of the other two transformations appear. But as has already been pointed out, these three different types of transformations again mutually determine one another. The *vipāka* transformations contain within them the seeds of the constructive instincts (*vikalpa-vāsanā*) of the selves as cognisers, the constructive instincts of colours, sounds etc., the substantive basis (*āśraya*) of the attribution of this twofold constructive instinct as well

appearances, had lost all their limitations it is called the *dharma-kāya* of the Buddha (*mahāmuneḥ bhūmi-pāramitā-dibhāvanayā kleśa-jñeyā-varaṇa-prahāṇāt . . . . . sarva-dharma-vibhutva-lāhhataś ca dharma-kāya ity ucyate*).

10. *tac ca vartate srota-saṅghavat*. *Ibid*., p. 21

11. *avaśyaṃ vijñāna-pariṇāmo vastuto'sty upagantavyo yatrā'tma-dharmo-pacāraḥ pravartate*, *Ibid*., p. 16.

as the sense-faculties and the localisation of space-determinations (*sthāna-vijñapti* or *bhājana-loka-sanniveśa-vijñapti*). They are also associated in another mode with sense-modifications involving the triune of the sense (*indriya*), sense-object (*viṣaya*) and cognition (and each of these triune is again associated with a characteristic affective tone corresponding with the affective tones of the other two members of the triune in a one to one relation), attention (*manaskāra*), discrimination (*saṃjñā*), volition (*cetanā*) and feeling (*vedanā*).[12] The *vipāka* transformations have no determinate or limited forms (*aparicchinnā-lambanā-kāra*) and there are here no actualised emotional states of attachment, antipathy or the like which are associated with the actual pleasurable or painful feelings. The *vipāka* transformations thus give us the basic concept of mind and its principal functions with

12. Feeling (*vedanā*) is distinguished here as painful, pleasurable, and as the basic entity which is neither painful nor pleasurable, which is feeling *per se* (*vedanā anubhava-svabhāvā, sā punar viṣayasya āhlādaka-paritāpaka-tadubhayākara-vivikta-sva-rūpa-sākṣātkaraṇa-bhedāt*). This feeling *per se* must be distinguished again from the non-pleasurable-painful feeling existing along with the two other varieties, the painful and the pleasurable. Here the *vipāka* transformations are regaded as evolving the basic entity of feeling and it is, therefore, undifferentiated in it as pleasure or pain and is hence called "feeling as indifference" (*upekṣā*) and undifferentiated (*avyākṛta*). The differentiation of feeling as pleasurable or as painful takes place only as a further determination of the basic entity of feeling evolved in the *vipāka* transformations of good and bad deeds (*śubhā-śubha-karma-vipāka*). Good and bad (*śubhā-śubha*) are to be distinguished from moral and immoral as potential and actual determinations of virtuous and vicious actions.

all the potentialities of determinate subject-object consciousness and its processes. There are here the constructive tendencies of selves as perceivers, the objective constructive tendencies of colours, sounds etc., the sense-faculties etc. attention, feelings, discrimination, volition and sense-functioning. But none of these have any determinate and actualised forms. The second grade of transformations called *manana* represents the actual evolution of moral and immoral emotions and it is here that the mind is set in motion by the ignorant references to the mental elements as the self, and from this ignorance about the self is engendered self-love (*ātma-sneha*) and egoism (*ātma-māna*). These references are again associated with the fivefold universal categories of sense-functioning, feeling, attention, volition and discrimination. Then comes the third grade of transformations which are associated with the fivefold universal categories together with the special manifestations of concerte sense-perceptions and the various kinds of intellectual states and moral and immoral mental states such as desire (*chanda*) for different kinds of sense-experiences, decisions (*adhimokṣa*) in conclusions firmly established by perceptions, reasoning etc., memory, attentive reflection (*samādhi*), wisdom (*prajñā*), faith and firm will for the good (*śraddhā*), shamefulness (*hrī*) for the bad etc. The term *ālaya-vijñāna* is given to all these three types of transformations, but there is underneath it as the permanent passive ground the eternal and unchangeable pure thought (*vijñapti-mātratā*).

It may be pointed out here that in this system of philosophy the eternal and unchangeable thought-substance undergoes by virtues of its inner dynamics three different orders of superficial changes which are compared with constantly changing streams and waves. The first of these represents the basic changes which later determine all subjective and objective possibilities ; the second starts the process of the psychosis by the original ignorance and false attribution of self-hood to non-self elements, self-love and egoism, and in the third grade we have all the concrete mental and extra-mental facts. The fundamental categories make the possibility of mind, mental processes and the extra-mental relations evolve in the first stage of the transformation and these abide through the other two stages of the transformation and become more and more complex and concrete in course of their association with the categories of the other transformations. In analysing the knowledge situation Vasubandhu does not hold that our awareness of blue is only a modification of the "awareness", but he thinks that an awareness has always two relations, a relation with the subject or the knower (*grāhaka-graha*) and a relation with the object which is known (*grāhya-graha*). Blue as an object is essential for making an awareness of blue possible, for the awareness is not blue, but we have an awareness of the blue. But Vasubandhu argues that this psychological necessity is due to a projection of objectivity as a necessary function of determinate thought and it does not at all follow that this implies that there are real external objects existing outside of it and generating the awareness as external agent. Psychological objectivity does not imply ontological objectivity. It is argued that if the agency of objective entities in the production of sense-knowledge be admitted, there could not be any-case where sense-knowledge can be admitted to be produced without the operation of the objective entities, but since in dreams and illusions such sense-knowledge is universally regarded as being produced without the causal operation of such objective entities, no causal operation can be admitted to the objective entities for the production of sense-knowledge.

DOGMAS OF INDIAN PHILOSOPHY*

The study of Indian Philosophy in modern times may be regarded as having a starting from Rājā Ram Mohan Ray. He was a religious and social reformer and in his attempts to purify the current popular forms of Hinduism he turned his eyes to the Upaniṣads. He pointed out that the Upaniṣads reveal a religion of the worship of one God, Brahman, and in his interpretations of the Vedānta doctrine he brought out the fundamental ideas of the Upaniṣads and he made them a corner-stone of his religion of Brahmoism. He also initiated a programme of social reform which he regarded as being a corollary of the Upaniṣadic faith. But though a great thinker and scholar, his interest was chiefly religious. Later on a few other Indians, Christians such as Banerjee, Gouray and others, also studied Indian Philosophy with the object of refuting Indian thought in favour of Christianity. In the meanwhile studies of Indian Philosophy were taken up by some European Sanskrit scholars such as Colebrook, Cowell, Wilson, Duff, Davies, Balantine, Venis, Hall, Max Müller and others. Many of these scholars published numerous articles on Indian Philosophy and translated some important philosophical texts, and Max Müller's *Six Systems Of Indian Philosophy* is probably the first attempt to give a brief survey of the general philo-

*Presidential address at the Philosophy section of the Lahore Oriental Conference, 1928.

sophical position of the six important systems of Philosophy. In the meanwhile Sanskrit manuscripts were being collected in several important cultural centres of India and of Europe, and Sanskrit philosophical texts were being edited and published by the Asiatic Society of Benares, the *Paṇḍit* Journal of Benares, the Bombay Government Publication Department, in the Chowkhamba Sanskrit Press series, the Vizianagaram Sanskrit Publication series and later on in Mysore, Travancore, Baroda, Nirṇayasāgar Press, the Veṇkateswar Press in Bombay, the Pāṇini Office of Allahabad, the Madhavilās Book Depot of Kumbakonam, by Jīvānanda Vidyāsāgar and many others in Calcutta and in other places. The European scholars were also not idle, and the Pāli Text Book Society had been gradually publishing the old Pāli Texts of Buddhism and important studies of early Buddhism and we have now almost the entire *Tripiṭaka,* which were wholly lost from India, published magnificently in Roman characters. Many important Mahāyāna Buddhist texts were published by the Pāli Text Series of Calcutta under the editorship of Rāy Śarat Candra Dās Bāhādur and Dr. Vidyābhūṣaṇ. Knowledge of Tibetan began to spread both in this country and in Europe, and this led to the publication of a number of Buddhist texts which were lost in this country but were preserved in Tibetan translations. Many European scholars began to discover through their knowledge of Chinese that a large number of Buddhist texts which were lost in India in their Sanskrit originals were preserved in their Chinese translations. Texts and studies were being published from several cultural centres of England, France, Germany, Italy and Russia and in the present day we have such great scholars as Thomas, Keith, Jacobi, Stcherbatsky, Suali, Lévi, not to speak of many other eminent writers, who have done excellent work in the field of Indian Philosophy either by way of translations or by the publication of texts or studies. On the side of the publication of texts, however, India has done very much more, as may naturally be expected, than any of the Western countries. In India also much work has been done in the way of translation of Sanskrit texts into vernaculars or into English such as the translations by Dr. Gaṅgānātha Jhā, Mr. Śrīś Candra Basu, Pramatha Nāth Tarkabhuṣan, and many others. Several important manuscripts on different systems of thought have also been edited in recent times.

One great difficulty that lies in the way of the study of Indian Philosophy is to be found in the fact that all the old living traditions of Indian Philosophy are now lost almost for centuries so that a study of Indian Philosophy, whether in the Paṇḍitic circle or in the Anglicised circle, is bound largely to be philological. The problems which were of vital importance to Indian Philosophy from age to age, in the solution of which they cheerfully spent all their lives, have in our present outlook and civilisation lost their value and significance. The Anglicised people who are now by far the most important in their influence are only nominally connecting themselves with the traditional faiths, but the problems of religion and philosophy, which were so much valued by their ancestors, have ceased to have any charm with them. The scholars in the Paṇḍitic circle also are only carrying on their work in a stereotyped fashion not for the intrinsic interest of philosophy and religion but merely as a learned occupation or for a living. The influence of Western education on the other hand has instilled into us newer ideals of nationalism, politics and patriotism ; and newer goals and newer interests of philosophy, life, social relations, social values and religious values are now appearing before us which are submerging as it were all the older, cultural and philosophical tendencies of the country.

The best people of the country are being gradually intimately associated with the Western Philosophy, literature, thought, culture and ideals. They do not know very much of their older ideals, nor are they in sympathy with them. A changed economical condition and the rising of the standard of life have increased the hard struggle for existence ; and as it is gradually being found that the claims of worldly life, worldly happiness, worldly prosperity, the civilization of the masses, honour, prestige and the like, are very much more important than the older goals of emancipation and self-abnegation, it is gradually being felt that the older methods of life will no longer do for us. Modern ways of life have their superiority over the ancient ways. For it is by the former only that all kinds of material success can be attained. There is the ancient thought that spirituality consisted in the destruction of desires, in the final realisation of a passionless self, of a pure consciousness for which all worldly prosperity has to be sacrificed. The dominant thought of the West is trying to discourage all these as silly fancies and is loudly proclaiming the need for a change in the ideal. This world is practically the only world with which we are concerned, we can only improve our material facilities and mental faculties individually or jointly, and we can make life easy and comfortable, more healthy and more progressive for the whole humanity. Our ideal, therefore, should be one of scientific progress for the material good of humanity as a whole. Religion is not an end in itself but is only a means to our own well-being as members of the society. We are not anxious now for catering to the needs of an abstract perfection but for the discovery of the needs of living practically a happy and contented life of intellectual and social progress. We now perceive that only those people, who are striving their utmost for this normal and practical well-being of worldly life in those lines, that are really thriving and growing powerful, whereas those who will shut their eyes to these will gradually become feebler and feebler and may be wholly exterminated. The Western spirit has thus naturally possessed us and we have been almost entirely cut asunder from the bonds of our old traditional life and culture, of philosophy and religion. Even the Paṇḍitic people, who are still with difficulty sticking to the old views, seldom get any vital sap from their loyalty to the past, for in doing so they are themselves torn asunder from the general progressive and dominant nature of life and from the rest of the cultural humanity. In the days of yore when the older ideals of India prevailed, it was not merely the ideal of the faith of a particular section of the people but of the Indian people as a whole and of Indian culture wheresoever it radiated. Even in other countries not within the zone of influence of Indian culture the spirit of supremacy of religion and the supremacy of the after-life, was felt almost universally. The Indian ideal, therefore, was then in consonance with the general tone of the world-ideal as a whole.

We have now, however, a new epoch of culture, progress and ideals in which the entire civilised world is participating. Whether we will or not, we are being directed into the whirlpools of our unknown destinies of continual movement and continual change of this new agc. We are thus naturally torn away from the spirit that dominated the philosophy and culture of India. It is no doubt true that here and there new thinkers are criticising the methods of this new age ; but whatever may be the value of these criticisms, it is difficult to find any tendency in them to lapse back into the idea of progress in the spirit of ancient Indian thought.

If we could completely transform ourselves by the newly introduced European culture our problems of life would be very much simplified. But howsoever we may be modified by Western thought we can never forget our traditional past and howsoever the foot-prints may have been obliterated, we are still intimately connected with it, and we can never wholly take ourselves away from the grip of the great ideals of our forefathers. We are thus in a very difficult situation ; we cannot identify ourselves with our forefathers, nor are our problems of life the same as theirs ; we cannot also identify ourselves with our Western brethren nor can we look at life wholly from their point of view. Westernisation has also been effected in very different degrees and intensity, not only amongst the different sections and communities of people but often also in the same family. It is a common fact that in the very same family some members are very strongly intoxicated with the Western view of life, whereas there are others who are as strongly loyal to the traditional faiths. Thus we cannot bind our faith to our traditional past nor can we heartily welcome the Western outlook of life. If the religious and moral problems of our forefathers are not our own, we cannot also wholly believe ourselves to be like the Westerners having the same view of life as they have. We are thus in a state of transition where both the Indian and Western ideals are fighting for supremacy and we do not know which to choose and where to stand. Nothing is more unsuitable for the creation and development of new thought than such an unsettled state of things. The Ancients believed in the Śāstric ways of life and the various problems that arose out of them, but we have moved far away from them and even those of us, who have been brought up in the Paṇḍitic atmosphere, cannot be said to be strictly loyal to the older ideals.

The bed-rock of old Indian culture and civilisation which formed the basis of our philosophy is fast slipping off our feet. The rush of waters is not, however, equally deep everywhere, but it is fast increasing. It may be waist-deep in some places, it may be shoulder-deep in others, but yet there are places where it is already passing over our heads. It would be a day-dream to suppose that we can ever arrest this torrential flow of inundating waters from the western seas. The new science of the West, with its daily increasing inventions of machineries and crafts of ever-increasing material power and advantages, is fast demolishing the barriers and insulations of time and space and of natural obstructions. The steam engine, aeroplane, telegraph, wireless and the like are fast removing all distances in land, sea and water. Through trade and commerce the machineries of advantage and articles of luxury in all departments of life are invading our country with an ever-increasing rapidity and are making them a necessity of life with us. The newspapers are broadcasting the bigger and smaller events for the whole world and as we swallow them with our tea, we fill in our mind with foreign materials of interests and build a mental constitution which is not so much Indian as cosmopolitan. Western thoughts, wisdom, ways and out-look of life, aspirations and interests are being shipped through their printed pages and fast assimilated by the youths of the country. Can we arrest this mighty inundation? Can we now turn to the old yogi's ideal of contentment with nothing, or restrict our needs to the bare necessities of life, and drive out the present civilisation, which is always tending to increase our material wants? Can we remain contented with being only a religious and spiritual people, and cease taking interest in politics, or in the development of our industries? Can we, in brief, go back to the past? Such a supposition seems to me to be an impossible and wild dream, which only an idealist can weave in his wildest fancy. The torrents that are coming are not merely a passing inundation. They indicate a rise of water which has come to stay and increase. If we try to hold fast to our old bed-rock and turn a deaf ear to the roaring rush we are bound to be drowned and suffocated. The very instinct of life would prevent us from taking any such foolish step, and any advice that would urge us to do it is too unpractical to be followed. We would rather be washed away, or clutch at a floating rafter, and save ourselves than hold fast to the old bed-rock beneath the waters. Our real chance of life, therefore, is neither to hold fast to the submerged rock, nor to allow ourselves to be washed away, but to build an edifice of our own, high and secure enough to withstand the ravages of all inundations. We want to avail ourselves of all that come floating to us and enjoy them at our home. Let the waters of the Western sea come and break themselves on the walls of our fortress with their foaming billows. Our only safety is thus to be with the sea and yet above it.

Philosophy with me is not mere Logic or Metaphysics, but the entire *epitome* of life. For me it stands as the collective and integrated whole of all that we think, all that we feel and all that we prize as high and great. Philosophy that sticks merely to verbal arguments and metaphysical dilemmas, and is not instinct with the reality of life, is no true philosophy, but a mere mockery of it. Philosophy is the formula of the entire spiritual existence of man, where by "spiritual" one understands all that is especial to man as man. It would be wrong to restrict the meaning of the word spiritual merely to a sense of God-intoxication or an ethical or religious inspiration. By "spiritual", therefore, as determining the meaning of philosophy, I should, therefore, like to mean the entire harmonious assemblage of the inner life of man, as all that he thinks, feels, values and wishes to create. A student of Indian Philosophy is, therefore, required not only to understand clearly in consonance with the spirit of the thinkers of the past, the details of the different strands of Indian philosophical thinking, but he must also realise their value and significance in connection with the totality of Indian culture as a whole, in the many-sided development of spiritual experience and spiritual creation. He must also realise what relation such spiritual achievements may have with the spiritual creations of our age, influenced as it is in diverse ways by world-thought as a whole. Our aims, therefore, are not merely to understand each strand of Indian philosophical thought of the past in true sympathy with the spirit of the past, but also to understand them in their mutual connection and contrast as representing the diverse phases of the development of the ancient Indian mind, and also to realise the way in which we can further advance our thoughts of the present age as a continuous prolongation of the spiritual impetus of the past into the bosom of the future. Philosophy cannot of course chalk out a path of future progress, but it must at least give us a concrete and enlightened feel of the spiritual impetus that guides and determines our progress.

The task of the proper study of Indian philosophy is indeed very great, in many ways very much greater than the study of Western philosophy. Indian philosophical systems have mostly developed side by side with one another. Most of the systems had in some form or other very early beginnings. They

O.P. 62/28

were not treated as mere vapourings of individual thought, but were regarded as the result of spiritual experience, which would not only give us intellectual satisfaction, but would also satisfy the highest ideals of life. Each system of thought had, therefore, its adherents, and these adherents of different schools criticised one another and mutually benefited themselves by reinterpreting and strengthening their positions, in the light of these hostile criticisms. This work of reinterpretation, this rise of new problems and their solutions continued to grow for hundreds of years in an atmosphere of mutual influence and in mutual give and take in the form of commentaries and sub-commentaries and independent monographs. Difficult and abstruse as the language of these philosophical texts and commentaries is, it is rendered very much obscure and incomprehensible through the constant references, allusions and refutations of unknown views of other systems of philosophy. For understanding any particular system of thought, one is required to know the fundamental problems and difficulties of almost every other system of thought, and this often leads to a vicious circle from which it is difficult to escape. It is also unfortunate that there should not be books which would make an easy introduction to the different systems of thought which could guide anyone in his studies in any particular system of thought. However strange it might appear, I should venture to remark that Indian systems of philosophy have very seldom been studied in detail, historically and in mutual interconnections, in an unbiassed manner. The study of philosophy, in the Paṇḍitic circles has often been limited to one particular system of thought, or at best, two, for the Paṇḍits take to philosophic studies not often as impartial philosophers, engaged in creating new thought, but as religious adherents of particular schools, holding particular dogmas and creeds of philosophy. Their interest in systems of thought, other than those to which they are loyal, is limited very largely to the prominent defects of those systems, in contrast with which they regarded their own systems to be superior. They are not generally interested in the growth and development of any particular system as a system of philosophy and the parts that are played and the contributions that are made by other rival systems in such a development. The best of them have a sound philological training and by life-long studies of some of the prominent works of a particular philosophy, they generally master the technical terms and expressions and they are used to the scholastic disputes on particular points of philosophical dogma, but they have seldom the philosophical interests as we now understand it. As a result of that, excepting the two tiny works of *Ṣaḍ-darśana-samuccaya* and *Sarva-darśana-sāra-saṁgraha* and Mādhava's *Sarva-darśana-saṁgraha* we have hardly any other work which deals with the different systems of Indian philosophy as a whole. Even these works are nothing but brief sketches of different systems of philosophy without any eye to their mutual interconnection, or their historical or rational development. They do not take any notice of the literature of the systems, nor do they separate the different schools that sprang up within each system or the earlier parts from later accretions. The materials collected regarding the various systems of thought are not also often based upon a comprehensive study of the literature of the subjects, but are often directly borrowed from important compendiums. Even the best Paṇḍits of our age follow the old traditional method, and are almost always profoundly ignorant of Buddhism and Jainism, the two great systems of thought which moulded in such an important manner the development of all Hindu philosophic thought in mediaeval times, and with few exceptions, they seldom publish anything which may be said to embody the results of their study and mature thinking. Their eminence, therefore, may be said to lie only in the fact that they are masters of the philosophical style and the technical language of the literature of the particular schools of thought, of which they are adherents, or which they have studied. But this much-vaunted Paṇḍitic learning is also fast disappearing, and as far as I can judge from my personal experience of Bengal Paṇḍits, among whom I have grown up, I can say that among the younger or the middle-aged generation, one can hardly find one out of dozens of title-holders, who understands the texts, or has studied the literature of the subject. The fact that the Paṇḍits are almost always unacquainted with any of the Western languages is another great handicap with them, as they are thereby excluded from profiting by the results of the learned researches and translations from foreign sources and also from romanised editions of Sanskrit and Pāli texts, by Western scholars. The great handicap with anglicised scholars is often their inadequate knowledge of Sanskrit. The short time that they can spare for

Sanskrit often renders it impossible for them to master the abstruse style and technique of Indian philosophical literature. Still, it is with them alone that our future hope of Indian philosophy lies.

If we want to construct the future philosophy on the basis of our own, we must at least thoroughly study our philosophy and know how and where it differs from the philosophy of the West and on which particular points and aspects it has its agreements. But before any such agreements or differences may be noted, before we can understand the spirit of our philosophy, in connection with the spirit of Western philosophy, it is the great necessity of our age to make a complete study of our achievements in philosophy as faithfully as we can, in consonance with the spirit with which it was carried on and the atmosphere that it breathed. There has of late been a tendency among some Indian scholars to interpret Indian philosophy on the models of the West. Technical philosophical terms have often been carelessly used to represent Indian concepts. Many of our scholars have breathed a sigh of relief if they could, by their manipulations, discover a Hegel in Śaṅkara, or a Hume in Buddha. Much as I would like to see particular systems of Indian thought compared or contrasted with other Western systems of thought, I should very much disapprove of the idea of forcing an interpretation of Indian philosophy through the inspiration of Western thought, for purposes of fruitless identification. If similarities are to be noticed, the reviewer of philosophy must also know his system thoroughly well to appreciate the differences. A philosopher who is inspired by Western philosophy and aims at providing that Indian philosophy is only like another revised edition of Western philosophy profoundly misses his part as an interpreter of Indian thought. In a lecture at the Fifth International Congress at Naples the present writer had an opportunity of pointing out that Indian Philosophy anticipates in a very large measure most of what is known as European thought. In illustrating this statement, the present writer analysed the principal features of Benedetto Croce's philosophy and showed how the most essential doctrines of this philosophy had been anticipated in the philosophy of Dharmakīrtti and Dharmottara. If one goes through the elaborate commentary literature of the different systems of Indian philosophy, one is astonished to notice how many of those philosophical and epistemological views, which pass as productions of modern philosophy, have already been worked out centuries ago by the thinkers of India. In the interests of comparative philosophy, it is indeed useful to bring out these anticipations of Western philosophy by Indian thought.[1] But before that can be done, it is necessary

1. Mm. Prof. S. Kuppusvāmī Śāstri in a short reference that he has made to my *A History of Indian Philosophy* says: "This learned Professor of Bengal endeavours in this work to give an account of the evolution of philosophical thought, strictly in accordance with the original sources in Sanskrit and seems to hold the view that there is hardly any need for an exposition of the doctrines of Indian philosophy, for the reason that they appear to him to be essentially the same as found in European Philosophy." *The New Era, Dec.*, 1928, Madras. This is, however, a gross misrepresentation of my views. Indian philosophy anticipates many problems and discussions of European philosophy; but in its history, structure, aims, ideals and concrete development

that the entire philosophical and religious literature of India should be explored and the materials discovered should be properly and faithfully collected and systematised in the proper Indian setting in which they appear. The task of faithful collection and right understanding must precede that of comparison. Not every student of philosophy can be a scholar of Sanskrit who can rightly interpret Indian thought by studying the original texts; it is therefore the clear duty of Sanskritists who understand philosophy to bring out all the materials of Indian philosophy from their inaccessible Sanskritic homes to our easy approaches of modern languages, Indian or Western. Indian philosophy ought not to remain any longer a special monopoly of a few expert Sanskritists; it ought to lay bare its treasures to all who can think, and it is in this way alone that our older philosophies can be made to work with us as a living force. The old ideal of reserving all higher knowledge for a few experts and qualified persons must have to be abandoned. The time when people took to Indian philosophy out of religious motives has almost passed away. If even now Indian philosophy is kept as a

as a whole, it widely differs from European philosophy. And it is exactly for this reason that I urge that Indian philosophy must first be faithfully interpreted and it is only after it has been faithfully interpreted that an attempt at a constructive comparison or construction should be made. It is because Indian philosophy is not European philosophy that the former cannot safely be reconstructed in the light of the latter. And it is only when a faithful exposition has revealed the real similarities, that these can be compared. It is regrettable that Mm. Kuppusvāmī Śāstri should make such a gross blunder.

proud possession of a few expert Sanskritists, it may as well lie buried in the moth-eaten pages of palm leaves and the whole world would move on without even noticing that it has missed it. Yet it is this philosophy which may be regarded as the highest achievement of the Brahmanic civilisation of India of which we are justly proud, and on the bed-rock of which we want to rebuild our future national culture. It is true no doubt that there may be parts of it which may be regarded as decayed and dead, but it is also certainly true that there are other elements in it which are universal and deathless. It is these which, while they would link us with our past, will yet allow us to continue our onward growth of progress and to assimilate all that is good, whatever may be the sources from which we receive them.

If we try to rise above all details of philosophical dogmas, views, opinions and disputes, and try to discover some of the fundamental results of Indian philosophical culture, a number of important propositions is seen to emerge. Indian philosophy has sprung forth out of ethical, eschatological and religious needs, and, with rare exceptions, has always been dominated or restricted by these considerations. The Upaniṣads reveal two different strands of eschatological ideas, firstly, the doctrine of *Devayāna* and *Pitṛyāna* (the views that the wise man at death passed away through the etherial regions above and never returned back to earth, while the man of deeds, after an upward course, was again showered down to live its prescribed life on earth) and the doctrine of re-birth. Throughout the entire course of the history of Indian philosophy, no one except the

Cārvākas raised any dissenting voice against this theory of re-birth. We do not know how this doctrine originally crept into Indian thought, but once it was there, it was accepted almost universally without a discussion. The few arguments that are sometimes adduced in its support (e.g., in the *Nyāya Sūtra* and the *Caraka Saṁhitā*) are trivial in their nature and may be regarded as offered in support of a faith and not as determining philosophical conclusions. The doctrine of re-birth is therefore a dogma of Indian philosophy. The Hindus believed in it; the *Jātakas* represent Buddha as remembering his past lives, but the Cārvākas denied it. It was a philosophical dogma or creed, which might safely be regarded as unproved. We next come to the theory of *Karma*. This also can be traced to the Upaniṣads, and it is not improbable that it originated from a belief in the magical efficacy of sacrificial deeds. It is supposed to explain the inequalities of this life by the unknown actions of the past lives, but it refuses to explain any question regarding original inequalities of circumstances and advantages by a clever dodge that there is no beginning in the series of lives. The difficulties of the theory of *Karma* are further realised in other directions also. If the fruits of the *Karmas* of the past cannot be avoided, how can, then, any one attain emancipation which must necessarily mean cessation of *Karma?* In reply to such a question, other dogmas regarding the fruition of *Karma* are introduced, all of which may be regarded as mythical. It is also held that when true knowledge is attained, or when desires are extinguished, the bonds of *Karma* are burnt up. So far as I can remember, I suppose, no attempt has been made, anywhere in Indian philosophy, to prove any of these propositions regarding the operation of the laws of *Karma* in a serious and systematic manner. The law of *Karma*, therefore, involves a number of unattested propositions, which have never been proved to be true, nor are capable of being proved so. This is, therefore, the second set of unproved dogmas of Indian philosophy, which has been almost universally acknowledged as true, not as a philosophical conclusion, but as an article of faith. It is only the Cārvākas who daied protest against it but no one ever cared to listen to them.

We next come to the doctrine of ***Mukti, Mokṣa, Apavarga*** or *Niḥśreyasa*, and *Nirvāṇa*. The Upaniṣads are full of the sages' experiences of an ultimate state of bliss, which is indescribable and indefinable and from which there is no return. The taste of this great realisation seems to be the most attractive and arresting feature of the Upaniṣads. But it is doubtful whether the Upaniṣads conceived it as a supraconscious psychical experience, or as a final state of realisation that put a stop to the cycle of re-birth. The former seems more probable. But all the systems of Hindu philosophy took it to mean the affirmation of an ultimate freedom of the self from mind and all that is mental and physical. Opinions differ in different systems of Hindu philosophy regarding the exact nature of this state, i.e., whether this is an inert state, or a state of pure thoughtless intelligence, or a state of intelligence which is also supreme bliss. But whatsoever may be the value of these differences, there is this general agreement that all systems of

Hindu thought have before them the ultimate goal of the absolute, perfect and final freedom of the soul from mind, and all that is mental and physical, and the ultimate cessation of the cycles of rebirth. It is not the place here to enter into any elaborate discussion regarding the exact concept and meaning of *Nirvāṇa* in the different schools of Buddhism, but whatever that may be, there is no doubt that *Nirvāṇa* means some kind of quiescence of finality, and the cessation of all desires, experience and the cycle of *Karma*. The Jainas also believes in the ultimate finality and the state of liberation of the souls in *Mokṣa*. But it does not seem that though this belief in a final and ultimate achievement, extinction or liberation was universal in all systems of Indian thought except the Cārvāka, no attempt seems to have been made anywhere in Indian philosophy to prove the reality of this state. In this case direct testimony from personal experience could not be available, for, he who attained salvation could not be expected to return back to normal life to record his experience. But in this case also another fiction was introduced and it was supposed that even after the attainment of this final liberation, one may with the help of another pure mind communicate his experiences for the benefit and instruction of other seekers after *Mokṣa*. This theory also has not been proved as a philosophical proposition anywhere. The doctrine of *Mukti* may, therefore, be regarded as another unproved dogma of Indian philosophy. The theory of rebirth, the theory of *Karma* and the theory of *Mukti* may thus be regarded as the three most important dogmas through which Indian philosophy has been made subservient to ethics and religion. The influence which these dogmas have over the moral and religious well-being of the Indian people cannot be over-estimated. Not all Indians are believers in God, not all of them believe in prayers, divine grace, or devotion as the best mode of approach to God, but all of them believe in these articles of faith. They have thus held together the entire religio-moral fabric of the Hindu-Buddhist-Jaina culture. Though they are but dogmas, yet they have fertilised Indian philosophy with life, and made its growth possible. For, Indian philosophy did not start from a sense of scientific curiosity or a spirit of scientific enquiry into the nature of truth, but from a practical religious need in the quest of the attainment of the highest spiritual good. It cannot, however, be denied that when philosophy began to grow, these dogmas did not in any way seriously handicap its free development. But the association of these dogmas has left their permanent stamp on the genius and character of Indian philosophy in the belief that a philosophy that does not ennoble man is but an empty vapouring. Science in this theoretic aspect seeks to investigate into the nature of truth with no other motive than the discovery of new laws, new principles and new relations. But on its practical aspect it is concerned to see how it can best employ its new discoveries to the alleviation of human sufferings and the attainment of new advantages for human well-being. Philosophy also is not merely a mental science of arguments and discussions, regarding the nature of reality and our modes of knowing it, but it must have a practical side as well. Whatever may be the result of our researches, our interest in a permanent well-being of our spiritual nature never lessens its sway. This spiritual well-being was conceived in India as self-control, or control of desires on the negative side, and the philosophic wisdom which directly revealed our spiritual nature as being above all desires and cravings on the positive side. The logic which sought to connect this moral or religious dogma with philosophy, demanded that this ascent on the spiritual scale must lead us somewhere, must end somewhere and have a finality. It was probably owing to such kinds of consideration that it was conceived that there was a deep chasm between our psychological nature and our true spiritual nature. Having made this chasm, Indian philosophy has always found it extremely difficult to explain the intimate connection between the two that is revealed in common experience. Philosophers have sought to explain it through the phenomenon of error, which is sometimes made to behave psychologically and at other times ontologically. There is a lot of confusion in this concept of error or ignorance, and the philosopher incapable of explaining it is content with leaving it untouched as the flourish of the irrational in experience. A necessary consequence of such a view is that ultimate spiritual attainment must mean the disruption of psychological experience. The moral conflict of the invasion of desires and their control and the strife for the ultimate spiritual attainment is the misery of all psychological experience which must abnegate itself in favour of the rise of spiritual enlightenment. Superior self-control is universally believed to be near to spiritual enlightenment, but opinions differ as to whether the true knowledge of this spiritual reality, being entirely different from everything else, leads to the final cessation of psychological experience of mind, or whether the control of desires ultimately produces it, or whether they do it conjointly. No philosophical arguments seem to have been adduced in favour of this bold proposition that the psychological and the spiritual lie entirely asunder, that the former is only related to the latter by a thin film of illusion or ignorance which has made it living and actual, and that the ultimate goal of all our moral and religious endeavours is to split asunder this thin film either by the complete disruption of the psychological stuff or by negating it through true knowledge. This is then another important dogma which has been produced through the logical tendency of setting a final limit to spiritual perfection. In the West, however, the nature of the spiritual perfection is kept delightfully vague and seldom defined with logical precision, and in consequence of that, philosophy is not inconveniently saddled with an unchangeable theory of mind and spirit. That philosophy should be concerned on its practical side through a better understanding of our own inner nature and our relations with the world and our fellow-beings, need not be contested. But whether spiritual advancement must have to be conceived as culminating in some kind of absolutism, may be open to doubt. Had philosophy started in this country out of a spirit of rationalisation and scientific enquiry, arising out of our intercourse with our fellow-beings, it would have remained content with setting a practical limit to spiritual advancement. But philosophy started in India out of a grave subjective anxiety for attaining our highest, and the validity of such a quest was attested and backed by the supra-conscious spiritual experience, epistemological discourses and dialectical discussions, and all that we call philosophy began to grow and accumulate through the centuries of their development, but they never contested the original dogmas which justified their practical significance. It is a fundamental characteristic of Indian philosophy that it not only tries to take its stand on reasoned and rational discourses, but it also wishes to profit by the results of the mystic and supra-conscious experiences of the sages. Indeed, one is often astonished to see in it a deep vein of anti-logical ideals, values and experiences that hold and support its logical frame. The experiences of the Yogins and the rapturous utterances of the Upaniṣads are incontestable. Philosophy, in its logical venture, has no right to come to conclusions which are contradicted by intuitional experiences. Mere logical consistency cannot guarantee truth, nor can it hold up a scheme which will be acceptable to us and which would satisfy the complex demands of our nature. But Indian philosophy not only admitted the claims of this supra-conscious experience in philosophy, but also accorded a superior validity to it. In one sense, it had its superior claims in this that it could only dawn as the result of superior self-control. But its superiority cannot be logically proved, and hence any proposition that affirms it can only be taken as a dogma. In this connection, it is not out of place to refer to another dogma that found currency with all systems of Hindu philosophy, viz., the dogma of the incontestable validity of scriptural authority. In some systems it is held that though the validity of the scriptures is incontestable, yet they are to be interpreted in such a way that they may not contradict the testimony of perception and inference. Other systems hold more extreme views and urge that since scriptural testimony has a superior validity, even the testimony of perception and inference should have to be modified in accordance with the testimony of the scriptures. Śaṅkara urges that since no finality can be arrived at by logical reasons, which behave differently in different hands, one must always depend on the scriptures for the final ascertainment of truth.

These are thus some of the important dogmas that have largely modified the direction of the purely philosophical and logical part of Indian philosophy. From behind these dogmas, one great truth emerges, viz., that philosophy owes its origin to the deep-seated human longing after some transcendent finality, and that philosophy must be expected to satisfy this longing by ennobling and elevating humanity to its high, moral and spiritual destiny. This ultimate optimism may in some sense be regarded as a bed-rock of Indian philosophical culture. All these dogmas have sprung out of the necessity of this optimistic nature of the Indian temperament. But how far these dogmas may be regarded as indispensable corollaries is open to doubt. In India the *Mukti* theory was also challenged by the devotional ideal of the Vaiṣṇavas and the older colourless ideal state of perfection involving the disruption of mind was replaced by an ideal of pure devotional enjoyment of the Vaiṣṇavas and the altruistic goal of the Mahāyāna Buddhists. The time has now come when keeping a steady eye on our fundamental optimism, we should examine how far the old accepted dogmas need hold their sway over us. Philosophy cannot dispense with dogmas altogether any more than science can dispense with unproved hypotheses. But if philosophy is to have any life, the older dogmas have to be criticised, modified, or dispensed with in the light of our new knowledge, and change of out-look. Philosophy which remains for ever encaged within its old bars, may well be taken as dead. It is, therefore, the imperative duty of Indian philosophy to rejuvenate and revitalise itself by a critical reformation of the fundamental postulates that have so long been guiding its destiny.

O.P. 62/30

SOME IMPLICATIONS OF REALISM IN THE VEDĀNTA PHILOSOPHY

The Upaniṣads contain the earliest philosophical speculations of the Hindus. Some of the earliest of these were written some time before 500 B.C. and it is only these which are considered as being philosophically most important. As these form the last part of those sacred works of the Hindus called the Vedas, they are called the Vedānta (literally the last part of the Vedas). It was probably about 200 B.C. that a systematic, but an extremely condensed, summary of the purport of some of the most important of these Upaniṣads was arranged by Vādarāyaṇa. This work is known as the *Vedānta Sūtra* or the *Brahmasūtra.* This important work did not attract the notice that it deserved until Śaṅkara wrote a brilliant commentary on it in the 8th century A.D. After Śaṅkara had written his great commentary, other forgotten commentaries on the work were revived by other thinkers and many other interpretations were made from the point of view of those thinkers who all claimed that this great work supported their philosophical views and religious beliefs.

Each of these different interpretations of the *Vedānta Sūtra* now claim that it and it alone represents correctly the ideas of Vādarāyaṇa and the Upaniṣads and claims to be called the Vedānta. But none of these other interpretations ever became as famous as that of Śaṅkara and his view is now widely known as the Vedānta Philosophy. Śaṅkara, however, did not himself work out a philosophy complete in all its parts. This task was completed by his eminent followers during a period of about 900 years. These followers all claim to be strictly faithful to the master, but they undertake to give satisfactory explanations of problems which were left untouched or make that explicit which was left implicit by the master. The superficially developed view of Śaṅkara has been made known to Europe as the Vedānta Philosophy by such writers as Deussen and Thibaut. But nothing has yet been published in Europe which gives an account of the system as developed and elaborated by Śaṅkara's followers.[1] The points of the Vedānta doctrine which I shall deal with in this short article are derived from the writings of Dharmarājādhvarīndra, the author of *Vedānta Paribhāṣā,* Rāmakṛṣṇa, the author of Śikhāmaṇi, and Madhusūdana Sarasvatī, the author of the celebrated work *Advaitasiddhi,* all followers of Śaṅkara. There are other followers of Śaṅkara whose views differ to some extent from that which I discuss here, but I do not deal with these.

The Vedānta takes a twofold view of things; the first refers to ultimate reality and the second to appearance. This ultimate reality is pure intelligence as identical with pure bliss and pure being. This is called ultimately real in the sense that it is regarded as changeless. By pure intelligence the Vedānta does not mean the ordinary cognitional states, for

1. For an abridged account of it the reader may consult my *History of Indian Philosophy* (vol. I). Cambridge University Press.

these have a subjective and an objective content which are extraneous to it. This pure intelligence is pure immediacy, identical with the fact of revelation found in all our conscious states. Our apprehensions of objects are in some sense events involving both a subjective and an objective content, but their special feature in every case is a revelatory inwardness or immediacy which is non-temporal and changeless. The fact that we see, hear, feel, touch, think, remember is equivalent to saying that there are various kinds of cognizings. But what is the nature of this cognizing? Is it an act or a fact? When I say that I see a blue colour, there is a blue object, there is a peculiar revelation of an appearance as blue and the revelation of the "I" as the perceiver. The revelation is such that it is both a revelation of a certain character as blue and of a certain thing called the blue object. When a revelation occurs in perception, it is one, and it touches both the object as well as its appearance in a certain character as blue. The revelation is not the product of a certain relation which happens to subsist at any time between the character-appearance and the object for both the character-appearance as blue and the object are given in revelation. The revelation is self-evident by itself and it stands unique by itself. Whether I see, feel or hear, it cannot be denied that there is a certain kind of revelation; for it is the intrinsic essence of seeing, feeling or hearing. The things that I see, feel, or hear, change but the fact that there is some sort of an awareness does not change. Awareness is ever present by itself and is not undergoing the change that its contents undergo. I may remember that I had seen a blue object five minutes previously, but when I do this, what I perceive is the image of a blue object with certain temporal and spatial relations, which arises or becomes revealed, but the fact of the revelation cannot be revealed again. I may be conscious but I cannot be conscious of my consciousness. For consciousness as such, though ever present in its immediacy, cannot become an object of any other consciousness. There cannot be any such thing as the awareness of an awareness or the awareness of an awareness of an awareness, though we may multiply such phrases in language at our pleasure. When I remember that I have been to Trinity College this morning, this only means that I have an image of the way across the common, through Church Street and Trinity Street; my movements through them are temporally pushed backward, but all this is a revelation as image at the present moment and not a revelation of a past revelation. I cannot say that this present image in any way reveals that particular time as the object of the present revelation. But the former revelation could also not be held to be distinct from the present one, for distinction is always based on content and not on revelation; revelation as such is identical and since this is so, one revelation cannot be the object of another. It is incorrect to say that "A is A" means that one A becomes itself back again. It is owing to the limitations of grammatical terminology that identity is thus described. Identity thus understood is different from what we understand by identity as a relation. Identity understood as a relation always presupposes some difference or otherness and thus is not self-contained. And it is because it is not self-contained that it can be called a relation. If it is said that A is identical with A, it means that on all the various occasions or contexts in which A appeared, it always signified the same thing, or that it had the same shape or that it was the same first letter of the English alphabet. Identity in this sense is a function of thought not existing by itself, but in relation to a sense of opponency or otherness.[2] But revelation has no otherness in it; it is absolutely ubiquitious and homogeneous. But the identity of revelation of which we are speaking does not simply mean that the revelation signifies the same thing amidst a diversity of contents: it is simply the one essence identical in itself and devoid of any numerical or other kinds of difference. It is absolutely free from "now" and "then", "here or there", "such" or "not such", and "this" or "that". Consciousness or self-shining self taken in this way cannot be regarded as the relation of an appearance to an object but it is the fact of the revelation or the entity of the self. If we conceive of revelation in this way it is an error to make any distinction in revelation as the revelation of the past or the revelation of the present moment. For moments are revealed as objects are revealed; they do not constitute revelation nor form any part of it. This revelation is identical with the self-shining self to which everything else has to be related in order to be known.

But let us return to our question. Is cognizing an act or a fact? Before this can be answered the

2. See Johnson's *Logic*, Part I, p. 186

point to be made clear is what is meant by cognizing. If we ignore the aspect of revelation and speak of mental states which can be looked at from the point of view of temporal or qualitative change of character, we must speak of them as acts or events. If we look at any mental state as possessing certain characters and relations to its objects, we have to speak of these as facts. But if we look at cognizing from the point of view of its ultimate truth and reality as revelation, we cannot call it either an act or a fact, for, as revelation, it is unique and unchangeable in itself. All relations and characters are revealed in it; it is self-evident and is at once in and beyond them all. Whether dreaming or awake, experiencing an illusion or a truth, revelation is always there. When we look at our mental states we find that they are always changing, but this is so only with reference to the contents. But apart from this there is a continuity in our conscious life. By this continuity the Vedānta does not refer to any sort of coherence in our ideas, but to the fact of the permanence of revelation. It may be asked what remains of revelation if the mental states are taken away. This question is not admissible, for the mental states do not form part of revelation; they are rendered conscious by coming in relation to revelation. This category of revelation is the ultimate reality. It is not self or subject in the sense in which self or ego is ordinarily understood. For what is ordinarily understood as the ego or the "I" is as much a content of the perception of the moment as any other objective content. It is not impossible that any particular objective content may be revealed at any time without the corresponding "I perceive" being explicitly revealed at the same time. The notion of ego or "I" does not refer to an everlastingly abiding independent self or person, for this notion is as changing as any other objective content. The "I" has no definite real content as referring to an existing entity it is only a particular mode of mind which is often associated as relatively abiding content in association with other changing contents of the mind. As such, it is as changeable as is any other object. "I know this" only means that there is a revelation which at one sweep reveals both the "this" and the "I". So far as the revelation appears as revealing the "this" and the "I" it is manifested in a subjective mental state having a particular conscious centre different from other similar centres. But since revelation cannot in reality be individuated, all that we may say about "I" or "mine", "thou" or "thine", falls outside it. They are all contents having some indefinite existence of their own and revealed by this principle of revelation under certain conditions. This principle of revelation thus has reality in quite a different sense from that which is used to designate the existence of any other object. All other objects are dependent upon this principle of revelation for their manifestation, and their nature or essence out of connection with it cannot be defined or described. They are not self-evident, but are only expressed by coming in some sort of relation with this principle of revelation. We have already seen that this principle of revelation cannot be either subjective or objective. For all considerations of subject or object fall outside of it and do not in any way qualify it, but are only revealed by it. There are thus two principles, the principle of revelation and all those that are revealed by it. The principle of revelation is one, for there is nothing else like it; it alone is real in the highest and truest sense. It is absolute in the sense that there is no growth, decay, evolution or change in it, and it is perfectly complete in itself. It is infinite in the sense that no finitude can form part of it though through it all finitude is being constantly revealed. It is all-pervading in the sense that no spatial or temporal limits can be said to affect it in any way though all these are being constantly revealed by it. It is neither in my head nor in my body nor in the space before me, but yet there is nowhere that it is not. It has sometimes been designated as the Self or *ātman* but only in the sense of denoting its nature as the supreme essence and transcendent reality of all—the Brahman.

Apart from this principle of revelation, all else is constituted of a substanceless indefinable stuff called *māyā*. This has often been misinterpreted in the sense that all is pure and simple illusion, that things exist only when they are perceived and dissolve into nothingness as soon as we cease to perceive them. This is however a mistake, though one school does interpret Vedānta from this point of view.[3] The Vedānta as explained by most of its illustrious exponents and particularly those whom I am following here, holds that things are as they are perceived though they are not *really* as they are perceived. Things which we perceive, whatever they may really be in themselves, are not my ideas, nor are they pro-

3. See Prakāśānanda's *Siddhānta Mutāvalī*. Published in the *Paṇḍit*, 1889, Benares.

duced by my perception, nor will they cease when I cease to perceive them, nor are they mis-perceptions, except in the sense that they have only a changeable and indefinable existence. They have no permanent substratum in the sense in which we speak of the principle of revelation as real ; they are ever changing and are revealed by the principle of revelation as they are and as they change. This leads to the confusion of identity of the principle of revelation with what is undergoing change.

Both the mind and external physical objects are composed of the same stuff, the stuff of *māyā*. Things that we perceive are but modifications of this *māyā*, somehow related to the principle of revelation. It will be seen that having admitted the principle of revelation and thereby rejected the theory that consciousness can be deduced from something else or be looked upon as the result of a certain interaction or relation, the Vedānta had no necessity of considering mind as being in any way superior in position. It definitely opposed that system of idealism represented by the Vijñānavādins who held that there was no external world or objects before us, but only the ideas appearing and disappearing in a series. The external world was present as perceived. For if we had any reason for believing that ideas existed, we should have equal reason for believing that the ideas referred to objects. We do not perceive ideas but objects. But the question arises that if the principle of revelation is not specifically situated with reference to any special object, how is it that things do not always appear as revealed? How is it that things cannot be known unless perceived by someone? To this question the Vedānta replies that the *māyā* stuff is characterised by two qualities, non-appearance (*āvaraṇa*) and variety of modification (*vikṣepa*). Revelation in itself is somehow associated with this obscure principle of *māyā* and thereby contributes to its being or existence, but is not itself opposed to it. The *māyā* stuff is associated (*āśraya*) with the changeless Reality in such a way that it remains itself non-apparent, and covered or veiled. Physical objects are but modifications of the *māyā* stuff remaining in association with changeless Reality and making the latter an object (*viṣaya*) to itself in the sense that it veils it in such a way that it (the principle of revelation—the Reality) cannot reveal the objects with which it is associated. It is for this reason that though the *māyā* stuff is always in some way associated with the Reality or the principle of revelation, yet objects are not revealed. Mind is as much constituted of *māyā* stuff as any other object, but the special modification of *māyā* as mind is such that its states do not veil the Brahman as do other things. This is not all. When any object comes in contact with the mind as transformed into a corresponding state, the principle of revelation, the Reality, the Brahman, reveals it. The non-appearance characteristic of the *māyā* stuff is overcome when any object constituted of it comes in close touch with mind-states (*antaḥkaraṇa-vṛtti*). It is for this reason that though the principle of revelation is always equally shining, the revelation of any particular object always depends upon certain conditions, dependent upon their contact with the mind, transformed into a corresponding state. Under normal conditions, the part that mind played is of a passive nature. Though itself a modification of the same stuff as that of which external objects are composed, the mind has a special quality of transparency by which its states can always reflect the self, the principle of revelation, the Reality or the Brahman.

But the question again arises as to the nature of the existence of the external objects or the mind, both of which are regarded as different types of the modification of the *māyā* stuff. Strictly speaking, the notion of permanent being belongs to the Brahman and not to the *māyā* and "being" as an independent entity is not perceived anywhere, though what is perceived is perceived as having "being" in it. Being is the fundamental essence which is referred to in all existents, whether physical or mental. In dealing with physical objects, to whatever characteristics we may refer, being is somehow always implied as belonging to them. Known or unknown, there cannot be anything which is not somehow attributed to being. An idea appearing in consciousness has both a revelatory or conscious character and an ontological character, but physical objects seem to have been without conscious character. Being is the common trait in both and reveals the Brahman or the reality which they possess in common as their underlying reality. Whatever is affirmed is affirmed of Reality or being manifesting itself either as external objects or ideas. Looked at from this point of view, the world of objects is a result of association of the *māyā* with the Brahman, in which the revelatory character is always hidden, whereas the character as "being" is always present. Thus the element of existence or being which we attribute to the external world is due to the Reality, which is held enwombed as it were within the *māyā* stuff forming its content and character. That the physical objects or the mind hold within them the Reality and thereby show themselves as existents is an accepted fact with the Vedānta. The mind however holds the same position as physical objects, for both derive their element of being from the Reality or Brahman or self held within them. But the being of any object is not thereby made dependent on mind. The existence of any object does not depend on its being perceived.

The question now arises that if the essence as being, which is found to underlie all our experiences, is the reality, the Brahman, what are we to say of the things and objects that are perceived? If a distinction is drawn between an object and its being, what is to be said of the status of objects, ideas, concepts, the mind, the ego—the products of the *māyā* stuff, if we wish to conceive them in themselves as unrelated to the Brahman which contributes to them their being? The plain answer of the Vedānta is that they can never be conveived as "this" or "that" when taken apart from Brahman. In themselves they are indefinite, indefinable and inconceivable. They are positive in their nature (*bhāvarūpa*) and yet they form the stuff of all that is negative as well. This positivity does not signify anything definite, but only non-negativity. The *māyā* stuff thus forms a category which is too elusive in its nature to be defined or made definite. For in order to make it definite permanent being has to be ascribed to it and permanent being is the essence of Reality or Brahman.

But if we abandon the attempt to penetrate deeply into the nature of the *māyā* stuff, we can accept a position of realism on most epistemological questions. We cannot indeed say that things "really" are as they are seen, but we may say that things are as they are seen. This is a distinction with which we are familiar in our own times. Thus Holt in defending his position against the idealists says that "as things are perceived *so they are*", Idealists have rather rashly misunderstood him to mean that "things are perceived as they are really", i.e., all perceived things are real things. But while all perceived things are things, *not* all perceived things are real things[4] . . . . "The entities of this universe have no substance, but if the spirit is too weak to grasp this, then let the flesh for a season predict a neutral subtance". In like manner, we might say that though things may in reality be regarded as a super-imposition of *māyā* on Brahman, yet they are present, just as they are perceived.

When I perceive an object, my mind comes in contact with the object, through the visual organs. This conception of an actual contact is not impossible, since the mind is also a modification of the *māyā* stuff of which the physical objects are also composed. When the mind thus comes in contact with certain colours existing in certain spatial forms, it assumes the same forms, just as water flowing into a vessel assumes the shape of that vessel. For the moment the spatially arranged patch of colour becomes one with the mind it becomes as transparent and lucid

4. *New Realism*, pp. 358—372.

as the mind itself. But the principle of revelation shines forth whenever the mind assumes any form, or in other words becomes transformed into a mental state. The result is that at that moment the perception and the thing being at one and the same place, the same principle of revelation illuminates them both and the awareness of the thing and the thing are both manifested at one and the same time. The perceptual event thus happens as much in my brain as outside in the thing, which is made the object of that perception. For the mind, though never out of touch with the body of the perceiver, is also somehow in touch with the object perceived, the shape of which it assumes in order to render it transparent for peceptual manifestation. The function of the mind and the senses is not to distort or create objects of perception, but to find them for manifestation by the principle of revelation which exists as the underlying principle both of objects and of the mind. It is on account of the non-appearance characteristic of the *māyā* that objects do not appear in awareness of themselves. But as soon as they are in contact with the mind they become as it were transparent and the *cit* or the principle of revelation, shining forth through the mental state, destroys the veil of non-appearance of the objects and the thing is manifested in awareness. The function of the mind is thus to give a correct expression of things as they are by affording them the opportunity of being illuminated by the *cit*. The real essence of all awareness is indeed the *cit* and it is only in an indirect way that the mental states are called states of awareness. The mind is a composite product of the *māyā* stuff, and cannot be regarded as being of the same nature as consciousness. What is meant by speaking of states of consciousness is simply this that the *cit* or pure revelation is manifested through particular forms into which the mind has passed by coming in contact with certain specific objects. As regards the association of the visual perception of colour with the perception of other senses, as when we see a piece of sandalwood and without smelling it call it fragrant, the effect is due wholly to memory, associating the present perception of a particular colour with certain smells previously experienced. This applies also to the perception of things as hard or soft, which is due to memory and implication. There is however no distinction between sensations and perceptions such that it could be said that we first get the sensations and that these are later coordinated into perceptions. For when the mind comes into contact with the object, perception directly and immediately arises and this involves no synthetic activity on the part of the mind in coordinating any elementary data which may be called the sensations. The objects are perceived as they are and not constructed from cruder materials supplied by the senses.

With reference to the objections raised by other Indian thinkers on behalf of the existence of indeterminate perceptions involving no qualitative relations previous to their development in the determinate perception (e.g., I see the jug), the Vedānta holds that the former can only exist in perceptions of identity, as when I am looking at a person before me who is pointed out to me as John or Henry. The perception of identity in this case does not involve any new qualitative addition to the perception of the man before me. For there is no new qualitative addition to the perception of John and yet there is the perception of identity.

It may be objected that since time is continually changing, we cannot correctly say that we are having the same perception of a thing when we look at it for a while, though there is no apparent qualitative change in it. To this the Vedānta replies that so long as the awareness of a particular object continues the same without change, there is no reason to think that we are having new knowledge at each moment. All that it involves is the perception of new elements of time, and there is no reason to suppose why perceptions of new elements of time should involve any change in the perception of the object itself. It may be objected that if the principle of revelation, the *cit,* is absolute and timeless, we cannot speak of an act of cognizing. To this the Vedānta replies that though the pure intelligence is timeless, yet the mental state which reflects it is produced by the mind-object contact taking place through the senses and the awareness *as associated with it* has a beginning and an end. The mental states, as we have already seen, are but composites of the *māya* stuff and are only called conscious in an indirect way, by virtue of the fact that they invariably reflect the principle of revelation. The Vedānta holds that not only the ordinary perceptual states, but desire, imagination, doubt, faith, shame, fear, and other mental feelings, concepts or ideas are all modes of the mind and are consequently constituted of the *māyā* stuff, and illuminated or revealed by the *cit* associated with the mind. The difference between these and the per-

O.P. 62/32

ceptual states of mind consists in this, that the former are inherent in the mind while the objects of the latter are outside the mind. What we ordinarily refer to as the ego is connected with out notion of the "I", is also a similar transformation of the *māyā* stuff. The difference between it and other mental modifications is that it is persistent throughout all our experiences. The reason why the mental feelings of pleasure, pain etc. are associated with the notion of the ego is this that the latter forms an inseparable feature of all mind-modifications and thus always gets illuminated in association with the illumination of all other emotional states subsisting in the mind. The result is that they get somehow combined together and instead of their being two separate notions of an "I" and a "pleasure" existing as different entities, the notion appears as "I am happy", as if the pleasure or happiness was a qualification or condition of the ego. But in the case of the perception of an external object, the revelation is in the object through the mind ; the mind by coming in contact with the object and assuming its form only helped to get its non-appearance character removed and its particular form revealed and hence it appears in an objective relation to the sense of the ego. Hence we say that we see the blue but are happy. The same principle of revelation illuminates in one sweep as it were the abiding mode of the mind as the perceiver or ego, the perceiving state of the mind of the form of the object and the object itself.

Thus we find that according to Vedānta not only are there external objects, independent of our perception, but even pleasure, pain, other emotions, and the logical concepts are all in the mind and are made known as corresponding awarenesses, when there are such modifications of the mind as can reflect the light of the *cit* on them. The reason why these mental feelings appear to be produced just at the moment of their perception is this, that they are not generated by any kind of activity, but are directly perceived in the mind as a mental state. As in the case of outside objects, the mind has to get itself transformed into a state before they can be revealed, so also in the case of the mental emotions or concepts, the mind must turn itself into those specific states before they can be revealed. But there is no reason to think that these mental feelings are only produced by our perceiving of them. They were there as a state of the mind already and made into an object of awareness.

The most important point with regard to realistic epistemology is its explanation of errors or illusions. What happens when I perceive a piece of conch-shell as a piece of silver? The silver does not actually exist in the shell and if perception reveals only that is present in the mind-object contact, it will not be applicable in this case. The answer that Vedānta gives to this difficulty is, that an illusory piece of silver is produced there at the time of error, with which the mind comes in contact and by this means effects its revelation in the ordinary way. It is true that the stuff of which this illusory silver is made, is somehow different from that which constitutes ordinary silver, but that does not mean that the illusory silver was not somehow existing. Vedānta holds that either through some defect of the eye, or on account of dimness of light or other accessory circumstances, there first arises in the perceiver a mental state as a "glittering this" with reference to the conch-shell before him, by virtue of the visual contact. The "being" involved in the conch-shell as a mere indefinite thing, as a mere "this", is then associated with the mental state as a "glittering this". At this stage, there is thus the appearance of a "glittering this", which hides the real conch-shell and takes its place. Then this false appearance in association with the subconscious impression of silver is roused into operation by a feeble suggestion of similarity between its present glittering character and the like character of silver and transforms itself into the illusory object of silver as well as into the illusory perception of silver. This explanation of error is however not as satisfactory as modern realists would wish. For although the Vedānta holds that in the case of this illusory perception of silver, an illusory silver has been created as the object perceived, yet the creation of this illusory silver requires for its accomplishment, although as an accessory, the perception of similarity and the sub-conscious awakening of the image of silver and hence the illusion would be non-existent when there were no perceivers. It is realistic only in the sense that the mental constituents of the perceiver and the external circumstances and the imperfectly perceived object, all contribute to produce a piece of illusory silver, which becomes the object of the illusory perception. Thus, though there is an object, which is referred to by the illusory perception, yet this object would not exist if there were no perceivers. Another interpretation of this situation suggests that the illusory silver is created by the accessory conditions of dim light, defect of the eyes etc., but that its stuff is such that it can only be rendered visible by certain subjective conditions, such as the rousing of the sub-conscious suggestion of silver etc. on the part of the perceiver. This explanation is more realistic, for the creation of the illusory silver is thus not regarded as dependent upon the perceiver and it might exist in the absence of perceivers. According to the former interpretation, when right knowledge dawns, it destroys the illusory silver, for the conditions which generated it having failed, the illusory silver also fails. But according to the latter interpretation, the illusory creation may still remain, yet the *knowledge* of the illusion may cease to exist when the mental conditions which contributed to its perception are removed. But the former view is that generally accepted, that the illusory silver only exists as an object so long as it is perceived. But so long as it is perceived, it is not a mere idea as Berkeley would have it, but an external object. The fact that it is soon destroyed is no reason why it should not exist as an object so long as it is perceived. Nothing ever appears as uncontradicted except the principle of revelation, the Brahman. In the case of dreams also, the dream-objects are there and are perceived. They are illusory only in the sense that they cease to exist when they are not perceived, yet they are there while they are perceived as external existents.

The question may naturally arise, that if illusions are possible in some cases, how can we know that there are no illusions in other cases? The Vedānta holds that there is no further criterion of truth than that of want of contradiction in experience. We must accept any fact as true so long as it is not contradicted, and this applies both to illusory perceptions and to those that are called real. There is nothing in our ordinary experiences of which we could be so sure that it would never be contradicted under any circumstances. Hence in judging whether any knowledge is or is not correct, we have only to see whether it is or is not contradicted. With this criterion of truth we may safely hold that our experiences reveal things as they are, however unthinkable, indefinable and indefinite they may be in their own nature.

MESSAGE OF BUDDHISM*

I beg to thank you most sincerely, ladies and gentlemen, and the organisers of this World Convention Of Buddhism for the honour they have done me in asking me to preside on such a unique occasion in the holiest and the most ancient living city of the world, the golden sands of which have been purified by the footprints and the life work of the Lord Buddha and the later Bodhisattvas, Pratyekabuddhas, Arhats and the numerous Hindu saints and Yogins, Tirthaṅkaras and the great savants who lived and worked here in unbroken succession from the oldest times. As I look back I fancy I see the populous and the prosperous city of Benares when the Brahmadatta line of kings were reigning or when the Upaniṣadic sages were roaming over in Kāśī in quest of *brahmavidyā*. The Vedic system of worship was established long ago. The Hindu people were divided into four castes and the four *āśramas*. The Vedic system of worship was almost entirely ritualistic in its character and directed to mundane ends. It was more a magic worship (in the scientific use of the term magic ; in the sense of mystic rites) than theism or polytheism. It was believed that if animals were sacrificed and the *mantras* were uttered and all the elaborate ceremonials extending over months and years were scrupulously observed and performed absolutely accurately according to the directions laid

* *Address delivered as President of the Buddhist Convention held at Holy Isipatana, Sārnāth, on the 12th November, 1931.*

down in the *Brāhmaṇas,* then any desired end could be achieved, be it a heavy shower of rain for the crops, the birth of a son or the destruction of a foe. The emphasis of this ritualistic religion was neither on a high elevation of morals nor on transcendental spiritualism which in a later age was regarded as its essence. A protest soon evolved in the Vedic circle itself and to it we owe the composition of some of the most important monistic and the monotheistic hymns of the Vedas and the Upaniṣads, and we note the criticisms of the Upaniṣadists in such phrases as *plavā hyete adṛḍhā yajñarūpāḥ* and *yajñiyā* are *paśavaḥ.* The fundamental emphasis of the Upanisadic religion consists in the intuitive grasp of a reality which was at the same time the highest and the truest self of man. The reality was the indivisible whole, absolutely homogeneous pure consciousness and bliss. The whole of the Upaniṣads reveals the history of the transition from the Vedic forms of worship to this higher call of spirituality in the quest of the sages after the highest reality and is permeated through and through with an exhilaration of joy and ecstasy at the realisation of the beatific truth which was not received from outside through the grace of any higher Being but was revealed as the true manifestation and perception of our inmost self. No ceremonial was necessary for its attainment and no God was to be worshipped. It naturally revealed itself to those true seekers who were pure in heart and self-controlled in their conduct.

The Vedic ritualistic religion was the religion of the Brahmins. The Śudras had no share in it. The two other higher castes could have the sacrifices performed in their behalf by the Brahmin priests and they themselves had to remain content only with the compulsory and occasional (*nitya* and *naimittika*) performance of certain rituals. The religion of the Upaniṣads was however still more restricted being only the religion of the philosophers and the seers, for it was only the select few who had risen above all mundane concerns and were filled with a zeal and yearning after the achievement of the highest truth that were deemed fit for this high philosophic religion. The observance of general morality called *sādhāraṇa dharma* such as non-injury to animals, non-stealing and the like was indeed a universal requirement, but yet each caste had its specific duties and if there was a conflict between the caste duties (*varṇadharma*) and the general morality, the *sādhāraṇa dharma*, the caste duties predominated. Thus, for example, the duties of a Kṣhatriya consisted primarily in fighting and in giving protection to those who sought it at any sacrifice. Instances are indeed rare where a Brahmin had given protection to any other caste at any considerable personal sacrifice. The Brahmins would indeed sacrifice their interests for the Gods as in the case of Dadhīci and they would also sacrifice their pleasures and comforts for the attainment of a higher spiritual goal but not generally for any lower caste. Whereas in the case of a Kṣhatriya the Purāṇas are indeed full of them. The whole of the Gītā is devoted in urging Arjuna to follow his caste duties of fighting and not to take to the *sādhāraṇa dharma* of *ahiṁsā*, and Lord Kṛṣṇa spared no philosophy at his command for this purpose. Thus none of the pre-Buddhistic religions of India may be said to have been able to formulate a code of ethics and religion that was universally and compulsorily valid for all. There were always boxes within boxes, branches and sub-branches based on the principles of scriptural competence or *adhikāri-bheda*. Even now though many tens of centuries have passed, the Hindus are divided and sub-divided into numerous castes, and even the Brahmins are so much sub-divided among themselves that in an orthodox Brahmin Hostel of twenty-five, six kitchens are considered as insufficient. Though the castes have all undergone a hopeless mixture through the ravages of time, we still see ineffectual efforts to re-establish them in their pristine predominance. The ritualistic codes which expanded in diverse ways in diverse provinces and localities under different conditions have again and again been put together and reinterpreted by ritualistic teachers, so that their hold on the people may not slacken and dry rituals are even now being offered in a wholesale measure as true religion. There is another important characteristic of the Vedic and Upaniṣadic religions that they are largely individualistic, not only in their scope but also in their ends. There was hardly anything in this religion which in the eye of the present generation would seem to contain any universal elements for the well-being and solace of the humanity at large. Human misery has often been the cause of the soul-rending cry for religion. It is after all the sinners and the sufferers who should be given some hope, some peace, some satisfaction, and the religion that would fail to do it would miss its primary vocation.

It was at this great world crisis that the Lord Buddha, the greatest and the noblest of all beings on earth, preached his great religion in the historic city of Benares in the Deer Park on the site of the *Mūla-gandha-kuṭi-vihāra*. He was born as a Kṣatriya prince in or about the year 560 B.C. and according to the legends, on successive occasions, issuing from the palace he was confronted by a decrepit old man, a diseased man, a dead man and a monk and this filled him with amazement and distress and realizing the impermanence of earthly things determined to forsake his home and try, if he could, to discover some means to immortality, to remove the sufferings of men. He made his great renunciation at the age of twenty-nine, and after six years of great struggle he was convinced that the truth was not to be won by the way of extreme asceticism and resuming an ordinary course of life at last obtained absolute and supreme enlightenment and preached his religion for over forty-five years travelling from place to place. At the age of over eighty years he entered into *dhyāna* and passing through its successive stages attained *nirvāṇa*. The vast developments which the system of this great teacher underwent in succeeding centuries in India and in other countries have not yet been thoroughly studied and it will probably take yet many long years before even the materials for such a study can be collected. This religion in the course of its growth and development spread in the North over Tibet and China up to the farthest border of north Mongolia, on the East and the South it spread in Siam, Burma, Japan and many of the Pacific islands and Ceylon and in the South-West up to Madagascar and in the West to Afghanistan, Persia, Turkestan and the whole of the now desert area near it, Syria and even to Egypt.

Even at the present day one third of the human population are Buddhists. But in the days of its prosperity when the greater portion of India had been converted into Buddhism at least half of the civilised world were probably Buddhists.

Nowhere in the history of the world before Lord Buddha do we hear of any teacher of religion who was ever filled with such an all-absorbing sympathy and love for the suffering humanity. Few centuries after him we hear of wise men in Greece, Socrates, Plato and Aristotle, but they were only dry thinkers and seekers after truth without any inspiring love for the suffering multitude. Centuries before the birth of Christ Buddhism was preached in Syria and it is not improbable that he might have been enkindled by the cardinal feeling of Buddhism of sympathy and love, the *maitrī* and *karuṇā* for our fellow-sufferers. But even in him it is more a spirit of godliness than the feeling for humanity that may be regarded as the motive spirit. Buddhism thus transcends all other religions by the very motive which permeates in and through it. When in the later days, different systems of philosophy were being offered as the panacea for all suffering, they only caught the catch-word of Buddhism but not the spirit ; for these systems of philosophy did not offer one universal food for all humanity. They were all within the pale of Brāhmaṇism and philosophic emancipation meant practically the emancipation of the higher castes. The only schools of thought which rightly absorbed the Buddhist feeling of sympathy for sufferers and reinterpreted it on lines of hygienic and mental well-being were probably the Carakean school of Medicine which regarded the preservation of a healthy body and a happy mind for all (*hita āyu* and *sukha āyu*) as the aim of all its teachings and the Bhāgavata Vaiṣṇavism.

For the first time in India Buddhism offered a universal religion based on the equality of rights and privileges of all mankind. I wish that in these days of communal and minority dissensions, Lord Buddha had once more appeared with his begging bowl and again preached his *dharma-cakra* and had shown us the way how a man can meet his fellow brother and embrace him with his religion of sympathy and love and not feel his religion a motive to thrust a dagger into his neighbour's bosom. Lord Buddha did away with castes and caste privileges and all kinds of ritualism and preached his religion to the masses of India not by appealing to scriptures or superstitions, but by arousing the dormant rationality in man by personal magnetism, above all by sympathy and love.

It is difficult at this distant date to point out definitely what were the exact words of Lord Buddha's teachings. They began to be collected through his pupils at least a hundred years after his *mahāparinirvāṇa*. Different traditional records give us different accounts of his religion and philosophy and the later adherents gradually developed the anticipations and implications contained in the *Buddha-vacana* and in this way there arose not only the Hīnayāna (the older Theravāda, the main branches of which were known from the 2nd century B.C. as the Hetuvādins and Sarvāstivādins and also identified with the Vibhajjavādins in the *Mahābodhivaṃśa*) and the Mahāyāna (the old Mahāsāṅghikas who seceded from the Vajjiputtakas at the first Council of Vaiśālī and branched out into different schools such as the Ekavyāvahārikas, Lokottaravādins, Kukkulikas, Bahuśrutīyas, Prajñāptivādins, Caittikas, Aparaśailas, Uttaraśailas and a number of other Yānas) and into a number of other schools. Hīnayāna of the Theravādins developed during the first and the second century B.C. into a number of schools such as the Haimavatas, Dharmaguptikas, Mahīśasakas, Kāśyapīyas, Saṅkrāntikas (also called the Sautrāntikas) and the Vātsīputtrīyas which later on was again split up into Dharmottarīyas, Bhadrayānikas, Sammitīyas, and Channāgārikas. In addition to these, other Buddhist schools also sprang up before the beginning of the Christian era. The Vaibhāśikas, who are identified with the Sarvāstivādins, have a vast *Abhidharma* literature, which is different from the *Abhidharma* of the Theravādins, which still exist in Chinese translations. These are (1) *Jñānaprasthānaśāstra* of Kātyāyanīputra, (2) *Dharmaskandha* by Sāriputtra, (3) *Dhātukāya* by Pūrṇa, (4) *Prajñaptiśāstra* by Mggaolāyana, (5) *Vijñānakāya* by Devakṣema, (6) *Saṅgītiparyyāya* by Sāriputtra, (7) *Prakaraṇapāda* by Vasumitra. In addition to these we have the vast literature of the *Mahāyānasūtras* (called also the *Vaipulyasūtras* which developed either the Śunyavāda or Vijñānavāda doctrines) which started probably in the second or the first century B.C. and continued to grow till the eighth century A.D. or even later.

But whatever may have been the different records or the interpretations of the teachings of Lord Buddha in the vast canonical literature excluding the well-known collection of the *Tripiṭakas* of *Sutta, Vinaya* and *Abhidhamma* and the countless writings of innumerable commentators and interpretors of Buddhistic thought in China, Japan, Burma, Ceylon and India and the many philosophical compositions of the Buddhistic faith by philosophers who are almost unparalleled in the history of human thought for their wisdom and logical analysis, it is not difficult to formulate the essential features of the doctrine of Lord Buddha as a religious teacher. He argued in the mind that since disease, old age, and death have to be prevented, what is it which not being there these would not be. He answered in his mind that if there was no birth there could not be disease, old age and death. But what being there, there is birth and he argued in his mind that if there was no *bhava* that is *karma* depending upon (*upādāna*) *tṛṣṇā* and that is a grasping and desire, depending in succession upon feeling (*vedanā*), the sense-contact (*sparśa*), the sense field (*ṣaḍāyatana*), mind and body (*nāmarūpa*), consciousness (*vijñāna*) and the psychological conglomerating forces (*saṅkhāra*) of another birth there could not be the event of the birth in the present life ; and those events of the past life again could not be without the determining cause of ignorance or *avidyā* of the third life. Thus the cause of all our sufferings in the present life is distributed over the past two lives and so in an infinite regression. There is no soul or permanent entity, which suffers transmigration or lives through the experiences as the followers of the Upaniṣads believed. When one says "I", what one does is that one refers either to all the psychological conglomerations or elements combined or any one of them and deludes himself that that was "I". Just as one could not say that the fragments of the lotus belong to the petals, the colour or the pollen, so one could not say that the sense-data were "I" or that the feeling was "I" or any of the other psychological elements were "I". There is nowhere to be found in the psychological structure or in the psychosis of our being any such permanent entities that could correspond with "I am". The forces of our *karma* actuated by *tṛṣṇā* and *avidyā* produce in successive stages the complex of our mind and the psychological experience of the moment and these change from moment to moment and the only difference that is produced at death is that they are associated with a visibly different body. At each moment we are theoretically suffering death and new psychological elements are originated by the forces of the past ones. And death is only visibly demonstrated as the destruction of the body and can only then be understood by inexperienced minds. Thus there is no entity that transmigrates but the psychological elements pass on in an unbroken series till they may be finally disorganised by the destruction of *tṛṣṇā* and *avidyā*. Since there is no permanent entity or reality, metaphysical discussions are wholly unnecessary; what we perceive in causation is not any transforming ground of evolution or any production through collecting conditions, but simply the fact that there being something, some other thing happens, there being *tṛṣṇā* or desire, there is a grasping tendency; there being the grasping tendency, there is the *karma* that produces rebirth. There is no conscious agent any where, causation is thus reduced to a mere phenomenalism of invariable antecedents and consequents.

This is the great Buddhist doctrine of *pratītya-samutpāda* (*idam pratītya idam utpadyate*). Buddhism in this sense is anti-metaphysical phenomenalism. The enlightenment of Buddha consists in the discovery that there is no real agent and no permanent reality and that our sufferings are caused by the twelve-fold phenomenalistic antecedents and consequents spreading over three lives (*trikāṇḍa*) beginning from *jarāmaraṇa* and going backwards to *avidyā* through the successive links through the happening of each one of which each of the others happens in an infinite *regressus*.

Karma indeed produces rebirth, the length of life and the condition of happy and unhappy experiences, but it can do so only when deeds are performed with covetousness, antipathy and infatuation. Deeds performed without covetousness are like a palmyra tree uprooted and pulled out of the ground and therefore virtually non-existent and incapable of producing future effects. *Karma* without *tṛṣṇā* is incapable of producing good or bad fruit. The cessation of sorrow can therefore only happen when the craving of *tṛṣṇā* entirely ceases. When the desire or the craving has once ceased, the sage becomes an *Arhat* and the deeds that he might do after that would bear no fruit for it is through desire that karma finds its scope of giving fruits, but yet an *Arhat* may like Moggalayana suffer the effects of the deeds done by him in some previous birth. We are all intertwined through inside and outside by the tangles of desire (taṇhājaṭā) and the only way by which these might be loosened is by the practice of right discipline (*śīla*) which consists in desisting from committing all sinful deeds, meditative concentration (*samādhi*) and wisdom (*paññā*). *Śīla* however does not only mean the actual non-commission of sinful deeds but those particular volitions and mental states by which a man who desists from committing sinful action maintains himself in the right path. It therefore not only includes all inner and outer negative control, but it also includes the watchfulness (sati-saṃvara) by which one can bring in right and good association when using his cognitive senses and the habit of remaining unperturbed under all conflicting conditions. By proper adherence to *śīla* all our bodily, mental and vocal activities are duly systematised, organised and stabilised. It is only then that the mind becomes fit for meditative concentration. The primary duty therefore for all those who seek relief from misery is the practice of increasing self-control on the negative side and on the positive side the preparation of the mind by continually habituating it to think of all beings as friends (*maitrī*), to sympathise and feel pity for all who suffer (*karuṇā*), to feel happy at the happiness of all beings (*muditā*) and to ignore the defects and short-comings of others (*upekṣā*) and thereby to free the mind from antipathy.

The most notable development of *Mahāyāna* consists in the fact that it gave a much greater emphasis on the practice of the positive virtue of benevolence, character, forbearance, tenacity of will, and energy and meditation called the *pāramitās*. There was also another point in which the Mahāyāna thought itself to be superior to the Hīnayāna. The former thought that the Hīnayānist wrongly interpreted the instructions of Buddha and thought that the ultimate good of a Buddhist was to attain his own *nirvāṇa* or salvation, whereas the Mahāyānist's creed was not to seek his own salvation but to seek the salvation of all beings. The Hīnayānist had only a short business of attaining his own salvation and this could be done in three lives, whereas a Mahāyāna adherent was prepared to work for infinite time in helping all beings to attain salvation and this is the vow of a Bodhisattva. Mahāyānism thus preached the doctrine of absolute altruism in a manner unprecedented in the history of human faiths. Its development of Nihilism and Idealism through the association of Brahmin converts, who brought a Upaniṣadic perspective with them, may also be regarded as the result of the tendency to elaborating the logial implications of the Buddhistic phenomenalism. For if there is no permanent reality anywhere and everything were mere phenomena none of these would be definable or explainable except in a mere relative manner and this is what is called *śūnyavāda*. Again, if everything were mere phenomena we need admit merely the cognative phenomena as that would be enough to explain experience. It is because the different schools of Buddhism had such an intimate relation among themselves that we sometimes find that the Buddhist writers might in the same book follow for better elaboration the Sautrāntika view that admits the existence of external objects and then quietly pass over in the other part of the book to a form of idealism that would deny the existence of external things. The conflict of the different schools of Buddhism had therefore only a methodological interest as it is largely due to a greater or less emphasis on this or that point.

The various ways in which Buddhism has influenced, modified, transformed and revitalised Hindu religion and thought, dogmas and myths, ideals and practices, are too elaborate a subject to be touched upon in a short lecture like this. But it may be pointed out that the Hindu systems of philosophy would have lost much of their depth, interest and value, if they could not assimilate much from Buddhism and if they were not forced to take an independent stand by its side. The Upaniṣads remained largely content with an ecstatic experience without the dynamic conceptualism that constitute philosophy in our modern sense. The Vedic ritualism was to a large extent magic. The Hindu thought could only grow when it came in touch with the sturdy universal rationalism of Buddhism through which alone the world-light of reason could flash upon it. In consequence of this almost all the philosophical *sūtras* of the Hindus may safely be admitted as being not only post-Buddhistic but post-Mahāyānic. It is difficult to say how much of the principal dogmas of Hindu philosophy such as the doctrine of *karma,* the doctrine of rebirth, the doctrine of *mukti,* the doctrine of *jīvan-mukti* were current before Buddhism, but it is in Buddhism and post-Buddhistic systems that we find the most comprehensive treatment of these pre-suppositions of Indian philosophy. The entire code of Yoga discipline, the doctrine of *tṛṣṇā* and *vāsanā* were probably to some extent in India in pre-Buddhistic time, but I believe it is undeniable that they attained their fullest development in the Buddhist literature. The Hindu thought has eclectically assimilated them but has not advanced them even by an inch. The whole of Patañjali's *Yoga-sūtra* with its *Vyāsa-bhāṣya* does not seem to me anything more than a Hinduised version of Buddhist Yoga. The essence of Hinduisation consists in the admission of permanent souls, *Īśvara* and scriptural authority. So almost the whole of the Budhdist tenets is accepted only with such modifications as to make it consistent with the admission of such permanent entities as are essential for the Hindu perspective of things. I yield to none in my profound respect for the great teacher Śaṅkara, but a careful analysis of his writings demonstrates indisputably that he largely borrowed his doctrine, his phraseology, his dialectics and his method of approach from Buddhism. Even his *saccidānanda Brahmavāda* reveals in it an echo of the *Triṃśikā* of Vasubandhu. His main contribution seems to be that where he could not prove his Brahma doctrine he appealed to scriptural authority of the Upaniṣads and he interpreted or interpreted away the Upaniṣads in order to show that he was giving us the philosophy of the Upaniṣads. Not only Śaṅkara but many of his followers like Śrīharṣa, Ānandajñāna and others who have constructed the Vedānta into a rational system of philosophy deliberately followed the footprints of Nāgārjuna and other Buddhist writers. It is only the Nyāya which tried hard to fight the Buddsists and those who have read the literature of this philosophy know how much of what may be called genuine philosophy in it has evolved out of generations of tussle with the Buddhistic opponents. The *Bhakti* cult of the Bhāgavatas is indeed an old system but it has assimilated so much from Buddhism that it has not hesitated to include Lord Buddha as one of the incarnations of Viṣṇu. Most of the highest teachings of the Purāṇas can be real almost word for word in the Buddhistic documents which preceded them and many of the myths and stories of the Purāṇas reveal their origin in the *Jātakas* and the *Avadānas*. Even when Buddhism degenerated in the later days into the *Vajra-yāna,* the *Sahaja-yāna* and the worst forms of Tāntrikism much of the literature of which is now lost in original Sanskrit and exists in Tibetan translations, it profoundly influenced the Tāntrikism of India particularly of Bengal and Assam on account of the intimate relation which then existed at the time of Pāla kings, between Tibet and those two provinces.

Buddhism has not only influenced the religious and philosophical literatures, manners, customs, and ideal of Hinduism, but it created a great art for the first time in India. Though other types of art have been created in course of time the remains of Buddhist arts in India, Burma, Ceylon, Japan and China may hold its own even at the present day with art creations in any other country. The institutions of democracy probably originated for the first time in India in the regulation of Buddhistic monastic order. It was the inspiration of Lord Budhda's religion that made a monarch like Aśoka who lived the life of a humble beggar for the good of his subjects. In these days of regrettable revolutionarism and the repression it has called forth it is refreshing to remember the conditions of India in Aśoka's time. We do not hear of policing, but of edicts and pillars of piety scattered through the length and breadth of India, where the chief concern of the king was to see not merely that the subjects should be law-abiding but that they should be virtuous. His *dharma-mahāmāttas* made it their business to see that subjects were dutiful to their parents, made gifts to the poor and deserving and practised non-injury and maintained the high standard of purity and character. He was not only anxious for his own people, his interest was not only national but it was international. He sent such messages to all those kings who were his allies far away from India. This is how an ideal government, actuated by love and sympathy, was set up by Aśoka. I ask you, ladies and gentlemen, if any other religion has produced any such kind in the history of the world.

Time is not yet ripe when a systematic account of Buddhism can be satisfactorily written and compared with the contributions of the philosophy of the West. But years ago I took the bold step at the Fifth International Congress of Philosophy at Naples of challenging Benedetto Croce, probably the most eminent continental philosopher now living, with a long paper in which I tried to prove that the essential portions of his philosophy were anticipated in the philosophy of Dharmottara and that where Croce differed he was exposed to serious contradictions and criticisms. Most of the eminent philosophers and orientalists of the world were present in the gathering. Croce himself was in the chair and the paper was previously circulated to him, but I am happy to tell you that I had no very serious opponents to reply to. The contributions of the Buddhist thought seem at the same time to be the most ancient as well as the most modern; its theory of causation, its relativism, its doctrine of sense-data, its pragmatism, its emphasis on morals—its disbelief in any permanent soul and its unconcern about God and its denial of the validity of scriptures, denial of rituals, its anti-metaphysical character and its appeal to experience—all tend to establish its superior claim to modernity. Theology is fast decaying in Europe. Russia declared itself to be godless, and it may be hoped that the Buddhist Academy which has been doing such valuable work under the guidance of Stcherbatsky will gradually supersede the Church of Christianity. I know from my personal knowledge that Buddhist scholars from Russia sometimes take their inspiration in *dhyāna* in Mongolian Monasteries and Grunwedel in Germany practised the *kālacakra*. On the whole the interest of European orientalists and laymen in Buddhism was never so keen as now. The present beautiful edifice at *Sārnāth* and the paintings that are to be made on the panel walls have been possible through the munificence of an American lady from Honolulu and the devotion of an Oxford Graduate. Not one out of the many millions of Hindus have done anything worth its name for the revival and propagation of Buddhistic studies, culture and religion. Even the Pāli texts would have been entirely lost to us if they were not printed and published in Roman character from the Ceylonese and Burmese editions by the efforts of the Pāli Text Society of Great Britain, and not a single manuscript of these was available in India. While Europe teams with Sino-Tibetan scholars who are trying to restore original Buddhist texts from Chinese and Tibetan sources, not even a quarter dozen of such scholars are available in India at the present day. The number of Indians who have made any serious attempt to study the Buddhist texts in Sanskrit and Pāli can be counted on the finger's ends.

We have seen what Christianity has done for its Teutonic and Latin disciples even after nineteen hundred years of development. We have seen how the fatherhood of God and the godliness of Christianity have failed in maintaining the normal standard of amity and friendship between neighbours, how in the name of ***dharma-yuddha*** each nation perpetrated on the others such atrocious cruelties which would have undoubtedly shocked a Changiz Khān for he had surely no such machinery of wholesale devastation. Godliness we may very well need as an ideal, but before that we must have at least a small dose of forbearance and friendship. The last war seems to have set some good people thinking in Europe if wars can be avoided. There has been a union of intellectuals and the League of Nations has been started, but it is bound to be a terrible failure if its members are not actuated by the superior Buddhist principle of forbearance and friendship for all. Science has given immense power in the hands of the westerners and power begets greed, greed begets enmity and enmity begets destruction. Power is an elusive demon and if it cannot be properly controlled and tamed it is bound to eat up the tamer. Only one man in India seems to have been convinced of the truth of Buddhism that violence cannot be stopped by violence. You have seen, ladies and gentlemen, what power such a conviction has given

O.P. 62/35

to this great man. He in his loin cloth has brought about a unification of the masses of India and is trying to dictate his terms to the greatest military power of the world. In no other country was such an experiment conducted and with so much success. We do not know as yet of the ultimate result, but what we have seen is sufficient to convince us that friendship and non-violence is at least as potent a force to combat violence as violence could be. It is in the exact fitness of things that the task of unifying India and of bringing about her regeneration should be in the hands of a man who is inspired by the true idealism of India. But what can one man do? Caste against caste, creed against creed, mutual distrust and jealousy, provincial bigotry and hatred are eating away our very hearts just as national jealousy and national hatred are drying up the fountain head of the life-energy of Europe. The ruled look upon the rulers with distrust and enmity and the rulers do the same to the ruled. How is this vicious circle to end at all? *Nahi verena verāni, sammantidha kadācana*—enmity can never cease through enmity. When shall we realise this golden truth of Budhism? It would be a pity if the opening of the *Mulagandhakuṭi Vihāra* was to be only the event of a day to be forgotten to-morrow. Let us on this memorable occasion invoke the blessings of Lord Buddha upon us that he may shower his mercy on us and we may be inspired by the noble example of his life and teachings, bind us together in amity and friendship and bring about a regeneration and a revival of our great culture and propagate the high principles of Buddhism to all our fellow-brethren in the world. When the western world is building up memorials for encouraging the killing of human beings and tariff papers are being prepared to take the place of costly cannon balls, while science is being enslaved for robbing the freedom and prosperity of others, let us on this memorable occasion build up a memorial of universal love, friendship, charity and peace and let us not for a moment distrust the universal testimony of the ages of the Hindu-Buddhistic culture of India, the ripe experience of all sages of the past—our inviolable inheritance—the conviction that friendship and forgiveness, sympathy and charity are the only doors through which peace and happiness can come either to a person or to a nation, and the victory will be ours.

AN INTERPRETATION OF THE YOGA THEORY OF THE RELATION OF MIND AND BODY*

The word *yoga* is used to denote either the union of the lower and the higher self (*Jīvātman* and *Paramātman*) or the arresting of the mental processes and states and all physical, mental and moral accessories connected with them. The word *yoga* is also used to denote mental energy by which the mind is disciplined and the goal of *yoga* attained. Patañjali defined *yoga* as the partial and complete or temporary and permanent arrest or cessation of mental states. Patañjali's main theories were elaborated by Vyāsa, Vācaspati, Bhoja and Vijñāna Bhikṣu. There are many important points of difference in the exposition of these scholars of the main theory of Yoga. But at the present moment we are not concerned with these. The theory that mental states can be arrested by our efforts is an extremely original one, and up till now we know of no country other than India where such a possibility was ever conceived. In an interview that I had with the famous psychologist Dr. Sigmund Freud, he expressed great surprise, in the course of a long discussion, that such a thing should be conceived possible, but he admitted that this experiment had always been made and that therefore it would be hazardous to deny its possibility. In

*The article cannot obviously be justified as an interpretation of the Yoga texts. It represents, however, the way in which some of the fundamental ideas of Yoga can be utilized in our present-day conceptions of philosophy and science.

India the *yoga* has always been practised from the earliest dawn of her civilization and carries with it the testimony of many decades of centuries.

Underlying the possibility of the fact of *yoga* there is a concept of mind and a theory of psychology. In spite of many differences in the attempts at the exposition of this psychology among the different thinkers of the school of Patañjali, there is a general agreement regarding the main position of the Yoga psychology. We shall try to give here a brief outline of this psychological theory.

This theory is based upon a metaphysical theory of causation, namely, that like causes produce like effects. A cause is regarded as a potential effect. Even before the causal operation the effect exists in identity with the cause. The function of the causal operation is not to produce anything new, but to actualize the cause as the effect or to exhibit manifestly in the effect what was already contained in the cause. There can thus be no interaction between unlikes, for in that case the interaction would have to be supposed to bring into being effects which were not contained in either of the two causal elements or in the interaction itself. Again, if interaction is supposed to be an extraneous relation, then being a relation it would be outside the causal entities, and whatever is outside the causal entities would be incapable of entering into them; so the relations will have to be conceived as having no relata at their two ends and this would baffle the very nature of relations. Thus relations cannot have any separate existence from the relata. It is the different aspects and manifestations of the relata that are interpreted as relations. Relations are thus certain constructions that are made by us by which the relata are held apart and connected in a certain manner which is called relation. This analytico-synthetic function of the mind which manifests the mere relata is related, and all relationed states of the mind are technically called *vikalpa*. Since the concept of relations is abolished, the problem of the relation of substance, attributes and motion does not also arise. Attributes are but modes of the substance and substance is also a mode of the attributes. The distinction of substances and attributes and their mutual relation of inherence are due to the constructive function of the mind, the *vikalpa*. They are one and the same. The apparent difference is only due to the different types of constructive emphasis of the mind. Now the whole universe, physical or mental, is a field of interactional relations. But if there are no extraneous interactions and no extraneous relations, it must be composed of a neutral stuff which is neither material nor mental. This neutral stuff cannot obviously be of a homogeneous nature, for in that case the diversity of the phenomenal effects cannot be explained. It is therefore supposed that this neutral stuff is composed of an infinite number of reals different in nature among themselves, though they may be broadly subdivided into three classes as *sattva, rajas* and *tamas*. Only some typical class characters of these reals can be mentioned and these innumerable characteristics exist only from the point of view of our phenomenal consciousness. As they hold within themselves the whole universe and all its characteristics in a potential form, it is impossible to determine the noumenal nature of these reals.

It is also wrong to call them either substantive entities or qualities or characters, for these distinctions are unreal. They have their value only to the constructive functions of a phenomenal mind. The only safe course, therefore, is to call this ultimate stuff neutral entities or neutral reals, whatever this may signify. It is said that the noumenal character or nature of these original entities called *guṇas* is unspeakable and indefinable. What appears as their characteristics in the phenomenal world is due to the constructive nature of the phenomenal mind and the phenomenal conditions. It is from these neutral reals that the mental and physical spheres have emanated through a course of evolution corresponding to their diverse kinds of aggregation, and directed by a tendency, inherent in them, which we may regard as teleological in the sense that it operates in such a manner that the universe is harmonious in its productive activity towards all its changes and all its later evolutions, and consequently towards the evolution of man and the shaping of his ultimate physical, intellectual, moral and spiritual destinies. That there is such a teleology is not a matter of *a priori* belief or any deduction from any such belief, but is an inductive truth based on observation, experience and the testimony of the wise men of the past.

It is obvious that a psychology based upon such metaphysical data cannot hold that mind and body or mind and matter are two distinct entities which act and react upon each other. The psychological view of interaction that the mental phenomena are the results of nervous changes in the cortex, or that the muscular changes are determined by mental changes of thought, emotion and volition, would naturally be quite inconsistent with its metaphysical background. The theory of parallelism with a metaphysical background of pan-psychism, though somewhat nearer to its metaphysical position, cannot also be admitted by it. The theory of parallelism holds that neither the mind influences the body nor the body influences the mind ; but though neither determines the other, the mental phenomena run parallel to the bodily phenomena. The pan-psychical parallelist would hold that the mental and bodily changes are the effects of some common elements present in the mind and the body. But we know that the introduction of certain drugs in the system almost immediately produces mental changes. Alcohol is a chemical compound of carbon, hydrogen and oxygen. When introduced into the body it is absorbed directly from the gastro-intestinal tract mainly into the portal blood and partly by the lymphatics, and within a short period of its introduction into the system it produces a sense of mental exhilaration. Now if interactionism is discarded, how are we to account for the mental change through the metabolic changes produced in the body by alcohol? The one explanation according to the pan-psychic theory would be that alcohol should not be regarded merely as a compound of carbon, hydrogen, and oxygen, but that in itself it liberates a psychical energy which directly affects the mind. If the body which is a conglomeration of material elements can have a mental counterpart, then even a compound like alcohol may have its own psychical counterpart which directly affects the mind. Such a view implies the metaphysical theory of ultimate entities which are double-faced ; on the one hand they behave in a physical manner and on the other they behave psychically also. But when we speak of physical and psychical energy, we miss the essential connotation of "psychical." If what we call psychical is merely a form of energy, then it may well be regarded as a product of nervous change. Physico-chemical changes are being always produced in the body and we should always have a corresponding influx of psychical energy all the time. The action of alcohol in the body is partly chemical and partly physiological. If the liberated psychical energy is to act on the mind, what would be the *modus operandi*? What would again be the relation between the psychical and the material energy as existing in an object? These and many other relevant criticisms are almost unanswerable in the above theory.

The metaphysical theory of the *Yoga* is a theory of neutral pluralism and not of pan-psychism, for both matter and mind and all their effects are nothing but diverse kinds of aggregates of the ultimate reals, the *guṇas*. The nervous changes that accompany the psychical states occur in the sphere of the body and are associated with various biochemical, mechanical or physiological changes which have a definite history with reference to the body in which they occur and in relation to the physical environment in which that body is located. In a remote manner each body-system is associated with the parents from which it was produced, the nourishment that it had, the climate, temperature, environment and the associated biological functions that are being discharged in the system. The psychical sphere or the mind also has its own

O.P. 62/36

history and is a universe in itself. What appears on the surface at any given time as a state of awareness is only a temporary phenomenon. But its conservation, repression, reappearance, its contribution towards the inner history of the mind and towards the determination of future psychical occurrences are associated with a peculiar definite history of its own. As the body-system develops in relation to mind and in relation to its external environment, but is always internally determined by its constitution and history; so though the mind develops in relation to the body and the external environment, it is always internally determined by its own history and constitution. The physical, biological or physiological and the psychical are essentially of the same stuff of neutral reals. But each sphere is internally determined by its own laws of emergence, evolution, order and correlation in consonance with the interrelation of the other two spheres. The contribution of the material to the biological is possible only because the two have the same essence. Such contribution simply means the participation of one in the history of the other. The biological, however, means only the stage where the material has come but partially within the history of the psychical. What we call biological force or life-functioning is nothing but the intermediate sphere where the psychical is partially adapting the material elements within its history. Such an adaptation is possible only because of the fact that there is an inherent tendency or teleology in the reals themselves to pass into the history of their others and thus to help the due functioning of the history of each of the different spheres. It is for this reason that the development of the psychical is in direct relation to the physiological organs, functions and structures in all animals.

The manner in which the neutral reals may combine among themselves has a limitation grounded in the very nature of the reals themselves as also of the particular combinations. As the reals themselves have their own inherent natures or qualities, so each of their combinations has special characters or qualities and the manner in which these combinations may enter into the history of other combinations is limited by the structural quality, character or nature of such combinations. In the spheres of theoretical science we try to discover the nature of such limitations through induction and such deduction as is associated with it, and try to formulate what are called the laws of nature. The uncertainty associated with all inductive propositions and laws relating to cause and effect and even to the uniformity of nature is grounded in the fact of our ignorance of the ultimate limitations of the noumenal reals and of their combinations in relation to one another. From the point of view of pure theoretic science or metaphysics it would be possible to overcome the limitations of any combination of reals and to transform one combination into another, provided we had the exact knowledge of the nature of the limitations of each combination and had the apparatus by which we could relate any combination with those other combinations in the presence of which each combination would change its history. A practical chemist not only studies the properties of elements and compounds but also tries to determine in the presence of which compound other particular compounds change their internal history. We know that a catalytic agent, either in the outside world or in the animal body in the form of enzymes, produces chemical change in other compounds without itself undergoing any change. A practical physicist not only studies the ultimate electronic structure of elements but also tries to discover the possibility of effecting such structural changes in the constitution of an atom of an element by the forces of heat, electricity or pressure that the atom may change its history as one element into that of another. Thus in the material world we find that in the presence of force as electrical, thermal, chemical or doubtfully chemical (e.g., in the case of a catalytic agent) chemical compounds or elements change their individual or mutual history. By history I mean properties or behaviours of an entity in the presence of other entities in determining or effecting change in itself or in those entities which form its environment, or which are copresent with it. History thus is self-determination and other-determination in the copresence of other entities.

The nature of this determination must be different in the physical, chemical, biological, physiological and the mental world. But history means the manifestation by a real of new qualities as actualization of the potential in copresence with others, participation in the history of others as their constituents or change of its own history in copresence with others. No case of causation is a case of external determination, but the elements that seem to determine a causal change or effect a causal operation are but the conditions under which a composite unity determines or changes its own history. The so-called other-determination mentioned above is also to be regarded as self-determination from the point of view of the composite unity that undergoes the change. The nature and ground of this self-determination are to be sought in the inherent tendency of the neutral reals forming the structure of any composite unity to change its history in copresence with other composite unities, in consonance with the mode in which alone the entire evolutionary process from the inorganic to the organic and from the organic to the highest development of man and his spiritual powers, has proceeded. The limitations in the behaviour of any composite unity are in consonance with this universal tendency with regard to the entire whole which has to emerge or evolve as an actualization of its potential career. Every individual history, be it of an atom, or molecule or compound, of the physical, electrical or thermal behaviour of inorganic substances, of living units, of mind, or of societies or nations, is only a part (abstracted mentally) of the universal history which is in a process of unfolding. Every individual history is at once its own self-determination as well as its determination by the universal history; it is an epitome of the universal history. The concept of causation is not one of production of change by an extraneous entity, nor one of assemblage of conditions or transformation of energy or of parallel changes in the causal conditions and the effect, but the self-evolution of an entity in copresence with its conditions from the proximate to the remotest. Such a self-evolution may mean either the unfolding of the nature of an entity, its contribution to the unfolding of the nature of other entities or its participation in the history of the unfolding of other entities. The tendency that guides the modes of self-evolution of any entity is on the one hand the actualization of its potentiality and on the other, its subordination to the history of development of other composite entities in the interest of the total cosmic development, of which every individual development is a part and towards which it has a tendency.

It may be remembered that, in accordance with the fundamental metaphysical position of this system, space and time have no separate existence ; they are not the general conditions of all occurrences, but are only the modifications or combinations of the ultimate neutral reals and are thus continuous with objects. Space is not like a box in which all things exist, but it is continuous with all objects. All matter has evolved out of space, and time has its first physical manifestation as a mode of space. The first physical category in the evolution of the neutral reals is space. Time is nothing but the constitutional or structural movement in space and in all space-products. Thus it may be regarded as a determining or structural mode of matter or space. In some older schools of Sāṁkhya-Yoga theory time is regarded as an original dynamic existing prior to space and determining the evolution or emergence of space, and also of the neutral reals in their active capacity, from an original hypothetical state of equilibrium in which their functions were inoperative. It is thus seen that time is not a separate entity, but is an original function inherent in the neutral reals, space, the psychical spheres, and all products of space as matter. When it is said that time is the first physical manifestation of space, what is meant is that since time in the phenomenal world means the structural movement of the ultimate reals, it exists even in the psychical sphere, as is realized in the apperception of time in the mind. Time exists as a structure of the mind or the psychical sphere as a pre-condition of its apperception which is a result of a process that may be either mental or physico-mental. Space is the first category that emerges in the physical plane as a result of the combination of the neutral reals. But since time is the dynamic in the structural changes of the reals and since space is the first result of structural changes in the reals, time may be regarded as manifesting first in the physical plane in space. But as the ground of the emergence of all other physical categories from space has the structural movements of the reals, time exists in all the products of space in the material and the biological world. There is a difference between our apperception of time as measurable moments of the phenomenal time and the noumenal time represented in the very nature of the structural changes of the *guṇas*. The phenomenal time or time as apprehended in consciousness has a measurable form. We may look forth for the finest, the smallest measure of such time and the limit of such smallness may be fixed in an imaginary fashion as the movement of an atom in the space of its own dimension. But even then such a unit of time or any time conceived by the addition of such units would not represent the real time either as the mode of space or as the structural changes of the neutral reals. Time as apprehended by us is thus false not only in its measure as a unit but also in its functional aspect; it is conceived as a flowing stream and as associated with the changes of matter and our experience of it.

It will be realized that such a conception of time is false as it does not show either the structural or the modal function of time. The apprehended time, therefore, is false both in its aspect as measurable and in its function as the locus of all experiential and material changes. It is, therefore, held that the apprehended time is a mental construction (*buddhi-nirmāṇa*).

Returning to the problem of causation and regarding the relation among the assemblage of conditions that effect a causal change, we find that these factors of the causal operation, apparently existing in different points of space and separated by the time-element involved in the process, are not in reality discontinuous from one another. The so-called primary cause and the conditions are to be regarded as forming one organized whole theoretically associated together with the entire organization of the universe. Individual organizations, when looked at from the standpoint of their separable or separate existence, are but the results of our mental construction (*vikalpa*) generally from the point of view of our practical needs and interests. When the potter makes a jug out of a lump of clay, we may say that the clay evolves itself into the jug by its self-evolving process through the contributions of its conditions, the energy of the potter, the wheel and the like. But the proper scientific view of causation would be to regard the clay, the potter, the wheel, the associated space and the associated time as one organized whole evolving forward in its self-evolving process. In this self-evolving process each element of the organized whole undergoes a change peculiar to its own nature, but none of these elements can be conceived as having existence by itself independent of other elements. None of the elements are in reality separable. They can all be taken together in relation to the organized whole as discharging a function with reference to the whole and also with reference to each and every constituent of the whole. The ordinary definition of cause as invariable unconditional antecedent is no true definition and has only a methodological value. It only serves to separate a certain entity in which we are directly interested from others in which our interest is more remote. In the Yoga view of the situation the difference between cause and conditions also ceases to have any real significance and has only a methodological value. The conditionals, the spatio-temporal elements of the mentally separated causal whole, are conterminous with the organization of the effect-whole constituting its own spatio-temporal and material elements. The differentiation of the effect-whole from the causal whole is also the result of a mental construction. The effect-whole exists in the causal whole as involved in its self-evolving process as its moments of self-expression.

The ordinary objection against the Yoga view of causation—that since the effect exists in the cause, the apparatus of the causal operation and its movement are inexplicable—arises from a misapprehension of the whole situation. It is not the so-called material cause that evolves by itself independently of every thing else, but it is the self-evolution of the entire organizd whole of the so-called material cause and all its conditions including the spatial and the temporal elements.

When it is said that oil exists in the sesamum, it does not mean that such an existence is ground for its self-evolution. Oil exists in the sesamum as much as the plant of sesamum exists in it. As a matter of fact the whole universe may exist in the sesamum, for it has for its constituents the natural elements which are the constituents of the universe. The Yoga theory of causation is not interested merely in the barren assertion of the existence of effects in the material cause. The true effectuating existence of the effect in the cause is with reference to the organized whole, and it is this alone that can be called the true material cause. In the Yoga theory of causation there cannot be any place for an extraneous entity as an outside agent. Such an internal organization is possible from the fundamental notion of the neutral reals which co-operate together for mutual self-evolution and the evolution of the organized whole. But when the different elements constituting an organized whole move forward for their own individual self-expression in consonance with the self-expression of the organized whole, which in itself is a unity and has its own specific self-expression, the contribution in the joint effectuation of any of the constituent elements may be regarded as extraneous from the point of view of the contribution of the elements which we emphasize from our practical interests. Thus when a seed is put under the moist ground, the moisture, the temperature, the pressure, the space, the mineral and other elements present in the soil, the contribution of the microbes as the fertilizers may be regarded as extraneous causes (*nimitta kāraṇa*) and the seed as the material cause. In the seed also, if we consider the function of the cellular walls which allow the passage of the proper nutrients through osmotic pressure, the cellular walls may be regarded as extraneous to the operation of the seed as a material cause. So, if we continue our analysis of the different physiological operations of the different structural elements inside the seed, we shall see that the so-called material cause, as apart from the extraneous causes, is reduced to a mere fiction as the tendency of the organization as a whole towards its specific self-expression. When a number of joint operatives work as an associated whole, which from our point of view seem to be more intimately associated in their operations, or which may somehow be regarded from our point of view as belonging to a different order in their modes of operation, we may ignore the internal, structural and functional activities of that integrated whole, regard it as one unit and as separate from the environmental influences and call it the material cause.

Thus the different structural elements have their independent existence and discharge independent functions through which new products come in and new bio-chemical and physiological operations set in. Such operations take place through the joint co-operation of the structural elements, their functions and products and signify the self-expression of the organized whole—as the seed of its growth. The joint operatives inside the seed may be regarded from the point of view of our separative intellect as being more intimately associated with one another than the environmental influences which may be more easily separated from them. It is from this point of view that the seed is regarded as a separate entity and the material cause. But in reality the seed in its production, existence, its effectuation as shoot and plant, its processes of growth and changes and variations of growth as well as in its destruction depends entirely on the environmental influences and their contributions. The potential and actual life of the seed is thus as much a function of the integral organization of the seed as that of the environment. It is for this reason that the fauna and the flora of a country are determined by its climatic and other conditions. Even the position of the earth in the limitless space determines the conditions of the production and growth of animals and plants. Thus the true cause is the organised whole, and it is from a purely methodological point of view that the separative intellect may introduce different concepts of causation, which may seem to be conflicting with one another when the true point of view is not held before the mind. Thus in the *Vyāsa-bhāṣya* (II. 28) we hear of nine kinds of causes, viz., cause as production or transformation by which the indefinite makes itself definite, cause as integral maintenance of the whole through inner teleology, cause as manifestation to consciousness of what is already existent, cause as determined in change of directions in a process, cause as determined in mental movement of syllogistic nature by deduction or induction, cause as attainment of a true state of consciousness negating the false ones, cause as negating the false state, cause as extraneous agent determining the transformation and cause as a sustaining agent. It will be seen that at least four or five of the above concepts apply in the mental field and the rest are of universal application. But it can be shown that these concepts of causality are drawn from the application of the fundamental principle of causality as applied in different spheres or as looked at from different points of view. As such, they are not in any sense exhaustive and have only a methodological value.

We have seen so far that causation means self-determination of an organized whole; each organized whole holds within it further organized systems and in tracing the subtle history of these related organizations and sub-organizations we may bring ourselves up to the limit of the assumption of structural determinations in space of almost an incomprehensible nature. The reference of these determinations to the ultimate neutral reals comes to the domain of metaphysical hypothesis. Each organization works in general harmony with all other possible organizations and in specific harmony with certain other organizations with which it may be more directly or proximately related. What is generally called force is an illusory abstraction and as such the enquiry into the association of force with a substance in which it is supposed to inhere is also an illusory attempt. The manifestation of the so-called force is but the behaviour of any organization or sub-organization or element with reference to its own self-expression or the self-expression of any other organized whole or wholes with which it is related. Electricity is regarded as a force, but in reality it is nothing but a behaviour. Thus Russell says: "Electricity is not a thing like St. Paul's Cathedral; it is a way in which things behave." The so-called force is a self-relationing process involved in all specific self-expressions which again cannot be distinguished from the very nature of any organization.

That there are no instances of simple entities in the universe may require a few words of explanation. If we start with a lump of matter, we find that it is divisible into molecules existing together in different degrees of cohesion and dispersion which determine the existence of solids, liquids and gases. These further determine along with other conditions the state of its existence as a solution, mixture, emulsion or colloid. The molecular structure of an object not only determines its ordinary physical conditions but is associated also with various physical properties of colour, texture, taste and the like and also with certain kinds of physiological characters. The molecule itself has in it a molecular structure of atoms of the same element or of diverse elements. Even when the atoms are of the same element, the molecular structure effects a great change in physical characters and possibly also in chemical characters. Diamond and charcoal may be cited as an instance. In the case of an inter-molecular structure of atoms of diverse elements, even when we have the same number of atoms of the diverse elements, the mere difference in their structure makes an enormous difference in the physical and chemical characteristics of the two molecules. Both organic and inorganic chemistry abound in instances of the formation of new compounds by such inter-molecular rearrangement. If we descend to the atoms, we find that they have a definite system of structure of protono-electronic arrangement. The exact nature of this arrangement is not definitely known, though it has been supposed with a fair amount of assurance that it consists of ellipses or circles, the complexity of which increases as we ascend from one group of elements to another in accordance with the Periodic Classification of Mendeleeff and Lothar Meyer. We know that the simple addition of one or two electrons in the outer ring of the atom of an element may result in the production of such intensely different chemical substances as carbon and oxygen. We know also that at least in some instances it has been possible to degenerate one element into another merely by the repulsion of one or two elctrons from the outer ring of electrons. Electron itself is identified with an electric charge, though it has a definite volume and a definite weight. Light is regarded as electronic and, as predicted by Einstein, it has been found to suffer from the influence of gravitation. Since electrons have weight it may be supposed that they also have a structure and an internal organization, and we are on the threshold of new discoveries and theories in which they are regarded as crossing points of millions and millions of sub-ether waves. The nature of these sub-ether waves is not definitely known and it is possible that they represent some indefinitely known structure of space. That space has a structure is one of the fundamental assumptions of Einsteinian Theory of Relativity. From where comes the structure of space may be left to the guesswork of metaphysical speculation. Coming to the domain of life we find that even the microscopic and the ultra-microscopic bacteria reveal in them the presence of chromatin granules which may be regarded as homologous in nature the the nucleus of higher organisms. It has been found that the bacillary bodies contain within them deeply staining structures. These structures show a preponderance of slender rods which are cylindrical with rounded ends. The development of a bacterial life shows separation, rearrangement and growth of these internal structures in a manner homologous with the growth on the cell-bodies of higher animals. The fact that the cellular bodies of higher animals contain an internal specialized structure and different kinds of internal apparatus, is too well known to need any elaboration here. Apart from the function of the chromatins and the chromosomes, I may refer here only to the Golgi apparatus. The Golgi apparatus is a centre of synthetic processes. It is engaged primarily in the production of secretory granules which are excretory in nature. These products are of a temporary character such as mucous, serous, lipoid granules, yolk, acrosomes, Nissl's granules, etc. The apparatus undergoes hypertrophy during the process and is not transformed into the various products. We need not enter into further details, but it will be evident from what has been said above that even in the crudest beginning of life we have definite proof of complex structures associated with complex functions. It can also be proved that the process going on inside the cell-life consists not only of localized actions at particular points but of a totalized action of the entire structural area, which is much more than merely additive. It is thus evident that both in the inorganic and in the organic sphere of plant and animal life we have to deal with structural organizations and sub-organizations which are constantly in an evolving process both in their specific interests and in the interest of other organizations. Their actions are both of a localized nature and also of the nature of a totalized whole transcending the limits of localized action. The localized actions are actions of sub-organizations. The action as a whole is the action of the sub-organizations towards the self-expression of the successive organizations of which the successive sub-organizations are constituents.

Causal operation cannot always be interpreted as involving definite functioning of each of the constituent elements, which may be interpreted as the exertion of force or as offering positive contributions in the parallel plane with the contributions of the other constituent elements. Thus in the case of a catalyst we find that a catalytic agent may in most cases excite chemical action in other compounds simply by its very presence in a measure quite incommensurable with the relative proportions of those compounds and without undergoing observable change in itself. Thus sucrose will act on at least two hundred thousand times its weight while rennin of the gastric juice will clot at least four hundred thousand times its weight of casein, the coagulable protein of milk. The very presence of the catalytic agent is the cause of the chemical change in the sucrose of the milk, though we are not aware of any definite contribution on the part of the catalytic agent in the same plane with the contributing actions of the constituents of sucrose and milk. No contribution of any definite force can be conceived as the catalytic agent itself remains unchanged, though only by its presence four hundred thousand times its weight of casein undergoes a change. Again a causal operation would not necessarily always be a prior event to the effect as may be expected from Hume's definition of cause as an invariable antecedent. When a planet approaches its perihelion its motion is accelerated. The cause of the acceleration is its specific position in the gravitational field which can be regarded only as a coexistent event, but not a prior one. Again from what has been said above it will be apparent that no cause can be unconditional. This view will be further apparent when we consider that the cause may also be defined as an assemblage of conditions, the remote conditions of which may sometimes be pressed backwards in an infinite regression. Thus we see that all the so-called defining characteristics of the causal concept have only a methodological interest. Causal operation is a process of self-emergence and self-expression or other-emergence and other-expression of organized wholes.

If we consider the nature of organizations in the non-living and the living world, we find that though their general nature is the same, yet there are remarkable differences in the specific modes of their operation. The behaviour of inorganic organizations is dominated by the law of inertia. The laws of force and their quantitative and qualitative directions are fixed. There is self-maintenance and self-expression, but there is no growth. There is aggregation and accretion, but no production. One atom of copper, one atom of sulphur and four atoms of oxygen produce the integral combinations of a copper-sulphate molecule. Two atoms of hydrogen, one atom of sulphur and four atoms of oxygen produce a molecule of sulphuric acid. There are processes inside the molecules of copper-sulphate and of sulphuric acid by which they hold themselves in *status quo* and which regulate their behaviour with reference to their environment and other substances contained within it. But no processes inside a molecule try to generate further molecules from it. A slight exception is perceived in the formation of crystals. We find that the electrical energies associated with the poles of a crystal help the formation of synchronously shaped crystals from a mother-solution. Here though a crystal supports the formation of other crystals, these crystals are not produced from a disintegration of one crystal through the operation of the materials absorbed within it. The contribution of a crystal towards the formation of its sister-crystals is through the adhesive and formative forces exerted in the peripheral regions of the crystal. As such, it is entirely different from the process of cell-division which secures the history of production and growth in the living world. The chief characteristics in which the living differs from the non-living may briefly be summarized as follows:

I. Persistence of a complex specific metabolism (comprising metabolism of protein, individuality of metabolism and persistence in spite of change) and the corresponding specific organization.

II. Capacity of growth, reproduction and development.

III. Effective behaviour, registration of experience and variability.

It was sometimes held, particularly in connection with the theory of vitalism, that the environment of an organism, physical or chemical, must be regarded as existing outside of it, that it may be explained independently according to the well-known physical and chemical principles and that even within the organism the same physical and chemical conceptions may be applied except in so far as there is interference by a peculiar influence within the organism by which the self-maintenance of the organism as a specific whole could be explained. We now know that the conception of life embraces the environment of an organism as well as what is within its body. The conception of life implies that the relations of the parts and the environment of an organism are such that a normal and specific structure is actively maintained. Thus the famous biologist Dr. Haldane says: "The environment is expressed in the structure of each part of the organism and conversely. When, moreover, we examine what appears to us as organic structure and the structure of organic environment closely, we find that it is the expression of continuous activity so co-ordinated that the structure is maintained. We cannot separate organic from environmental structure, any more than we can separate the action of the environment from the reaction of the organism. Moreover, the spatial relations of the parts do not imply their separate existence from one another, since we cannot define them as existing separately when their very existence expresses co-ordination with one another. The coordination extends over surrounding environment, and the spatial relations of parts and environment express unity, not separation. They also cannot be described as existing within space ; for the co-ordination embodied in them is not limited to a certain position in space, but extends indefinitely beyond any spatial position which we might attempt to assign to it."[1]

Even the Darwinian theory of hereditary transmission implies the fact that life is a unity and it constantly maintains and reproduces itself. Such a self-maintenance is consonant with variation involving adaptation of an organism as regards structure and activities to new circumstances. Structure expresses the maintenance of function and function expresses the maintenance of structure, and a physico-chemical environment cannot be separated from the living organisms, as if the former was the content and the latter the container. The environment and the living whole together form one whole, one organization. Morphology cannot be separated from physiology and no physico-chemical theories can explain the self-maintaining and reproductive nature of life. The science of life is an exact science, the concepts of which are original and are not in any way applications of or deductions from physico-chemical concepts. The time when it was thought that physico-chemical concepts could explain the concept of life is fast passing away, and we have indications of a new era when explanations of physical concepts will be attempted on the analogy of biology. Thus a hard-boiled scientist like Whitehead says that science is taking on a new aspect which is neither purely physical nor purely

1. *The Philosophical Basis Of Biology*, pp. 14-15.

biological. It is becoming the study of organisms. Biology is the study of larger organisms whereas physics is the study of the smaller organisms.[2] According to him an event may be taken as the ultimate unit of natural occurrence and it contains within it two aspects, an aspect of self-maintenance and an aspect in which it holds itself in unison with the self-maintenance of other events. An event corresponds to two patterns, namely, the pattern of aspects of other events which it grasps into its own unity and the pattern of its own aspect which other events severally grasp into their unities. There is thus an intrinsic and an extrinsic reality of an event, namely, the event in its own prehension and the event as in the prehension of other events. The ordinary scientific ideas of transmission and continuity are details concerning the empirically observed characters of these patterns throughout space and time. Considered from these points of view, the biological and the physico-chemical events are in one sense alike and on that account we get a peculiar insight into the nature of physico-chemical events when we look at them from the point of view of biology. The idea of self-expression in the interest of other expressions is most prominent in biological studies. The idea of the universe as an interrelated organization in the interests of one another receives an important justification from a biological outlook. We have seen so far that biological organizations belong to an order different from physico-chemical organizations. Yet they are conterminous with the physico-chemical organizations which

2. *Science In The Modern World*, Chap. VI.

form their environment. Plants seize the radiant energy of the sun and utilize it in building the compounds they use. Animals digest them to build their own. The complex activities of the animals have three powerful groups of governors, the ferments, the endocrine secretions and the vitamins, all chemical compounds and all acting chemically. All the processes of life are governed by the same quantitative laws that have been proved to hold for non-living matter. Life can neither create energy or matter nor cause their disappearance. The two great laws of physics and chemistry are conservation of matter and conservation of energy, and all living processes conform rigidly to these laws. An organism carrying on an active metabolism accounts for all matter taken within itself during a measured period of time, so that the difference in weight between the matter ingested and that excreted is exactly balanced by a gain (or loss) of weight by the organism itself. So the total intake of energy from the potential energy of the food ingested and the actual energy acquired from food hotter than the organism is equal to the total energy output consisting of (a) radiation, conduction and convection, and (b) actual and potential heat lost with the excreta and the work done by the organism. Many of the chemical compounds and elements are directly produced and stored up by the endocrine glands. Thus the thyroid stores up iodine and forms definite iodine compounds. The para-thyroid glands secrete compounds which assist in the control of calcium metabolism. The pancreas secretes compounds which help the catabolism of glucose and so on. Many other acids and salts are prepared in the body by a mechanism entirely different from that in which they may be prepared outside the body. Many of the compounds prepared in the body are such that we have no indication as to how they are produced inside the body by the chemical processes that are known to us. Some of the compounds which may be produced outside the body by the application of considerable heat and various chemical reagents are produced in the body in a very simple manner under entirely different conditions. It will thus be seen that though ultimately the constituents of our body are homogeneous with the radiant energy of the sun or the electrical conditions of space indicated thereby, our organism is an organization of an entirely different nature from all other non-organic organizations. It uses non-organic methods and assimilates and transforms non-organic matter and energy for its own interest in its own peculiar way. Whatever is taken inside the body is made to enter into the specific processes of the organism and to obey the laws of the organism which are different and yet consonant with the loss of non-organic nature. When an organism fails to do so in any respect we have diseases. Thus the larger protein-molecules do not under normal condition reach the circulation, but when by any chance they do reach the circulation they act toxically producing certain reactions which may reveal themselves by definite symptoms. The cells of the organism then form and excrete compounds which can unite with them and de-toxicate them and these are called anti-bodies or anti-gens.

The mechanistic view of life implies that if at any instance of time we were to know the precise distribution of the matter and energy which are present in an organism, we should have a complete understanding of all its properties. In other words, the behaviour of living systems can be completely defined in terms of laws that are fundamentally similar to those which describe the behaviour of inanimate systems. But the theory of the spontaneous evolution of the animate from the inanimate, though it may give us a comfortable feeling of continuity of thought, is on the whole untenable. It is just as probable for a piece of stone to leap spontaneously from the surface of the earth as for a living organism to evolve spontaneously from inanimate matter. The probability of simultaneous co-ordinative movement such as we find in living organisms is extremely small on the assumption of a purely physico-chemical arrangement. The organization of the simplest living organism is clearly more complex than that of a stone or of a motor car and it carries out processes that are infinitely more complex than what can be explained as chance coincidences. No chemist can seriously think that protein can spontaneously originate from carbon-dioxide, water and simple salt, any more than a physicist can admit the spontaneous origin of a motor car. Biology itself provides not one shred of observational evidence to support the spontaneous origin of living matter. There are a few biologists, however, who postulate the spontaneous origin of the intermediate stages between the living and the non-living world. But the physical events that have to be assumed in such a theory are such that our present concept of physical "laws" can hardly be applied there. It may be said that in past ages events which are now very improbable were, in fact, of common occurrence. But no man of science can give any credence to such a supposition unless he had some assurance as to the nature of those events and conditions which made the origin of life inevitable or even probable. The distribution of energy and of matter in past epochs may have been different, but if there were conditions prevalent at the time which could produce the living organisms through the spontaneous co-ordination of matter and material energy, it would be extremely strange that every attempt to reproduce them in the laboratory should fail so completely. If the spontaneous origin of the animate from the inanimate cannot be held as a plausible theory, there is no ground for hoping that we shall ever be able to express all the properties of an organism in terms of physical laws. Under the circumstances it would be more logical to accept the existence of matter in two states, the animate and the inanimate, as a fundamental initial assumption. Some properties are naturally common to matter in either state and it is therefore legitimate to study the so-called physical properties of living matter. But just as the fundamental concepts of physics must be based on observed facts, so the fundamental concepts of biology must also be based upon observation in that specific sphere.

From one point of view a mass of protoplasm may be regarded as a very fine colloidal emulsion, the fundamental units of which are extremely small. The properties of the whole may thus in some sense be regarded as being essentially those of each individual. There is some evidence to show that even a single differentiated cell represents an aggregate of very small living units. Even a single spermatozoon shows the growth and decline of its mechanical and respiratory activities in such a manner as if it represented the joint behaviour of a large population of much smaller units of activity. Yet when we try to think of the mechanism whereby the cell differentiates itself as a whole, we have to postulate some form of co-ordinated relationship which is more than additive, and which cannot be explained except as an organized behaviour of a total indivisible agent. If so long physical concepts were fruitlessly applied for the explanation of biological facts, the time has come when biological concepts are being employed to explain physical behaviour. M. Poincare and others really define physical phenomena in terms of biological conceptions when they say that "modern physics is presenting us with apparent examples of spontaneity and foresight." When the dividing cells of a molluscan egg rotate in order to reduce their centripetal pressure, the rotation in the clockwise direction would be as effective as the counter-clockwise direction. But in every case it takes one direction rather than the other, though no mechanical difference of the inside force-arrangement can be observed. The cells of a molluscan egg turn one way or another for intrinsic reasons quite independent of any external influence. This and many other considerations of a similar nature show that the cell has an individuality of its own which is free from the limitations of the statistical laws of physics. Probably this may be extended to the minutest living components of the dividing cell. We are now in a position to assert that a living organism—or even the minutest parts of it —behaves as an individual and determines itself in consonance with both its own nature and its immediately associated life-entities and probably also with its external environment. Every case of its self-determination is also a case of other-determination. The variability of Darwin's law is the function of this self-determination. The concept of self-determination does not imply the exclusion of the need of others, but it involves within it both its own self-expression and the expression of others. Its individuality is not negative and abstract, but is positive and concrete in the sense that its very consideration for itself is also a consideration for others with which it is associated.[3]

Coming back to the problem of causation, we find that though from the ultimate point of view the determination of all causal operation is based upon the fundamental nature of the neutral reals, yet each individual organization, be it material or organic, may be regarded as different individual organizations each of which involves the relevant 'other' of it within itself. This also has its ground in the very nature of the different reals which co-operate together for self-expression, other-expression and whole-expression. Thus the statement that like co-operates with like or like is produced from like is as true as that like co-operates with unlike or that like is produced from unlike. All dialectical discussions on the subject prove to be barren simply because of the fact

3. Cf. Presidential Address of the Zoological Section of the British Association, 7th September, 1933, and *Nature*, 1933, pp. 661-664.

that the concrete nature of the process is ignored and emphasis is put upon abstract generalities which exist nowhere excepting in the brains of the quarrelling metaphysicians.

From the above considerations we come to the important conclusion that the sphere of the living is in a very relevant sense an independent sphere which has its own concept and own laws that may be known by observations and experiments, just as the laws of the inorganic world may be known. We know also that all the higher forms of life contain within them as integrated in their history the dominant potential tendencies and functions of the lower forms of life, just as even the most complex inorganic compounds contain within their history the tendencies and functions of electronic matter. The behaviour of any higher form of life can be revealed in its historical aspect only as involving within it all the lower forms as also a tendency towards further history in its further higher forms. Each form below the highest represents within it a process of events which can be interpreted only by a backward and forward oscillation of the mind in search of an integrated meaning.

Just as in the case of life it has been shown that it is a definite and independent world by itself having its own growth, function, structure and reactions to environment determined by itself, so in the case of mind also, we have to assume its existence as an independent world having its own inner history integrated within it which regulates its growth, function, structure and reactions to environment determined by its own specific laws. There is a difficulty, however, in making any definite assertions about the nature of 'mind' and its definite conception. In the case of living units, their processes consisting of physico-chemical changes are directly observable. The inference in their case is with reference to their specific inner urge that regulated their co-ordinating movements. But in the case of mind we have no sensual evidence of any organized whole. The phenomena of mind as thoughts, emotions and volitions can be observed by introspection or can be inferred from the manner in which they induce physiological changes or changes in the movement of the organism in consonance with changes in the environment. These may be studied to some extent, using the methods of exact science which involve definite measurements made under standard conditions. These experiments may be performed by oneself or by two persons, the observer who makes the introspection and the experimenter who handles the instruments and makes the record. But even in these there are obvious difficulties in carrying out the introspective work. There is always a chance of its being unduly affected by the temperamental characteristics of the observer and the association of ideas and feelings on the part of the observer at the time of the experiment. Then, again, what we may observe is almost always the phenomenal behaviour of mind, an idea, an emotion, an image or the like. There have been philosophers and religious teachers who have denied the existence of any organized whole as 'mind'. Thus the Buddha said that there were the petals, the pollens, the corolla, the stalk and the like but there was no lotus ; similarly, there is this or that passing idea, passing emotion, images and their momentary aggregate, but there is no organized whole behind them which can be called the mind or the ego or the self. Again there have been philosophers on the other side who, judging from the fact that all our assertions regarding extra-mental objects are dependent upon our various modes of awareness as sensations, ideas, emotions and relations, denied the existence of the extra-mental entities and regarded them either as wholly non-existent or as modes of our thought. It has been supposed by many of them that all our knowledge of the objective world is of a relational nature enunciated in an ideational form and regulated by the fundamental laws of thought of identity and contradiction. Sensations, images, ideas and relations are mental and as such it is only the mind that exists. There are others who think that relations have both an external and an internal reality and the mind is like a window. The perception of an event is the occurrence of a relational event both inside and outside the mind. The presence of the occurrence in the mind does not in any way involve any change in the nature of the occurrence and it leads only to the phenomenon we call awareness. There are others who are prepared to regard mind as a combined totalized concept of the various physiological functions which express themselves in the behaviour of the organism.

These divergences of opinion are due to a fundamental advantage and disadvantage of the mind-situation. On the one hand the mind has this great prerogative that all assertions regarding mental or extra-mental existence can only be made by the peculiar phenomenon of awareness which we call mental. From this point of view there is nothing which is outside the mind. Though intimately associated with a physiological organism the processes of which take place in a definite spatio-temporal situation, the mind apparently has no such limitation. The modes of its working, the laws of its relationing, retaining, reviving, discriminating or assimilating, determine the nature of all our scientific knowledge and its acquisition. It is true that most mental phenomena are associated with physiological, neural and biochemic changes in the body, but these changes are so very different from the associated mental factors that even by the wildest stretch of imagination they cannot be regarded as their modifications. If the biological entities cannot be regarded as the functions of the physico-chemical process, it is infinitely more impossible to regard the mental phenomena as the functions of the biological world. It is not possible to give any reply to the question as to what may be the ultimate nature of the mental phenomena, and we know that it is equally impossible to say anything about the ultimate biological units or the ultimate units of matter. We cannot define anything except in terms of behaviour. We know that probably each and every conscious mental phenomenon has its correlative in the physiological condition of the body, particularly in the neural substances in the brain. In our bodies there are two more or less distinct systems, the relation of one of which to the mental phenomena must at any rate be distant. Thus the normal movements of heart, respiratory muscles, blood vessels and intestines are generally regarded as being largely unaccompanied by any kind of conscious emotion. But even in their case we know that strong emotions or deep concentration produce great changes in the functioning of these processes. The other system, namely, the neuro-cerebral, undergoes great changes along with conscious processes. The muscular processes, however, undergo changes by the volitional behaviour of the mind by which we can move our limbs according to our will.

Studies in biochemistry show that corresponding to the various phases of our emotions there are probably produced various kinds of secretory chemical compounds. We know that when there is a strong emotion or mental excitement, it affects the adrenal glands through certain nerves and leads to the secretion of an increased amount of adrenine from the *medulla*. This output of adrenine has its twofold effect, a general "stringing up" of the organism through the increasing blood-pressure, and mobilization of liver-glycogen to produce a heightened level of blood sugar. The animal is thus conditioned, but as yet we know nothing of the mechanism by which adrenine is produced in the gland. It is known to us to be present in the poison gland of the tropical toads. Thus we see that the mental processes of emotion, attention and the like produce physiological and biochemical changes which are in consonance with them. We know also that though the neuro-cerebral system is more directly and intimately associated with mental phenomena, the muscular system of the body and the organism as a whole are also influenced by the mental changes. If we try to find any criterion of mind even in levels lower

O.P. 62/40

than the human mind, we see that the introspective process by which the mental phenomena are revealed to the perceiver cannot be of any avail. As regards the presence of mind in human beings other than ourselves we have also no direct evidence, but we have to accept their testimony as supported by corroborative behaviour and observable behaviour, physical and physiological changes. If we have to observe the objective existence of mind in other fellow-beings or in animals, it can only be done by the joint application of the deductive and the inductive methods. The objective test of volition is attainable from a comparison of the universal nutritive and sexual impulses. It is only as a result of sensory excitations that the animal changes its behaviour, which implies voluntary actions. We have to call these actions voluntary, because they do not appear in mechanical regularity in response to external stimuli, but they are variable in accordance with the inner conditions of the living being. Judgements in individual cases may remain doubtful, for most biological processes are largely automatic and unconscious, and are selective towards the adoption of means with reference to particular ends. But a close observation of the nature of living beings may enable us to decide between the two alternatives, that is, whether the determination is primarily biological or mental.

The observation of experts on the subject leads almost unanimously to the view that consciousness is a universal possession of living organisms from man down to the protozoa.[4] In the lowest stages the

4. *Principles Of Physiological Psychology* by Wundt, London, 1910, p. 29.

processes of consciousness are restricted to very narrow limits and the will is determined by the universal organic impulses in the very simplest manner; yet the manifestations of life even among the protozoa are explicable only upon the hypothesis that they possess a mind. The amœba, which morphologically is only the single cell with a nuclear protoplasmic body, will return after a short time to the starch particles that it accidentally came upon and will take in a new portion of it for the nutrition of its body. The infusoria pursue others which they kill and devour. This shows that the choice of means for the furtherance of their biological satisfaction is determined inwardly by some kind of mental process as it cannot be explained as a result of any mechanical or chemical influence. We cannot however say anything definitely as to whether mind emerges only at the stage of protozoic life or whether it can be supposed to extend to still lower stages, that is, whether mind can be affirmed of every living organism. There are some grounds for asserting the fact that wherever living protoplasms occur there are certain phenomena which are akin to mental, which possess a determining activity not explainable by physico-chemical influences. It is evident that mental characteristics other than voluntary cannot be demonstrated in these lower forms of life where there are no means of communication. Thus Wundt says that from the standpoint of observation we must regard it as a highly probable hypothesis that the beginnings of the mental life date from as far back as the beginnings of life at large. Fechner goes even further in expressly attributing consciousness to the earth and the other heavenly bodies, making the cosmic consciousness the whole, of which the individual forms of consciousness in plants and animals are parts. Such hypotheses emphasize the intrinsic impossibility of the view that mental life suddenly appears at some point of time and space as a new thing and that we need not seek for its general conditions in the universal substrata of the vital processes. Such theories imply further metaphysical speculations into which we need not enter.

But from what has been said we may assume that the psychosis of mind as such has to be admitted as having a sphere of its existence which, on the one hand, is associated with the physiological and physical substrata and, on the other hand, is an independent existence having its own inner laws of determination. The concept of the psychical sphere has to be formed on the obvious analogy of the biological sphere and the biological sphere is associated with the physico-chemical sphere. As the biological sphere is on the one hand associated with the physico-chemical sphere and yet has its own independent determinant principle in accordance with which the former maintains its relations with the latter, so the psychical sphere or the mind is also an independent sphere which can manifest itself in its diverse forms and ways only in association with a definite physiological system and physico-chemical environments. The psychical sphere in accordance with our theory has a definite substratum and reality, being the result of the modification of the neutral reals. As such it has its own existence by itself, but it can manifest itself only with the help of suitable physiological and physico-chemical organizations. The fact that things may exist without manifesting themselves is so obvious that it is not necesasry for us to enter into any long discussion about that. A ray of light and an eye may both exist, but the condition of visibility can arise only when the former is reflected from a surface to the latter. The sound-waves may be there, but it is only within a certain range and in the presence of the ear that they can manifest themselves. The long waves of wireless or the short waves of X-ray manifest themselves only under the conditions of suitable mechanical apparatus. According to our assumption, then, the psychical sphere and the living sphere have been both existing, for aught that we know, even when the earth was undergoing nebular changes. The material, the living and the psychical may all three be independent organizations of which the last may manifest under the conditions of the first two and the second may manifest under the conditions of the first, or it may also be that the second is a relative function due to the varying degrees of co-operation of the first and the last. But we need not enter into the further metaphysical implications or discussions of such a situation for our present purposes. What we are interested to affirm is that mind or the psychic sphere does not consist of passing waves of consciousness and emotion, but that these constitute together an integrated whole which has its own laws of behaviour and operation in consonance with the operation of its internal laws and constituents and with its intimate physiologcal, biochemical and physico-chemical environments. Mental efforts determine metabolic changes, metabolic changes involve expenditure of energy and expenditure of energy is dependent upon the intake of energy through the assimilation of physical food. Thus mind determines not only physiological conditions but also physical conditions. On the other hand metabolic changes may induce various types of mental states. The consumption of alcohol may produce exhilaration and the smelling of chloroform may induce a semi-conscious or unconscious state. From the superficial point of view one system of organization may seem to be determining the other and be determined by it ; but a keener appraisal of the entire situation shows that each system works independently by itself according to its own constitutional laws only under the co-operative conditions of other systems of organization.

According to the *Sāṁkhya* we have the concept of the *prakṛti* which, on the one hand, covers all that is physical and, on the other, all that is mental. The mental events and the physical ones are both abstractions if they are taken as entirely separate and distinct from each other ; for they are both the manifestations of the same ultimate reals behaving towards one another according to their own specific laws. The mental and the physical are not two distinct worlds, as it is ordinarily supposed, but they are two co-operating wholes within one whole, the *prakṛti*. The ordinary difficulty as to how two entirely dissimilar wholes can come in contact with each other vanishes when we look at the point from the *Sāṁkhya-Yoga* perspective. From what we have already said it will appear that the relation between the mind and the body or the physical world is not one of interaction or parallelism, but one of co-operation. As it is a case of wholes within a whole, the operations in each whole follow certain universal laws in such a manner that the operations in other wholes follow a course of correspondence in co-operation, so that from a methodological point of view one may regard the operations in one whole as determining and conditioning, in a large measure, the operations of the other. In every sphere operations are self-determining and yet other-determining. That the operations in any sphere, by being self-determining, can also be other-determining satisfies for us the concept of co-operation or teleology or mutual determinism. When through the operation of the physical phenomenon of light the mental functions so determine the organ of the eye as to facilitate its co-operation with them, or when through the operation of light change is produced in the operative functions of the eye so as to secure the co-operation of the mental functions, we have the perception of an object which is regarded as a mental fact. But this mental fact is, on the one hand, continuous with the sense organ, the physical object and its environment, and, on the other hand, with the final illumination by its association with *puruṣa* or its incorporation in a final scheme of meaning which is the ultimate end of the knowledge process. There is an apparent duality between the physical and the physiological, the physiological and the mental, and the mental and the meaningful conscious. But this duality is only an apparent duality, for there is a continuity of process from the mental to the physical, signifying the functioning of one whole within the other, each following its own law in consonance with the law of others. Even the meaningful conscious event is regarded as neither similar (*sarūpa*) nor dissimilar (*virūpa*) to the other events, for it is a final emergent fact which arises out of the conditioning processes of the other wholes. Even the universal and particlar are not mental ; but the objective things are themselves of the nature of universal and particular and in accordance with diverse kinds of mental processes either the universal or the particular may be more or less predominantly manifested as facts of consciousness. Thus in perception the notion of the particular is more predominant and in inference the notion of the universal. So the relation of mind and body is no special problem in the *Yoga* theory, but is deducible from the general metaphysical position of the system.

AN ANALYSIS OF THE EPISTEMOLOGY OF THE NEW SCHOOL OF LOGIC OF BENGAL

Cognitions may be determinate or indeterminate

Leaving aside the problem of indeterminate cognition, if we turn to determinate knowledge, it is easy to see that determinate knowledge must refer to an object with reference to some of its characters and qualities. When I know a book, the knowledge refers to it as "bookness". In all cognitions there is a specific relation between the cognition and its object, for it is only the existence of such specific relation that can account for the knowledge of specific objects. This relation of specific objectivity is called *viṣayatā*. This being a two-term relation, it must exist both in the subject and in the object. The object and the objectivity being the same entity, the relation of objectivity exists in the object in a relation of identity (*svarūpa-sambandha*). For if another relation was required to relate it to the object then there would be an infinite regressus of relations. But yet the relation of objectivity is admitted to be different from the object itself, for our cognitive experience refers to the object as a term in which the relation subsists. But if the relation is in the object in a relation of identity, then it becomes difficult to distinguish the relation and the object as two different entities. It is therefore that the *Naiyāyikas* refer the relation to the special characteristic of the object which becomes directly revealed

O.P. 62/41

in cognition. Thus when a book is known, the cognition refers to the "bookness" the special cognitive characteristic of the book in the cognition "I know the book" and this characteristic of "bookness" subsists in the book in a relation of identity (*svarūpa-sambandha*) and may therefore be regarded as different from the book and also as a relation of objectivity. This special aspect of the relation of objectivity (*viṣayatā*) is called *viṣayatāvacchedaka*. But even in this view there may be this objection that here also the "bookness" and the relation of objectivity (*viṣayatā*) have to be regarded as identical, and in that case the characteristic of "bookness" cannot be regarded as determining (*avacchedaka*) the nature of the relation of objectivity, which is the same as saying that the bookness is not the *avacchedaka* of the relation. This difficulty can be solved only by the supposition that objectivity (*viṣayatā*) is not a relation, but a separate category which forms the extra-subjective term of the cognitive relation. This category can then be regarded as specifically determined by the characteristic of the object (e.g., bookness) which exists in the book in a relation of identity.

This objectivity as a separate category determining the subject-object relation is produced by the conglomeration of the same conditions that produced the cognition itself. It remains only as long as the cognition remains and it is destroyed also along with the cessation of the cognition. This category of objectivity is different in accordance with the different kinds of *pramāṇas*, as they all involve different kinds of causal conditions for their production. It is also different according as the cognition refers to the past, present or the future. One can remember a past event or thing and imagine a future event or thing ; the category of objectivity (*viṣayatā*) is such that in the present memory of past, event or thing, it may abide in that event or thing, which is no longer existent, or it may abide in a future event or thing which has not yet come into being. No other entities which are separated in time can have the relation of the container and the contained excepting that of the object and its objectivity (*viṣayatā*). In all cases of inference and memory the object may be past but its objectivity which is revealed in the present cognition is subsistent in that past object. Some say that there are as many categories of objectivity as there are objects of knowledge ; others hold that so long as the objects are of similar nature their numerical difference would not constitute a ground for admitting different categories of objectivity.

So far for the objectivity and the object. But there is also a specific relation between the objectivity (*viṣayatā*) and the cognition (*jñāna*) viz., that of the determiner (*nirūpaka*) and the determined (*nirūpita*); for it is the nature of an objectivity that determines the specific nature and characteristic of the cognition. But this relation is a reversible relation and one can also say that it is the cognition that is the determiner, and the objectivity the determined, and they two are mutually dependant on each other for their subsistence and nature, and each leads to the other. One can thus define a cognition through its objectivity and the objectivity through the corresponding cognition. The specific defining characteristic of objectivity is technically called *avacchedaka* as it limits and defines the specific nature of the objectivity, but this specific characteristic (*avacchedaka*) may have a further defining characteristic and in that case the second defining characteristic is called *avacchedakatā-vacchedaka*.

When there is a cognition "the hill is fiery (*parvato vahnimān*)", the cognition of the hill has an objectivity (*viṣayatā*) associated with it, defined by the characteristic of the class-concept "hillness", and the cognition of the fire has an objectivity defined by the class concept "fireness". There is here no further defining characteristic (*avacchedaka*) of hillness or fireness. The defining characteristic may be either a quality (*dharma*) or a relation (*sambandha*). In the former case the defining characteristic may have a further limiting condition of some sort (*kiñcit-sambandhā-vacchinna*) where as the latter being of the nature of relations cannot have any further limiting condition of any kind (*kiñcit-sambandhā-navacchinna*), for if relations are admitted to have further relations that would involve an infinite regressus. Thus in the cognition "this book", the "this" refers to an object before the perceiver and both the "this" and the "book" are objects of cognition. Though the two are identical, yet they jointly qualify the nature of the cognition, for if we take the "this" to be the object of cognition then the "book" is to be admitted to be associated with the "this" in a relation of identity. The cognitional objectivity of the book is thus defined by a relation of identity with the "this". "Identity" being a relation, it cannot have any further defining characteristic or relation. In the cognition "this book", the cognitional objectivity of the book is defined only by the relation of identity with the "this" and this relation of identity, being a relation, cannot have any further defining characteristic, and this explains the view stated above that relations are no further limited by other defining characteristics. Again viewed from a somewhat different point of view, one may arrive at the same kind of result. Thus the objectivity of the book in the cognition of a book is "bookness" and this "bookness" again is in the book in a relation of inseparable inherence (*samavāya*). Viewed in this way the "bookness" has for its defining characteristic the *samavāya* relation, but this defining characteristic, being a relation, cannot have any further defining characteristic. The objectivity of the book may, on the one hand, have for its defining characteristic a relation of identity, or on the other hand as "bookness", a relation of inseparable inherence (*samavāya*). The objectivity of the book is thus the determinant (*nirūpaka*) of the relation of identity further unencumbered with any other relation and of "bookness" in a relation of *samavāya*. In other words, the "bookness" and "the relation of identity" have in them the determinedness (*nirūpitatva*) of the objectivity of the book in a cognition of the book.

Now it is well-known that the word "book" is equivalent to the expression "possessor of bookness" or "the locus of bookness". So the expression "the table which has a book on it" is equivalent to the expression "the table which has the possessor of bookness on it". But in the latter expression though the possessor of bookness may be associated with the table in a relation of contact (*saṁyoga*), the notion of bookness which is a constituent in the above cognition can only be determined by a further reference to another characteristic of it, such as the quality of bookness or bookness-ness, for an object of cognition must have a characteristic through which it is known ; and when "bookness" as a constituent of the complex cognition "the table which has the possessor of bookness on it" is an object of cognition, it must be admited to have a further defining characteristic, the quality of bookness or the bookness-ness. The table has a complex defining characteristic "contactual association with the possessor of bookness". Here the first-grade relation of the possessor of bookness with the table is a relation of contact, the second grade relation is that between the bookness and its possessor or locus, the book—i.e., the relation of inseparable inherence (*samavāya*) ; none of these relations requires further defining characteristic. But this complex cognition cannot start with the cognition of bookness ; the bookness, it may be remembered, is a defining characteristic of its possessor, the book. In the cognition of the book, the book was known by its defining characteristic, the bookness ; but when the bookness is the primary object of cognition, it must be admitted to have a further defining characteristic—bookness or the quality determining the nature of bookness. Here the objectivity (*viṣayatā*) of the book (*pratiyogī*) has for its defining characteristic (*avacchedaka*) the bookness, and this bookness has a further defining characteristic (*pratiyogitā-vacchedakā-vacchedaka*) the bookness, and from this point of view the book may be said to be defined by two grades of *avacchedakas* or defining characteristics.

The quality of defining characteristic (*avaccheda-*

katā) is not however the only point of view from which the objectivity, (*viṣayatā*) can be looked at. There are at least five other ways from which the notion of objectivity can be discerned, such as *viśeṣyatā, prakāratā, vidheyatā, uddeśyatā* and *dharmitā*. Take, for instance, the cognition of "a man with a stick". The objectivity of this cognition has for its constituents manness, man, stickness, stick and the contactual relation of the stick and the man. Though they are all within the scope of the objectivity (*viṣayatā*) of the cognition, they are not so in the self-same relation. Thus the notion "man" (which is equivalent to that which is possessed of manness) is expressed as subject (*viśeṣya*) in the cognition, while the notion "stick" (equivalent to what is possessed of stickness) is expressed as a predicate (*vidheya*) or mode (*prakāra*) of that subject (*viśeṣya*) ; the notion "manness" is expressed as the defining characteristic of subjectivity, and stickness is expressed as the defining characteristic of the mode or the predicate and the contactual relation is expresed merely as a relation. Thus the different constituents of objectivity are expressed in different notional variations. In other words, these different objects of cognition have different types of objectivity towards the cognition. It is useful, however, to note in this connection that the notion of "mode" and the notion of "predicate" are not identical, for there are instances of "modes" which cannot be called predicates. Thus, for instance, in the cognition "the book there", "the book" is the subject (*viśeṣya*) and the notion of thereness which may be regarded as a determining mode (*prakāratā*), cannot be regarded as being in any sense predicative ; for the predicative force (*vidheyatā*) is in the book. The case would be reversed in the proposition "that place is occupied by a book", for, in that expression the term "the place" is both the subject (*viśeṣya*) and the subject of affirmation (*uddeśya*) and the "book" presents the mode as well as the predicate. So though there may be instances where the modality (*prākāratā*) and the predicative character (*vidheyatā*) may exist in the same identical entity, the two concepts are different. The concepts of the character as an object of affirmation (*uddeśyatā*) and of "subjectness" are also different, and though in certain cases they may be found to exist together they need not necessary do so. Thus, for instance, in the cognition "the book there", it is the book that appears as the subject and it is the "there" that is the "object of affirmation" (*uddeśya*), for here the entity of place, which holds in it the mode (*prakāratā*) defined by the character of spatiality (*deśatva*), as defined by the character of relatedness of the corresponding relation of being limited by the contactual character, has in it the character of being the object of affirmation (*uddeśyatā*). Here though the book is the subject (*viśeṣya*) yet it is not the object of affirmation (*uddeśya*).

Viśeṣya has here been translated as "subject"; *dharmitā* may be translated as the possessingness of a quality or characteristic ; and since in any idea the subject is also often the possessor of the qualifying characteristics it may sometimes be mistakenly held that the subject character (*viśeṣyatā*) and the *dharmitā* character are one and the same. But this is not so ; though these two are often found to co-exist together in the same entity, they are not identically the same concept, for they do not always mean the same thing. Thus in the idea "the hill is fiery", the hill appears both as *viśeṣya* and as *dharmin,* but in the idea "the fire is in the hill", the fire is the subject (*viśeṣya*), but the hill is the *dharmin,* for, the phrase "in the hill" is a predicate to the "fire"; but it is the hill which in the objective world contains the fire as qualifying itself. *Dharmitā* is the real possession of a character in the objective world, whereas *viśeṣyatā* refers to a subject (in thought) of which something is predicated. Again in the idea "this book", the term "this" (referring to something before) is the object of affirmation and "book" represents the way in which it is affirmed (*vidheya*), but yet the "this" is not a *dharmin* which possesses the "book" as a quality or a character. Thus an object of affirmation (*uddeśya*) is not necessarily a possessor of character or quality.

The elements that form the object of an awareness may either refer to the separate elements such as "the tabular place", "the book", "the bookness", "the tableness", "the contactual relation" (*saṁyoga*), or these may appear combined in a particular form and may become the object of awareness in that combined form as in the idea "the table having the book on it." In the second case the awareness is qualified principally by the subjective character as limited by the concept of tabular placeness (*deśatvā-vacchinna*) as determined (*nirūpita*) by the mode (*prakāratā*) with the double defining characteristic of the concept of bookness (in the *samavāya* relation) and the contactual relation (*saṁyoga-sambandhā-vacchinna*). Here the tabular placeness is not directly the object of cog-

O.P. 62/42

nition but as modified as the subject of the defining characteristic of bookness. The place (where the book is) is limited firstly by the defining characteristic of placeness as modified as the subject of the defining characteristic of bookness. The place itself has two kinds of objectivity (*viṣayatā*) ; one is the primary substantial characteristic (*mukhya-viśeṣyatā*), as limited by the concept of placeness and as determined (*nirūpita*) directly by the mode (*prakāratā*) as limited by the concept of bookness and the contactual relation ; the other objectivity is that which is represented by the mode limited by the concept of placeness as it is and unqualified by other relations. According to Gadādhara Bhaṭṭācārya, the latter is to be regarded as being limited by the former. But according to Jagadīśa Tarkālaṅkāra, there is no difference between these two objectivities—they are one and the same. Similarly the book has one objectivity purely as limited by "bookness" and secondly, as limited by other relations as involved in the complex objectivity of the idea as understood from the phrase "book on the table".

If we inquire into the nature of the objectivity contained in the phrase, "the place with a book", we notice the following different objectivities: firstly, the objectivity residing in "bookness", otherwise called the defining characteristic of the mode (*prakāratā-vacchedaka*), secondly, the relation of inseparable inherence (*samavāya*) which is regarded as of the nature of the associative (*sāṁsargika*) defining characteristic (*avacchedaka*) of the objectivity as the defining characteristic of the mode (*prakāratā-vacchedakatvā-khya-viṣayatā*) ; thirdly, the universal of the relation of inseparable inherence (*samavāyatva*) which is to be regarded as the defining characteristic of the mode of objectivity. But fourthly, there is a further objectivity in that relation of inseparable inherence which stands as the objectivity of the substantial character underlying the former. Fifthly, there is the objectivity as the book. Again, sixthly, there is a further objectivity which is of the nature of the substance of the objectivity as the defining characteristic of the mode (*prakāratā-vacchedakatvā-khya-viṣayatā*) as defined by the *samavāya* relation underlying the universal of bookness and undefined by any other relation. There is a further objectivity underlying the contactual relation and there is a further objectivity in the universal of the contactual relation which is the subject characteristic (*viśeṣyatā*) of objectivity as the defining characteristic of the specific associative character (*sāṁsargikā-vacchedakatā*); eventually there is a further objectivity which is in a relation of identity with it which is of the nature of the defining characteristic.

MĀYĀ OF ŚAṄKARA AND HIS FOLLOWERS

(*An interpretation on the basis of textual study.*)

Referring to Śaṅkara's interpretation of *Brahma-sūtra* I. 1. 2, Rāmānuja says that those who believed in Brahman as characterless (*nirviśeṣa*) cannot do justice to the interpretation of the attributes of Brahman as affirmed in the above *sūtra,* for, instead of saying that the creation, maintenance and absorption of the world are from Brahman, they ought rather to say that the illusion of creation, maintenance and absorption is from Brahman. This raises an important question as regards the real meaning of Śaṅkara's interpretation of the above *sūtra.* Did he really mean as he is apparently ascribed by Rāmānuja to be saying that, that from which there is the illusion of creation, etc., of the world is Brahman, or did he really mean that Brahman and Brahman by itself alone is the cause of a real creation, etc., of the world? Śaṅkara as is well-known was a commentator of the *Brahma-sūtras* and the *Upaniṣads* and it can hardly be denied that there are many passages in these which would directly yield a theistic sense and the sense of a real creation of a real world by a real God. Śaṅkara had to explain these passages and he did not always use his strictly absolutistic phrases, for as he admitted three kinds of existence he could talk in all kinds of phraseology, only one had to be told about the sort of phraseology that Śaṅkara had in view at the time and this was not always done. The result has been that there are at least some passages which appear by themselves to be realistically theistic, others which are ambiguous and may be interpreted in both ways and others which are professedly absolutistic. But if the testimony of the great commentators and independent writers of the Śaṅkara school be taken, Śaṅkara's doctrine should be explained in the purely monistic sense and in that alone. Brahman is indeed the unchangeable, infinite and absolute ground of the emergence, maintenance and dissolution of all the world-appearances and is the ultimate truth underlying it. But there are two elements in the appearance of the world phenomena, the ultimate ground, the Brahman, the only being and truth in them, and the element of change and diversity, the *Māyā* by the evolution or the transformation of which the appearance of the many is possible. But in passages like those found in Śaṅkara's *bhāṣya* on the *Brahma-sūtra*, I. 1.2, it might appear as if the world-phenomena are no mere appearance but are real, inasmuch as they are not merely grounded in the real but are also the emanations from the real—the Brahman. But strictly speaking Brahman is not alone the *upādāna* or the material cause of the world but Brahman-with-*avidyā* is the material cause of the world and such a world is grounded in Brahman and is absorbed in Him, and Vācaspati in his *Bhāmatī* on Śaṅkara's *bhāṣya* on the same *sūtra* (B.S. I. 1.2) makes the same remark.[1] Prakāśātman in his *Pañca-pādikā-vivaraṇa* says that

1. *avidyā-sahita-brahmo-pādānaṃ jagat brahmaṇy evā'sti tatraiva ca līyate. Bhāmatī*, 1.1.2.

the creative functions here spoken of do not essentially appertain to Brahman and an enquiry into the nature of Brahman does not mean that Brahman is to be known as being associated with these qualities.[2] Bhāskara had asserted that Brahman had transformed himself into the world-order and that this was a real transformation—*pariṇāma*—a transformation of his energies into the manifold universe. But Prakāśatman in rejecting the view of *pariṇāma* says that even though the world-appearance be of the stuff of *māyā,* since this *māyā* is associated with Brahman, the world-appearance as such is never found to be contradicted or negated or found to be not existing—it is only found that it is not ultimately real.[3]

Māyā is supported in Brahman and the world-appearance being transformation of *māyā* is real only as such transformation, and it is grounded also in Brahman, for its ultimate reality is only so far as this ground or Brahman is concerned ; and so far as the world-appearances are concerned they are only relatively real as *māyā* transformations. The conception of joint causality of Brahman and *māyā* may be made in three ways: that *māyā* and Brahman are like two threads twisted together into one thread, or that Brahman with *māyā* as its power or *śakti* is the cause

2. *na hi nānāvidha-kārya-kriyā-veśā-tmakatvaṃ tat-prasava-śaktyā-tmakatvaṃ vā jijñāsyaṃ viśuddha-brahmā-ntargataṃ bhavitum arhati. Pañca-pādikā-vivaraṇa,* p. 205.

3. *sṛṣṭeś ca svopādhau abhāva-vyāvṛtatvāt sarve ca svopādhika-dharmmāḥ svāśrayo-pādhau abādhyatayā satyā bhavanti sṛṣṭir api svarūpeṇa na bādhyate kintu paramārtha-satyena. ibid.* p. 206.

of the world, or that Brahman being the support of *māyā* is indirectly the cause of the world.[4] In the latter two views *māyā* being dependent on Brahman, the work of *māyā*—the world—is also dependent on Brahman and these two views by an interpretation like this pure Brahman (*suddha-brahma*) is the cause of the world. Sarvajñātma Muni, who also thinks that pure Brahman is the material cause, conceives the function of *māyā* not as being joint material cause with Brahman, but as the instrument or the means through which the causality of pure Brahman appears as the manifold and the diversity of the universe, but even in this view the stuff of the diversity is the *māyā*, only such manifestation of *māyā* would have been impossible if the ground cause, the Brahman, is absent.[5]

In discussing the nature of the causality of Brahman Prakāśātman says that the monistic doctrine of the Vedānta is upheld by the fact that apart from the cause there is nothing in the effect which is speakable or describable.[6] So in all these various ways in which Śaṅkara's philosophy has been interpreted it has been universally held by almost all the follwers of Śaṅkara that though Brahman was at bottom the ground cause, yet the stuff of the world

4. *traividhyamatra sambhavati rajjvāḥ saṃyukta-sūtra-dvayavat māyā-viśiṣṭaṃ brahma kāraṇam iti vā devā-tma-śaktiṃ svagunair nigūḍhām iti śruter māyā-śaktimat-kāraṇaṃ iti vā jagad-upādāna-māyā-śrayatayā brahma kāraṇam iti vā. Ibid.*, p. 219.

5. *Saṃkṣepa-śārīraka I, 332, 334*, and the commentary *Anvayārtha-prakāśikā* by Rāmatīrtha.

6. *upādāna-vyatirekeṇa kāryasya anirūpaṇāt advitīyatā. Pañca-pādikā-vivaraṇa*, p. 221.

was not of real Brahma material but of *māyā*, and though all the diversity of the world has relative existence it has no reality in the true sense of the term in which Brahman is real.[7]

Śaṅkara himself says that the omniscience of Brahman consists in its eternal power of universal illumination or manifestation.[8] Though there is no action or agency involved in this universal consciousness, it is spoken of as being a knowing agent, just as the Sun is spoken of as burning and illuminating though the Sun itself is nothing but an identity of heat and light.[9] Before the creation of the world what becomes the object of this universal consciousness is the indefinable name and form which cannot

---

7. Prakāśātman refers to several ways in which the relation of Brahman and *māyā* had been conceived, such as—Brahman and *māyā* as his power, and the individual souls were all associated with *avidyā*,—brahman as reflected in *māyā* and *avidyā* was the cause of the world (*māyā-vidyā-pratibimbitaṃ brahma jagat kāraṇam*)—pure brahman is immortal and individual souls are associated with *avidyā*—individual souls have their own relations of the world and these through similarity appear to be one permanent world. Brahman undergoes an apparent transformation through its own *avidyā*—but in none of these views the world is regarded to be a real emanation from Brahman. *Pañca-pādikā-vivaraṇa*, p. 232.

Regarding the question as to how the Brahman could be the cause of the beginningless Vedas, Prakāśātman explains it by supposing that Brahman is the underlying reality by which all the Vedas imposed on it were manifested. *ibid.* pp. 230, 231.

8. *yasya hi sarva-viṣayā-vabhāsana-kṣamaṃ jñānaṃ nityam asti.*

9. *pratatauṣṇa-prakāse'pi savitari dahati prakāśayatī'ti svātantrya-vyāpadeśa-darśanāt. . .evam asaty api jñāna-karmaṇi brahmaṇaḥ tadaikṣata iti kartṛtva-vyāpadeśa-darśanāt.*

be ascertained as this or that.[10] The omniscience of Brahman is therefore this universal manifestation by which all the creations of *māyā* become the knowable contents of thought, but this manifestation is not an act of knowledge, but a permanent steady light of consciousness, by which the unreal appearances of *māyā* flash into being and are made known. That Brahman is the creator of the world is true in the same sense as it may be called the material cause of the world. Brahman being the support of *māyā* which has transformed into the world-appearance is called the material cause, and it being the support of *māyā* in all its various transformations as will and activity is at the same time regarded as the creator. So it is in the same sense of underlying reality that Brahman is called both the producer and the material cause of the world (*abhinna-nimitto-pādānakaṃ brahma*).[11] The Buddhists had asserted that all that we see and know were mere phenomenal appearances and that there were nowhere anything which could be called truly real, absolute and unchangeable, ultimate and ever-existent. Śaṅkara tried to rebut this view by affirming that the entity denoted by the term Brahman in the Upaniṣads was the ultimate reality which was the underlying ground of all our

---

10. *kiṃ punas tat karmma yat prāg-utpatter īśvara-jnānasya viṣayo bhavatī'ti tattvā-nyatvābhyām anirvacanīye nāma-rūpe-avyākṛte vyācikīrṣite iti brumaḥ. Śaṅkara-bhāṣya*, I-I-5.

11. *ekam eva caitanyam avidyo-pahitatvena upādānam avidyā-pariṇāme-cchā-kṛtyā-dy-āśrayatvena kartṛ ca iti siddham idaṃ nirviśeṣaṃ brahma nimittam upādānaṃ ca.* General drift of the argument in *Advaita-siddhi*. *brahmaṇo' bhinna-nimitto-pādānatve pramāṇo-papattiḥ.*

experience and of all phenomena as such. Śaṅkara emphasised the importance of the realisation of this Brahman as the pure contentless consciousness, the ultimate reality or being, which was also identical with pure and contentless happiness. The concept of change or appearance was irreconcilable with the notion of being or reality and though the latter was the basis of the former, yet no independent meaning could be attributed to the former. So he in a manner agreed with the Buddhists that the world of appearances was false, mere magic show or *māyā*. He himself however did not do much to elaborate philosophically the full significance of this concept of *māyā*. He tried to explain it by means of commonplace analogies of perceptual error or illusion, *e.g.*, the illusion of snake in rope, or of silver in conch-shell. Either on account of the defect of the eye or dim light, or mental inattention or preoccupation with other ideas, one may falsely perceive a snake where there is only a rope, and at a later moment when he is told that it was only a rope, he attends to it more carefully, and correctly perceives it to be a rope. This positive perception has with it, however, a negative implication as well—this is a rope and not a snake. This leads to a third stage of reconsideration of the matter which convinces us that the snake did not at any time exist in the rope, it does not exist in it now and it will not be in it in future. What is meant by saying that the snake does not exist in the rope is that the snake is not of the same stuff as the rope and is by no means a real transformation of the rope, but is only an appearance which was only hanging on the entity of the rope when we were ignorant of its true nature as rope. This contradiction or negation (*bādha*) of snake in past, present and future is called its falsehood or illusoriness. It is held that the appearance of the world phenomena is also hanging, as it were, on the Real—the Brahman, but when the true nature of Brahman is realised, this world-appearance will also be found negated in the same way as the illusory perception of snake was.

It may naturally be asked, what is then the nature of these phenomena. Are they mere impositions of our corrupt imagination,—mere ideas of the mind having no objective existence outside of us as perceivers as the subjectively idealistic school of Buddhists asserts? Śaṅkara emphatically denies any such suggestion. Things which we perceive, whatever they may really be in themselves, are not my ideas, nor are they produced by my perception, nor will they cease when I cease to perceive them, nor are they mis-perceptions except in the sense that they have no permanent substratum in the sense in which we speak of the principle of pure consciousness to be real; but still they are somehow there. Śaṅkara definitely opposed the *vijñānavādins* who held that there was no external world or objects before us, but only the ideas appearing or disapearing in a series. The external world was present as perceived, though it may not have a reality as such. We do not perceive ideas but objects. The Buddhists held that things which are invariably found together are identical and that since 'blue' and the idea of 'blue' were always and invariably found simultaneously they were identical (*saho-palambha-niyamād abhedo nīlataddhiyoḥ*). Śaṅkara rebutted this epistemological view and held that 'blue' and the knowledge or the idea of 'blue' were entirely two different things and they could not be identical. I perceive the 'blue,' have an idea of the 'blue,' but neither my idea nor my perception is blue. Corresponding to each external perception there is an external object that we perceive, the pillar, wall, jug, cloth.[12] These objects are perceived by sense-contact and one cannot say that they are not perceived or that they do not exist.[13] These external objects are certainly different from my ideas of them or perceptions, for no one thinks that his perception of a wall is a wall or that his perception of a pillar is a pillar (*yataḥ upalabdhi-vyatireko'pi balād arthasya abhyupagantavya upalabdher eva ; na hi kaścid upalabdhim eva stambhaḥ kuḍyaṃ ca iti upalabhate*). If the things did not exist externally, why should they appear that they were existing outside, whereas my ideas were felt to be my own. So the "awareness" and its object are different from each other (*tasmād artha-jñānayor bhedaḥ*). Dr. Moore had asserted in his well-known article in "Mind"—Refutation of Idealism—"that the main defect of idealism is that it cannot distinguish between "awareness" and its object, "blue" and the knowledge of "blue," and this is his refutation of idealism that the object and its awareness are different—we are aware of blue but blue and awareness are not identical. Here in Śaṅkara we have a form of idealism where this

12. *upalabhyate hi pratipratyayam bāhyo'rthaḥ stambhaḥ, kuḍyaṃ ghaṭaḥ, paṭaḥ iti.*

13. *indriya-sannikarṣeṇa svayam upalabhamāna eva bāhyam arthaṃ nā'ham upalabhe naca so'stīti bruvan katham upādeya-vacanaḥ syāt.*

distinction is realised and where it is definitely maintained that knowledge and its object are different and which agrees with Moore in holding the view that we are aware of "blue" and our awareness is not blue. We cannot indeed say that things "really" are as they are seen, but we may say that things are as they are seen. This is a distinction with which we are familiar in our own times. Thus Holt in defending his position against the idealists says that "as things are perceived so they are," and the Idealists have rashly misunderstood him to mean that "things are perceived as they really are", *i.e.*, "not all perceived things are *real* things."

But a question might then naturally arise, what then is the nature of the falsehood of the world-appearance? If it is urged by any interpreter that the world-appearance is simply felt to be given but when this is corrected it will be found that it was absolute nought (*tuccha*), it did not exist, it does not exist, and it will not exist and so are all illusions, I must at once point out that such an interpretation is entirely false and against the universal tradition of Vedāntic interpretation and also against the evident intention of Śaṅkara's view. When an error is corrected then the third stage of reflection does not show that the illusory object did not exist at all, but it only certifies that the illusory object was never partly or wholly any part of the entity which was perceived as the illusory object. The "snake" perceived never was, nor is, nor will be, any part of the "this" of the rope which was mistaken as the snake—*pratipanno-pādhau traikālika-niṣedha-pratiyogitvaṃ mithyātvam*. This definition of falsehood means that falsehood of an appearance consists in the fact that its existence may be denied, in all the three possible temporal relations, in the locus or the entity (*upādhi or adhikaraṇa*) where it is perceived (*pratipanna*). This latter qualification (*pratipanno-pādhau*) is purposely given to rule out the suggestion that the falsehood of the world-appearance may be regarded to be of the nature of the absolutely non-existent like the round square or the hare's horn (*śaśa-viṣāṇā-dya-sad-vyāvṛtty-arthaṃ pratipannatvaṃ upādhi-viśeṣaṇam*).[14] This has been said in a slightly different way when falsehood is again defined as that which appears to exist in an entity where it does not exist (*svāśraya-niṣṭhā-tyantā-bhāva-pratiyogitvaṃ* or *svā-tyantā-bhāvā-dhikaraṇe eva pratīyamānatvaṃ* i.e., the illusory object is that which appears in an entity (*adhikaraṇa*) where it (*sva*) does not exist (*atyantā-bhāva*). When it is said that the illusory object is both existent and non-existent, it may again well be argued that according to the principle of excluded middle what is existent cannot be non-existent and what is non-existent cannot be existent (*sattvā-sāttvayoḥ paraspara-viraha-vyāpyatayā*); but the answer to such a question is that the word 'non-existent' has been used here in a special sense; it means here a denial of that 'existence' which remains uncontradicted in all time; an illusory object is then that which appears as existent, but is yet not such an existent which remains uncontradicted in past,

14. *pratitpannaḥ, mithyātvenā'bhimata—(sva)'prakāraka-dhī-viśeṣaḥ ya upādhir adhikaraṇaṃ tanniṣṭho yas traikālika-niṣedho' tyantā-bhāva-pratiyogitvam ity arthaḥ—Gauḍa-brahmā-nandī* and *Viṭṭhaleśopādhyāyī*.

present and future. So the principle of excluded middle has no application to the co-existence of such existence and non-existence. Brahman is known to us on the strength of the testimony of the Upaniṣads to be the unchangeable pure existence, but the world-appearance cannot be admitted to be such existence, but yet it appears to be objectively existent, it is therefore a denial of unchangeable pure being and is at the same time to be admitted to be objectively existent; the world-appearance is therefore a different category from both existence and its denial, the non-existence; if an animal is a horse it cannot be cow, if it is a cow it cannot be a horse, but if it is an elephant it need not be either a cow or a horse. So between absolute existence and absolute negation one has to admit separate category which is not absolute existence like Brahman because it is not permanent and uncontradicted in all times, and is not also the absolutely non-existent like the hare's horn (the absolute nought—*tuccha*) for it appears as objectively existent and excepting the fact that it is not uncontradicted at all times it is existent for all other purposes.[15]

The main point about the world-appearance is that it depends entirely on Brahman or pure consciousness or absolute being for its existence and it is this that constitutes the difference between reality and unreality. That alone is real which does not depend on anything else for its self-manifestation, whereas unreal is that which cannot manifest itself

---

15. *sattvā-tyantā-bhāvavatve sati asattvā-tyantā-bhāva-rūpaṃ viśiṣṭam.*

without the help of the real; it is therefore that though being is different from appearance all appearance is manifested only as associated with being or as revealed by the underlying being. One of the most essential characteristics of the Vedānta philosophy is that it distinguishes between being and all manifestations which appear to have being, consciousness and all states which appear to be conscious and these manifestations or states cannot be supposed to have any independent existence but yet they are not non-existent; only when considered as separate from being they are unspeakable, indefinable and substanceless. It is this dependence on pure consciousness or pure being that constitutes the perceivability (*dṛśyatva*), the materiality (*jaḍatva*) and the limitedness (*paricchinnatva*) of the world-appearance.

Disregarding the subtle technical difference between *avidyā, ajñāna* and *māyā*, *avidyā* or *māyā* is defined as that which is a positive entity from beginningless time but which ceases with the rise of the true knowledge.[16] This positivity means merely the denial of negativity or nought.[17] But though this positivity does not mean pure or absolute existence, yet it may be the material cause of the transformations through which it passes, for it continues through all its transformations.[18] So *māyā* is regarded as the

16. *anādi-bhāva-rūpatve sati ajñāna-nivartyā.*

17. *bhāvatvaṃ cā'tra abhāva-vilakṣaṇatva-mātraṃ vivakṣitam.*

18. *ajñānasya bhramasya ca bhāva-vilakṣaṇatve 'py upādāno-pādeya-bhāvo-papatteḥ, na hi bhāvatvam upādānatve tantram, kintu anvayi-kāraṇatvam upādānatve tantram.*

upādāna or the substance-stuff of the world-appearances and Brahman is only the support of this substance, for it is such that it has always to hang on Brahman in order that it may remain or that it may produce all its illusory transformations as the world-appearance (*viśva-bhramo-pādāna-māyā-dhiṣṭhānaṃ brahma*).

Appearances and illusory objects have therefore objectivity, but not reality, and one of the special features of the Śaṅkarite Vedānta is to distinguish the two concepts, and the acceptance of a third category of that which is neither being nor non-being. On the right understanding of the nature of *avidyā* as accepted by the Śaṅkarites, there is an illuminating passage in *Nyāya-makaranda* of Ānandabodha-bhaṭṭārakācāryya which I translate, "It cannot be said that *"avidyā"* is mere false knowledge (*mithyā-jñānaṃ*) or absence of knowledge (*vidyā-bhāva*) and that in neither of these senses can *avidyā* be regarded as material cause (*samavāyi-kāraṇa*) for in neither of these senses can it be regarded as a substance (*adravyatvāt*), for *avidyā* is accepted as beginningless and indefinable. Its nature is to be determined by the nature of the effect that it produces and it is not something fictitious (*apramāṇikatā*). The occasional happening of an effect necessarily requires the operation of a cause ; without a material stuff no effect can be produced merely by the instrumental cause, for all effects (except destruction—*dhvaṃsa*) are produced by material cause ; an untrue effect cannot be due to a true material cause, and that which does not exist and which is devoid of all capacity cannot be called material cause, so since neither being nor nothingness can be the substance-stuff of the illusory objects, we are forced to admit a cause which is neither being nor nothing.[19] So it is for admitting such a wholly different kind of cause that a beginningless cause of the type of *avidyā* has to be admitted." "That which is the indefinable substance-stuff of the illusory object—silver—is what is termed *avidyā*."

That this view was almost universally accepted by the Śaṅkara school of thinkers is apparent from the account of the origin of the illusory silver as found in *Saṁkṣepa-śārīraka*. In that work Sarvajñātma Muni thinks that the substance-stuff (*upādāna*) of the illusory silver is the ignorance (*ajñāna*) of the determinate qualities of the "this" perceived before, *i.e.*, the "this" underlying the conch-shell, for so long as this specific ignorance of the qualities of the conch-shell remains, there is the illusory perception of silver in the "this" of the conch-shell, and as soon as this ignorance is removed the "this" of conch-shell appears in its true state as conch-shell. This view has also been emphasised in *Pramāṇa-mālā* and *Nyāya-dīpāvalī*, and Vācaspati also supports this view in his *Brahma-tattva-samīkṣā*.

It is only Nṛsiṃha Bhaṭṭa who denies the two processes (*vṛtti*) in illusory perception and takes a somewhat subjective view of it and thinks that illusory perceptions are due to defects in the sense organs due to associations and other causes which

19. *tathā cā'nupapādyamānāyāṃ sad-asad-upādānatāyām tad-vilakṣaṇam eva kāraṇaṃ pariśeṣataḥ kāryam anumāpayet*—*Nyāya-makaranda* p. 123.

become operative when their functions are not opposed by the specific nature of the object baffling all suggestions of similarity and the like which when aroused generally corrupt the proper functions of the sense organs. But even in his view it is the *avidyā* inherent in the object that is affected by its association with the defective sense organ and undergoes a modification towards being turned into an effect and at the succeeding moment transforms itself into the form of the illusory object (e.g., silver).[20]

But it may well be asked what is meant by this transformation of ignorance? Ignorance is only absence, or negation, of knowledge and there is no meaning in saying that negation can undergo any positive or objective transformation. But the answer of the Śaṅkarites on this point is that ignorance or *avidyā* as used in this connection is not negation, but is a positive entity which can be directly experienced by perception and established by inference. When one says "I do not know what you mean" (*tvaduktaṃ na jānāmi*), it is not the negation of something that is meant, but a perceptual experience of ignorance as a positive entity. For, if it was simply a negation that is denoted, such a negation must be a specific negation negating a definite object, but in the above cases it is only indefinite negation that is meant and negation cannot be indefinite; what is said an indefinite negation is the positive experience of ignorance. The awaking memory of deep sleep

20. *idam arthā-vacchinna-caitanye rajata-pariṇāmiṇi avidyā duṣṭe - ndriya - samparka - rūpād adhyāsa-nimitta-kāraṇa-bhūtāt kṣobhaṃ kāryā-bhimukhyaṃ prāpnoti, uttara-kṣaṇe ca rajata-rūpeṇa pariṇamate.*

that I slept so long and did not know anything (*etāvantaṃ kālaṃ na kiñcid avediṣāmiti parāmarśa-siddhaṃ sauṣuptaṃ pratyakṣam api bhāva-rūpa-jñāna-viṣayam eva*) also refers to a similar kind of perception of positive ignorance. For, in such cases though there is an experience of ignorance as referring to the particular import that is meant, there is no specific negation that is implied.[21]

The only difficulty, however, is with regard to the conception of the dissolution of *avidyā* with right knowledge, and commentators use all their ingenuity to explain the nature and characteristic of such a dissolution. Ānandabodha Bhaṭṭārakācārya after discussing all sorts of views, says that such a dissolution cannot be regarded as 'real,' for then the doctrine of monism fails (for, then both this dissolution of *avidyā* and Brahma would be real and that would be duality), it cannot be regarded as unreal in the sense of absolute nought or non-existent, for then how could it be removed by right knowledge (*nā'pyasati jñāna-sādhyatva-yogāt*), cannot be both existent and non-existent in the same sense, for that would be self-contradictory (*nā'pi sad-asad-rūpa-virodhāt*) ; it cannot also be considered to be indefinable in its nature (*anirvācya*) for it may well be contended that there is no reason why it should not then exist even after

21. *viśeṣa-jñānā-bhāvasya tvaduktā-rtha-jñānā-bhāvasya vā'-nābhyupagame tad-viṣaya-jñānasattvena tad-vyavahārā-patteśca ; na caivaṃ dṛśyate ; svataḥ-prāmāṇya-pakṣe tu tat-prakārakatve tad-viśeṣyakatve tu gṛhyamāṇe tadvattva-grahaṇasya āvaśyakatyā-tadaṃśe tat-prakāraka-tad-viśeṣyakatvasya tādṛśa-pratiyogi-jñāne sambhavāt spaṣṭa eva vyāghātaḥ bhāva-rūpa-jñāna-pakṣe tu sarvasyā'pi sākṣi-vedyatayā na vyāghātaḥ. Advaita-siddhi*, p. 556.

emancipation (*mukti*) or why it could after all be removable by true knowledge (*tad-upādāna-jñānā-nuvṛtty-upapatteḥ jñānā-nivarttyatvā-patteśca*). It is therefore to be regarded as being of an altogether different type, different from all these four possible kinds of conception, a fifth and a different kind altogether. This is known as the *pañcama-prakāra-vidyā-nivṛtti*. Sureśvara in his *Brahmasiddhi* says that the dissolution of *avidyā* is nothing but the pure self (*ātmaiva iti*). Others think that *avidyānivṛtti* or dissolution of *avidyā* is also indefinable (*anirvācyā*).[22]

---

22. See *Siddhānta-leśa*.

THE MEANING OF CULTURE

We use the two words culture and civilization but we are not always conscious of their exact connotation and distinction. In ordinary usage the distinctive trait of the concept of culture is hardly brought clearly before the mind. Sometimes the word culture is also used in the sense of civilization ; thus, the German word Kultur-Stosse is used in the sense of "grade of civilization." But still there is an obvious difference between the two terms.

By civilization we understand all that we have externally achieved by way of self-protection and self-satisfaction as men, as members of a society and of a nation. Thus, from our semi-animal condition we learnt the use of weapons. The invention of different kinds of weapons, the methods of cultivation, cooking and weaving and the discovery of various metals and beasts of burden and the invention of the various means of locomotion mark the advent of a superior type of civilization. Such a state of civilization naturally implied the development of certain tribal institutions, including diverse kinds of vocational instruction. As the conditions of civilization gradually improved and city-life developed, we had various types of political, legal and educational institutions, together with the development of various kinds of arts and industries. Emulation of civilised communities for supremacy in politics or in trade led to the development of the art of warfare and of diplomacy and statecraft. We thus have a continuous history of the development of civilization in various countries among various nations.

From the commencement of the Renaissance we notice an extraordinary desire for the knowledge of the secrets of nature among certain notable persons in Europe which led to the discovery of many new scientific truths. The parallel development of technology led to a quickening of scientific investigation and discovery. These discoveries could often be utilized in the service of man for the alleviation of human misery. The enterprising activity of the Europeans led to the discovery of America and India and to the exploration of many new countries. This led to the opening of new markets. The scientific truths that were discovered led to the manufacture of many commodities which were used either for daily needs or for luxury. The capitalist and the politician were in alliance and came to the aid of the technologists and the scientists for the devising of new methods of transport and communication and the satisfaction of ever-increasing needs. Thus the discoveries of science, pursued and achieved through purely scientific enquiries, began to be transformed into various commodities which benefited the scientists, by the production of various scientific instruments, and also benefited societies and nations by the exchange of products, easy communication and easy transport. But side by side with the production of commodities of comfort, transport or communication, there are also produced deadly weapons, poison gases and the like for the destruction of neighbours and the exploitation of the weak and the helpless.

Civilization in the main has been the product of our efforts for self-protection and self-satisfaction. Within a particular society and nation it has resulted in the exercise of control in the interests of mutual protection and mutual satisfaction. Legal, political and educational institutions train up the people of a community to desist from the transgression of mutual rights and privileges and punish those who commit any actual violence. But the progress of civilization has not yet been able to produce any institutions which are effective in controlling the relations between two or more different nations. In unfortunate countries where there are diverse religious sects which are more or less equal in strength, or in countries where there are different parties contending for supremacy in different ways we have a similar difficulty in evolving institutions which would work for mutual benefits. The evolution of civilization of a scientific type, such as we now find in Europe, has contributed immensely to the welfare and well-being not only of the people of Europe but of the whole world. But side by side with such contributions, the civilization of the Europeans has been a menace to themselves and to the people of the whole world. The power of science, the might of accumulated wealth and the energy of virile nations are being made subservient to motives of fear, greed and ambition. If our civilization is thus baffling us, may we seek our salvation in any other quarter?

In the Oxford Dictionary 'culture' has been defined as the intellectual side of civilization and also as the refinement produced through training and education. If we take the first meaning, culture would imply subjective intellectuality of which the objective institutions and products of civilization are external manifestations. But the mere intellectuality is a power without the necessary supervision and direction. Such a power may have produced the civilization, but by itself it is incapable of giving us any help towards emancipating us from the bonds of civilization or of attaining our salvation from its evils. The intellectuals of the nation may, unless they are controlled by moral considerations, produce organizations and instruments for the destruction of others which may ultimately be disastrous to themselves. Obviously then we cannot seek our salvation from the merely intellectual apparatus which is responsible on the subjective side for the production of civilization. The other definition of the Oxford Dictionary of culture as refinement produced from training and education is extremely vague. It is difficult to ascertain the limits of the connotation of the concept of refinement. On the one hand, it has a shade of meaning tending towards aesthetic apperception; on the other hand, it may signify moral and humanitarian considerations for the well-being of others. Ultimately the two senses are closely associated with each other. We are reminded in this connection of Shaftsbury and Hutchison's conception of morality. Hutchison adopted avowedly from Shaftsbury the widened use of the word 'sense' to denote certain mental feelings other than those incident to know changes in the bodily organs; and it is through his school that the term aestheticos, though still kept true to its proper meaning in the strict nomenclature of Kant, has been made to yield the modern conception of Aesthetics.

O.P. 62/45

According to Hutchison the single quality of a body, *e.g.*, its shape or colour, produces in us a simple sensation. He regarded the sense of right to be in its nature as simple as the sense of beauty. It is this common element that induced him to apply to purely ideal states a word previously limited to affections through perception. Thus, according to him, the appeal of good actions was as simple and as unanalysable as the appeal of beauty of a flower. The contiguity of the notions of the good and of the beautiful is also well-known in Indian thought. It is said that the apprehension of beauty and the awakening of moral tendencies are grounded in the excitation of the *sattva-guṇa.* Thus the notion of refinement involved in the concept of culture may be supposed to involve within itself the notion of moral elevation becoming simple and instinctive like the apprehension of beauty. Refinement means fineness of feeling, taste or thought. Such a fineness necessarily involves a delicate and tender consideration for the feelings and interests of others—a consideration which no longer appears in intellectual modes but which has transformed itself into a simple sense-organ as it were.

The word culture is derived from the Latin word *cultura,* which means cultivation, tending and, in Christian authors, worship. Among the primitive meanings of the word we have the dominance of the sense of cultivation. Thus the word means cultivation or rearing of plants or crops, the rearing or raising of certain animals such as fish, oysters, bees, etc., or natural products, such as silk. It also means the artificial development of microscopic organisms, such as bacteria, the training of the human body, the cultivating or development of the mind, faculty, manners, etc., the general improvement or refinement of mind, taste and manners. It also means a particular form of intellectual development. Passing in review the various meanings of the word, one is reminded of the fact that the mental improvement signified by culture is a composite product under various influences. If it involves the inward will or intellect of a person, it also involves the influences to which one is subjected through education by coming in contact with great minds and the general effect of the civilizing influence and atmosphere that may be all around us. A seed shoots forth not only by its own inner power but by the composite influence of its environment—the air, water, light etc. So the mental improvement signified by culture which is produced in a man as if it were a new organ can only do so under the most beneficent influences of internal gifts and external environment. Culture as refinement of tastes and manners shows itself in the spontaneous observance of good manners and etiquette in society which are all ultimately based upon a due consideration for the feelings of others and may therefore be regarded as being ethical in their nature, as has been well established by Wundt in his Ethics.

There is yet another important sense of the word culture. It means the entire spiritual asset of an individual or a nation. Thus when we speak of Hindu culture, we mean by the term not merely the intellectual achievement but the moral and religious ideals, the nature of the sense of value and the goal of conduct, the relative sense of the subordination of intellect to the moral will or mystical intuition and the spiritual value of life as a whole being the sole determinant of all our actions. A study of the culture of the Hindus would not mean merely the study of the intellectual achievement of the Hindus, the study of their philosophy, their literature, their sciences and mathematics, their arts and crafts; but it would mean a study of them all or even a part of them as illustrative of the fundamental value-sense of the Hindus. To appreciate Hindu painting from the point of view of the tone and the blending of colours is not enough; it is necessary to go beyond the painting into the mind of the painter which conceived the work and to trace within him the value-sense of the nation that operated through him and quickened his artistic genius.

If we look at a human body or at an animal body we find there not only the flesh and the bones and the skin but we find them distributed over in definite proportions. It is this proportion that gives the man and the animal his distinctive form and beauty. If we look at various plants and trees, we do not find there merely the trunk, the branches and the leaves but find there also the form and rhythm which are unique to every plant. The distribution of the branches and the trunk, their proportion and harmony, the distribution of the leaves in a methodical manner—all manifest a restraint and subordination to some fundamental principle that determines the rhythmic grace of plant and animal body. When the plant grows its leaves round its trunk or branches, it seems as if it were conscious of some determining principle which it must follow in its outflow of the green of life. So also many are the ways in which the spiritual life of a nation manifests itself. Behind the actual products of civilization, there is a spiritual grasping which represents not only the intellectual side of civilization but the entire spritual life involving the superior sense of value as manifested in morals, religion and art and the diverse forms of social and other institutions and forms and ways of life. The nature of this inward principle cannot always be definitely formulated but it can be realized in an intuitive manner in the various ways in which it may manifest itself. The charm of a beautiful poem cannot be located in any of the words or the sentences that form the structure of the poem, nor can it be defined and described; but yet it can be felt as forming the essence of the poem and as giving its very life and form.

So the cardinal principle or the soul of culture that manifests itself in the various spiritual activities of the self is grasped and intuitively felt but cannot be defined. It is this, however, that gives the distinctive uniqueness of every culture. It may be indefinite in the sense that it cannot often be definitely described and yet it is so definite in itself that there is hardly any chance of its being confused with anything else. If you read two poems of two master poets or see two paintings of two master painters, the distinction and individuality are unmistakable, yet they are indescribable. So also the cultures of two nations may not be definitely described but may easily be distinguished, traced and illustrated in their concrete spiritual activities. Even in the same nation it is sometimes possible to discover two distinctive cultures which are different in character, temper and expression. Thus among the Aryan Indians for over a thousand years two distinctive cultures, the Hindu and the Buddhist, sometimes operated together in union and in other times came into clash or conflict. Looked at from this special point of view one may say that a particular culture signifying the animating spirit of a particular type of civilization, art, or religion may behave almost as an individual having its own uniqueness and peculiarity of expression. As one individual may influence another, so it is possible that a particular culture may influence another. It is also found that particular cultures sometimes become saturated with a militant self-consciousness and destroy other cultures and reinstate themselves in their place. The Muslim culture in the days of the Khalifat may be cited as an apposite example. In modern times a near approach to it may be found in the notion of the German ***kultur***, particularly in the life of the Kaiser and also under the present despotism of Hitler. With Mussolini in Italy we have the beginnings of the youthful days of another aggressive culture, namely, Fascism, and in Russia we have communism, socialism and Bolshevism.

If we compare the older notion of culture as represented in Hindu culture, Buddhist culture, Egyptian culture or Greek culture, or the culture of the Chinese, we find that it represents a special refinement or psychic improvement, the production of a mental harvest due to aesthetic, religious or moral impulses which saturate the mental grounds and make them rich and fertile. In modern times, however, the spirit of nationalism produced largely by the demands of selfishness and self-interest of a group of people living under particular geographical areas has to a large extent spoilt the refinement of culture and made it subservient to itself. In fact national jealousy and national hatred, national ambition and greed are trying to destroy any culture that may oppose them. At the time of the last war even Bertrand Russell was imprisoned for giving expression to his pacifistic views. In Italy and Germany one can hardly give expression to his independent views or appreciation of internationalism or of cosmopolitan culture without running the risk of grave legal consequences. I hear that conditions are still worse in Russia, where it is difficult for a Russian even to come out of his country without paying heavy penalties for the same. Almost every Russian is a prisoner in his own country and every man is forbidden by the State to think in any other terms or manner than that prescribed by Stalin and his party. Thus intoxicated nationalism may not only try to defeat the possibility of international rapprochement through international cultural influences, but it also may be subversive of the evolution of any true culture in any country.

Nationalism in modern times is in a large measure economic in its concept. The securing of economic advantage for a special country, the maintenance and furtherance of its economic interests are probably the strongest arguments in favour of nationalism. But in critical situations, nations, like individuals, may become nervous and defeat their purpose through anger and hatred, like a man in the street. This is particularly possible because of the fact that in international dealings for peace and war, nations are not represented by cool-headed philosophers but by administrators who have seldom learnt to be generous and self-controlled through refinement of culture. I shall give one example—the peace deliberations of 1919. The peace council was a council of four, Clemenceau, Signor Orlando, President Wilson and the Prime Minister Lloyd George. Clemenceau felt about France what Pericles felt of Athens, unique value in her, nothing else mattering. His principles for the peace can be expressed simply. He thought that the German understands and can understand nothing but intimidation, that he is without generosity or remorse in negotiation, that there is no advantage that he will not take of you and no extent to which he will not demean himself for profit, that he is without pride, honour or mercy. Therefore you must never negotiate with a German or conciliate him; you must dictate to him. On no other terms will he respect you or can you prevent him from cheating you. Keynes remarking on the subject says:

"Clemenceau's philosophy had therefore no place for sentimentality in international relations. Nations are real things of whom you love one and feel for the rest indifference or hatred. The glory of the nation you love is the desirable end,—but generally to be obtained at your neighbour's expense. The politics of power are inevitable and there is nothing very new to learn about this war and the end that it was fought for ; England had destroyed, as in each preceding century, a trade rival ; a mighty chapter had been closed in secular struggle between the glories of Germany and France. Prudence required some measure of lip-service to the 'ideals' of foolish Americans and hypocritical Englishmen ; but it would be stupid to believe that there is much room in the world as it really is for such affairs as the League of Nations or any sense in the principle of self-determination except as an ingenious formula for re-arranging the balance of power in one's own interests."

The councillors of the old world believed that, being based on human nature which is always the same, the old order cannot change. If France and England had been victorious now, they might not be so in future. If now there is an opportunity of crushing Germany, the situation must be fully exploited. A peace of magnanimity or of fair and equal treatment based on such an idealism as the fourteen points of President Wilson could only have the effect of shortening the interval of Germany's recovery and hastening the day when she will once again hurl against France her greater numbers and her superior resources and technical skill. Hence the necessity of "guarantees," and each guarantee was taken by increasing irritation, and thus the probability of a subsequent revenge by Germany made necessary yet further provisions to crush. Thus a Carthagenian peace was concluded. The idealistic President Wilson was almost a puppet in the hands of Mr. Llyod George, who watched the company with "six or seven senses not available to ordinary men, judging character, motive and sub-conscious impulse, perceiving what each was thinking and even what each was going to say next and compounding with telepathic instinct the argument or appeal best suited to the vanity, weakness or self-interest of his immediate auditor." The peace thus concluded out of a spirit of revenge and future fears will be the cause of many devastating wars in future. 1870 was replied to in

1919 but 1919 must be prepared for its catastrophic reply in future. It is this peace that was responsible for the manner in which Germany and Italy are making all their higher cultures entirely subservient to the demands of nationalism. Any one who has travelled through the continent in recent times must have noticed how even in the best and most advanced University circles the demands of nationalism in its narrow and aggressive sense are gradually clouding the illumination of cultures.

We thus see that, as there are different races, countries and nations, there are individual cultures which are often opposed to one another. In ancient times these cultures were closely associated with religion, morality and arts. But in modern times this culture is being impregnated by materialism as it appears in the current economic tendencies, and the spirit of nationalism in a higher sense as the welding together of the spirits of a group of people may be a spiritual fact, but it is always liable to grosser invasions of materialism from our lower natures. As such, nationalism may often be prejudicial to the interests of higher culture, which being internationalistic in spirit may be in conflict with nationalism in a narrow sense of the term. The invasion of nationalism into culture has been so large and so frequent that it is often difficult to distinguish the former from the latter, as in the case of German nationalism and German *kultur*. In the case of the religious culture of the past we see that a line of thought impregnated with humanitarian or God-intoxicated emotion as initiated by a religious prophet like the Buddha, Jesus or Muhammad, was gradually elaborated by the disciples inspired by them whose life and manners reflected the religious cultures of their minds. Such was the fire that enlivened their hearts that whoever came in contact with them caught the flame and immediately became the participants of that culture. These religious cultures not only inspired those who were particularly of a religious temperament but by their very presence induced a mental temperament around them that responded to the bugle call of the enthusiasts ; new recruits flocked in and each contributed to the forward march in his manner. Thus art, industry, rituals of worship and even politics and political organizations and ways of thinking were all affected and coloured by the fundamental spirit of a religious culture. Aśoka was a typical Buddhist emperor and the solicitude of his mind for the well-being of his people, as manifested by his appointment of religious superintendents and the publication of religious edicts, is almost unique in the history of the world.

That the religious culture of India, be it of Jainism, Buddhism or of Hinduism, affected even the temperaments of her kings is apparent from the lives of the three greatest kings of India—Candragupta, Aśoka and Harṣa. Candragupta retired and became a recluse, Aśoka was a recluse even while he was a king and Harṣa used to give away his all in charity after particular periods of accumulation. The system of Hindu, Buddhist and Jaina cultures in spite of their differences have this common feature that they all attach a higher value to the demands of the spirit than to the demands of the flesh. If the old Vedic culture with its system of sacrifices set the well-being of life and happiness as the ultimate goal, the culture of the Upaniṣads and all that followed it, repudiated it in an emphatic manner. The result of this repudiation was the production of an oscillation which accepted the demands of the spirit either in a proportionate manner as may be consistent or consonant with the other demands of life or in a superlative manner almost ignoring all other demands of life. The oscillatory movement describes, as it were, a course between the normal satisfaction of the demands of the flesh and the supreme and all-denying satisfaction of the spirit, and this course represents the varying character of the Hindu culture. The spirit of Islamic culture seems to recommend the satisfaction of all normal demands subject to the restrictions imposed upon them by the religious commands of God or His prophet. But here also the demands of the spirit have often been over-emphasised at the expense of life on earth. The culture of the Sufis is often almost indistinguishable from the Upaniṣadic culture. Thus Jili says:

> Thine is the kingdom in both worlds ; I saw therein none but myself, that I should hope for his favour or fear him. Before me is no 'before' that I should follow its condition and after me is no 'after' that I should precede its notion. I have made all kinds of perfections mine own and lo, I am the beauty of the majesty of the whole. I am nought but it. Whatsoever thou seest of minerals and plants and animals together with man and his qualities. And whatever thou seest of elements and nature and original atoms whereof the substance is a perfume. And whatsoever thou seest of seas and deserts and trees and high-topped mountains. And whatsoever thou seest of spiritual forms and of things visible whose countenance is goodly to behold. . . . . .
>
> Lo, I am that whole and that whole is my theatre: 'tis I not it that is displayed in its reality.

The same mental approach is also to be found in Hallaj and Ibn'l-Arabi and others.

Even Omar Khyyam, who has been so wrongly delineated in Fitzgerald's version, describes the nothingness of the world in terms which would suit a Nāgārjuna, a Vedāntist, or a Bāul:

> *"Duniya didi o har ch didi hic ast*
> *Oan nij kh gufti o shunidi hicast*
> *sar ta sare afak duidi hic ast*
> *oan nij kh dar khanah khijidi hic ast."*

> "You see them, but all you see is naught
> And all you say and all you hear is naught,
> Naught the four quarters of the mighty earth,
> The secrets treasured in your chamber naught."

It is important, however, to notice that the intimacy and the feeling of fraternity that existed among the members belonging to a particular culture were not often extended to the adherents of other faiths and cultures. Thus Abusaid said:

> "Whoever goes with me in this way is my kinsman, even though he may be many degrees removed from me and whosoever does not back me in this matter is nobody to me even though he be one of my nearest relations."

In the Hindu, Buddhist and Christian cultures also we seldom notice the feeling of fraternity extended to one another in the same manner as it was extended to the adherents of the same culture. In Islam also it is a fact of great importance that, though whole-hearted fraternity is recommended among "the men of faith," it was done in a very remote measure among the people of the Book and was almost wholly denied to others.

It is thus seen that the different religious cultures did not observe a spirit of supreme friendship and amity among themselves. It was of course due to ignorance that the adherents of any culture found fault with those of other cultures. But it cannot be said that even when the adherents knew well the contents of one another's cultures, they would also appreciate it, for culture means a new outlook, a new orientation, a new angle of vision, which may not have its appeal for another. The psychological differences, tendencies and temperaments are by themselves sufficient to explain this. But yet it has to be admitted that familiarity with different cultures may remove the primary feeling of hostility due to ignorance and consequent undesirable misattribution.

New types of culture may grow under various conditions and causes. Thus in modern Europe the growth of science and the consequent advance of knowledge have produced in us a faith in the application of the methods of science, namely, that of accurate observation, experiment and deduction, which is of a different nature from the faith possessed by a man of religion. It is often said that there is no opposition between science and religion. But such a proposition can only be true in the sense that science may be supposed to discover many new facts which may increase the scope of religion. But it cannot be denied that the angle of vision of science is widely different from that of religion. Religion proceeds largely from our faith in the prophets or books of revelation or from *a priori* inclination of our hearts which influences our powers of reason. The scientific culture may thus be regarded as greatly antagonistic to religion in its accepted sense. The former is not satisfied with the optimistic inclination of the heart and the articles of faith deduced therefrom but insists on accurate and tangible proofs and pins its faith on their results or on suppositions which are consistent with them. We have seen in our days how in order to keep pace with science some older religions have been re-interpreted in such a manner that they have become almost indistinguishable from the scientific spirit. The only concession demanded has been the association of some emotion of wonder and awe for the mighty unknown and unknowable towards which both science and religion are directed. It happens that a certain idea which in a distant epoch may have remained merely as an utopian ideal, may, in the course of time, continue to gather force in such a manner as to assert its supremacy over all things and show itself as the determinant of a mighty culture.

Let us take an example: Plato in his *Republic* drew the picture of aristocratic communism and a dictatorship of philosophic communism. In adition to communism of property, Plato advanced the startling proposal that all should possess their wives in common. "No one shall have a wife of his own; likewise the children should be in common and the parents should never know the child nor the child the parents." Both sexes should be given the same education and should share the same responsibilities of the state. From Plato to Sir Thomas More of the sixteenth century we find that equality and common ownership were urged by philosophers, poets, theological writers and agitators in the belief that a communistic state of society was the first and 'natural state' and that civil law, creating inequality, private ownership and class divisions, had arisen as a debased substitute for the reign of God and nature. Thomas More in his *Utopia* strove to hold before men a commonwealth which honoured its citizen neither for wealth nor for ancestry but for their service to society. He attacked the institution of private property and gave a scheme of government and commerce from which all money and money-transactions were abolished. Side by side with the English Utopians, we have the German and Italian Utopians like Andrea and Campanella, who wanted to abolish both riches and poverty and preached in favour of communism. The writings of Hobbes, Locke, Harrington and Chamberlain, as well as those of Babeuf, Cabet, Saint-Simon, Fourier, Louis Blanc, Proudhon, all moved in the same direction, though each of these writers had his own distinctive peculiarity. The ideal of all these writers was the establishment of equality. They all thought that the aim of society is the happiness of all and happiness consists in equality and that every man has an equal right to the enjoyment of all goods. Proudhon put forward a scheme in which he proposed to do away with all kinds of government which involved inequality and forced men to degrading levels. He also proposed that every man should have equal advantages with other men, whether he worked or not. It is unnecessary to go into further details, but throughout the influence of Owen and other writers in England and France and through the influence of the left wing of the Hegelians we come to Karl Marx and Engels. Karl Marx by his speculations in economics and knowledge of history attacked the Utopian socialism of the past and based it upon economic principles such as the conception of labour, value and the like. The communistic party organized by Marx could be distinguished from other parties in this that in the national struggles of the proletariats of the different countries, the communists point out and bring to the front the common interests of all proletariats independent of all nationalities and that in the various stages of development which the struggle of the working class against bourgeoisie has to pass through, they always and everywhere represent the interests of the movement as a whole. The communistic principle enunciated by Marx and Engels passed through many vicissitudes and sometimes departed largely from some of the main tenets of Marx but yet it followed different lines of progress in Russia, Italy, Austria, Germany, France and even in England.

The idea of communism enunciated by Marx differs from that of the Utopian communists of the past in this that here the central idea of the doctrine of equal rights and equal happiness is no longer an idle desire or an inactive ideal but it assumes here a new role of controlling the social and political activities of the people. There is another important point about this communism. It actively professes to be a scheme of unity which is much wider and broader than the schemes of religion and nationalism. A true communist works not for the people of his nation or for the people of any particular religion but he works for

O.P. 62/47

establishing throughout the world the fundamental principles of communism by which alone it can have safe existence.

It may, however, be pointed out that the central notion of communism is being exploited in the interests of nationalism, such as the Bolshevism of Russia, National Socialism of Germany and Fascism of Italy. Marx's philosophical contention was that in every historical epoch the prevailing mode of economic production and exchange and the social organisation necessarily following from it form the basis upon which is built and from which alone can be explained the political and intellectual history of that epoch ; that consequently the whole history of mankind has been a history of class struggles, contests between the exploiting and the exploited, the ruling and the oppressed classes. Such an unqualified assertion is in my opinion as incorrect as to say that the quality of the mind depends upon the quality of the body. There is obviously some connection between the well-being of the mind and that of the body, but it will be foolish to suppose that the talents of a person are in any sense a function of his muscles. Again, Marx's ideal was the overthrow of the bourgeoisie, the rule of the proletariat, the abolition of the old bourgeoisie society which is based on class antagonism and the establishment of a new society without classes and without private property. Thus, whatever may be the nature of the ultimate aim, the way in which this was to be attained involved class war. Though Marx himself wanted it to be bloodless, his followers would not have it so. Nevertheless the central idea of socialism and communism as it is going to affect the world today has a note of universality which transcends the bounds of nationalism.

We have made a brief review of some of the main types of culture. We have so far emphasised their distinctiveness, uniqueness and hence the aspect of separation. We have also seen that the word culture is often used in different senses. We have also seen that the pure content of culture becomes often associated with elements which are of alien origin. But inspite of the diversity of the different cultures due to different ways of the flowing of the mind and the diverse circumstances and conditions through which they show themselves, there is a fundamental spiritual content—their attitude to humanity and their human interests. In whatever ways a particular culture might manifest itself in art, literature and religion or in diverse social institutions, manners or behaviour or in whatsoever ways the expressions of a culture may differ from that of another, there is one fundamental content which must be common to all cultures worth the name. This content consists in the delight that is felt by a spirit in expressing itself to another spirit and in realising another spirit as one with itself. The feeling of the spiritual fellowship of mankind, its expression and realisation, may thus be said to form the vital element of the concept of culture. It is true that nationalism, classism and the like, so far as they reflect the fleshly part of our nature as represented in the concepts of utility and advantages, greed or jealousy or ambition, will always try to vitiate the impulses of true culture and usurp its place. But still the spirit must always assert its need of self-realisation in and through other spirits and try to resist the invasion of flesh and dominate over it. The struggle between the true cultural instinct and the instinct for other types of federation represents the central strife between the spirit and the flesh. Many have been the failures of the spirit, but it is through the continual self-assertion of the spiritual that man has often succeeded in transforming many unspiritual elements into the spiritual and also in elevating himself from the level of animality.

Never has there been in the past greater opportunities for understanding and realising spiritual expression of man in diverse countries and ages and under diverse circumstances and conditions as in our modern times, when the whole world has been brought to our door and the separation of space and time has been dissolved.

The lower parts of our nature will no doubt still continue to create the limitations and barriers, divisions and classes, and may raise nations, classes and religions against themselves. Still there will be some who in the milk of human sweetness will not only think that every man is equal but will regard him as a friend, and in the splendour of spiritual light will dissolve the darkness of all divisions and realise all cultures and all nations and people, the torch-bearers, as the diverse expressions of the same divinity that exists in all.

It is our egoism and self-conceit that obscure our view and separate us from God and our fellow-beings and is the cause of the miseries that are brought by us.

"Iya rab ji kabuli, orj dum baz rahan
mashgule, khudat kun, ji khudam baj rahan
ta hushiarani ji, nik o vad nidonam
mastam kun o az, nik a badam baz rahan."

"O Lord, from self-conceit deliver me,
Sever from self and occupy with Thee.
This self is captive to earth's good and ill.
Make me beside myself and set me free."

There is one thought, one culture, one religion that flows through all the ages, and all cultures and all religions, whatsoever may be their diversity in outward expression, must lose themselves in it. It is only through the supreme union of all cultures and religions that their claims to our acceptance can be recognised.

yathā nadyaḥ syandamānāḥ samudre
astaṃ gacchanti nāma-rūpe vihāya,
tathā vidvān nāma-rūpā-di-vimuktaḥ
parātparaṃ puruṣaṃ upaiti divyam.

"Just as the rivers flowing into the ocean are lost in it, losing their names and forms, so the wise man emancipated from names and forms passes on to the highest divinity."

Or, as Omar Khayyam says:

"katre vagirist kh, aj vahar juda im hma
vahar var katre vakhandid, kh ma im hma
dar hakikat digri nist khuda im hma
lik aj gardishe iknuktha khuda im hma.'

"The drop wept for its severance from the sea.
But the sea smiled, for, 'I am all," said he.
"The truth is all, nothing exists beside.
That one point circling apes plurality."

A HINDU VIEW OF RELIGION

Religion implies the spiritual expression of our personality in a much higher sense than Art, as it is generally understood, does, though in some of its special aspects Art approaches religion, passes into it or is an important aid to it. Art as spiritual expression may be distinguished from its material translation in audible and visible forms. As spiritual expression it represents the creative activity that manifests itself in sensuous forms, implying an immersion of the inner being in an exhilaration of emotion. The object of representation may be a landscape, beautiful scenes, or figures, any emotional complex or character ; the sensuous content, be it of colour, sounds, tune or rhythm which gives it its form, is spun out of the creative activity of the mind under the spontaneous direction of an outflow of joy which suffuses the whole creation. When the genius of the artist is such that it can manifest this joy and translate it in sensuous forms in such a manner that it can be enjoyed by others, we have an immortal work of art. The creation of the artist may imitate nature, but it exists on an entirely different plane. The artist's joy in his creation emanates from an inner spring which is free from all animality and dissociated from all animal needs. There is a parable in the Upaniṣads—the most sacred literature of the Hindus—in which two birds take part in the same action, mutually helping each other. They sit amicably on the same tree ; yet one eats the fruits of the tree while the other tastes nothing but feels the joy spontaneously. The poet may sing his song on the bitterest experience of his life, but as soon as the sorrow takes the artistic form it ceases to be personal, or, rather, it becomes personal to all and therefore universal. Thus the universality of art is no abstract universality. It signifies the presence of a concrete spiritual reality in all to whom the appeal of art is made. It is this spiritual reality in the poet that transforms his animal feelings, be they sorrowful or pleasurable, into the artist's joy, and utilises the materials of his experience, intellectual, technical or sensuous, for the creation of the artistic form through which it may manifest itself. The creative activity, order, method, choice of materials, their manifestation, due proportion and form, though they manifest themselves through the intellectual apparatus, are all guided and controlled by the inner spiritual being whose content is always beyond the intellectual plane. But though this spiritual being continually manifests itself in moulding the elements of our experience complex, in the interest of the creation of the artistic form, yet it is always not only beyond the animal man, but also beyond the intellectual man. Being in thought and sense it is superior to them. The internal logic of artistic activity is thus transcendental or mystical. It is the inner controller (*antar-yāmin*), of which the *Kenopaniṣad* says that it "weaves the functions of the mind, but the mind does not know it."

The artistic form conceals within itself the life of the inner spirit. When it passes over to another through some channel it creates in him a corresponding form. Through it his inner spirit manifests itself in joy, and this joy overcomes the animal and intellectual obstruction of the individual that had separated him from the artist, so, in the manifestation and enlightenment of the spiritual joy he becomes one with the artist and with all others who may be appreciating the artistic work. Thus the secret of art-communication lies in the revelation of the spirit in joy, which, like a burning torch, is carried to the heart of another and sets free his spirit, and in the effulgence of illumination burns away his egoistic self, which had separated him like a shell from the artist's person and created an obstructive individuality. In artistic creation and appreciation we have a field in which spiritual realities become awakened, we are suffused with radiant joy and beauty, and come into communion with kindred spirits. All sense of utility, personal advantage and the craving for egoistic satisfaction ceases for the moment, and we feel ourselves to be in an entirely different world. But this illumination of the spirit through art is by means of the sensuous content of the moment and the awakening of spiritual joy and fellowship is therefore bounded by the limitations of the sense and touches our whole being only remotely.

The presence of a spiritual principle in man so well illustrated by art-experience is the bedrock of Hinduism, and the fundamental aim of religion is to secure a supreme awakening to this principle. In religion, however, it is not, as in art, a momentary flash produced by a sensuous content, but exists through all the complexities of our whole being, in our conscious and sub-conscious mental states, and in all our emotional and volitional manifestations and determinations. Religion is art in the deepest and widest sense of the term. It is an activity of the spirit in its self-expression through the whole of our personality. By personality, I mean here our entire complex structure, including our biological or animal tendencies and cravings, temperament, character, emotions and emotional outlook, will and conduct, in fact the totality of our interrelated experiences. This personality has in it a potential and an actual aspect, and in religious activity the spirit strives to reveal itself in and through the entire personality. Just as in art-activity the sensuous content involving the ideas, images, words, colours and their complex order must be so arranged or transformed that the spirit may find in them a proper form of self-expression, so in religion, the entire personality must be so worked upon and transformed that it may prove itself to be a suitable vehicle for self-expression, even as a creeper blossoms into beautiful flowers and a tree sweetens itself into its fruits.

One of the chief characteristics of art is sympathy. A poet or painter is in sympathy with nature and with man. By sympathy here I mean attachment or love. A poet surveys tenderly the scenes and events in the life of nature and the characters and situations in human life. To him inert nature is pregnant with spirit and he dallies with it as with human beings, and he transports man from amidst the economic and animal struggle to a higher level and invest him with a spiritual meaning. The affairs of men and their conflicts of character and interests appear to him in a new perspective and he clothes them with his own joy. He rejoices in the

O.P. 62/48

revelation of his own spirit and invests with a like joy all those through whom, or in association with whom, the revelation is made. The Upaniṣads say that a brother, sister, wife, or son is dear because the Self is dear. The joy of all things is through their association with, and revelation through, the self. When this association is through the animal self, we have animal or egoistic pleasure, and when it is through the higher spiritual self we have disinterested, æsthetic pleasure or art-joy. The Upaniṣads say that when one wakens the spirit within the Self then are the winds honeyed, honeyed the rivers flow, the nights and days are honeyed and even the very dust is sweet.

The spiritual principle revealed in artistic experience may well lead to belief in the concrete spiritual principle revealed through religious experience, and we may, through it, get additional insight into the method through which the spiritual principle works to transform our personality and determine our attitude towards nature and man. The difference between the mode of activity of the spirit in the two spheres is primarily with regard to the materials for transformations ; for, in art the spiritual principle transforms merely a sensuous content and reveals itself under its limitations, but in religion the transformation affects the whole personality. Thus art, from one point of view, is only imperfect religion and is utilised in its service in the form of various kind of rituals, images, altars, songs, dances, music, stories and the like.

The fundamental purpose of religion is the spiritual fellowship of man on a non-utilitarian plane, but this is only imperfectly secured through the sensuous content used in the services of religion by the members of any religious fraternity.

When the unification implied in rituals is misapplied for utilitarian or other ends religion may descend into fanaticism or worse forms of egoism so well illustrated by the religious history of the world. Though most forms of Hinduism employ rituals, the fact is continually emphasised that the sensuous representations of such rituals must always be inspired by the ultimate concept of religion, without which all ritual loses its significance and becomes false. Rituals without the true spirit of religion are like a lifeless body; the purpose for which they are employed must continually advance, until the sensuous contact becomes unnecessary.

The subsistence of a spiritual principle in man is testified not only by religious experience but also through artistic expression, as shown above. Like the artistic genius its revelation may manifest itself in a greater or less degree in this or that religious genius, but its reality, as a dominating influence in moulding the lives of us all, cannot be denied. It is true that its defining content cannot be looked for within either the sense-data or the purely intellectual elements of our mind; but that only shows that it belongs to another plane. The Upaniṣads demonstrate in parables the fact that things may exist even though they may not be grasped by the senses of the intellect. The seed of a banyan tree is very small and when we split it up we can see nothing inside it, yet it contains the principle which can unfold into a great tree; a lump of sugar when dissolved in water cannot be seen, but it is still there and can be tasted. So the spiritual principle of man is revealed through inner experience and in the moulding influence that it exerts on his entire personality by transforming it into a suitable vehicle for its expression. It is neither knowledge, nor emotion, nor will, but it expresses itself through them all as their inner controller and moulder. Being in them, it is beyond them.

The concept of immortality cannot be applied to our bodies or the sensuous and intellectual elements of the mind, but only to the spirit which reveals its nature through an inner intuitive enlightenment. It lies deep in the cavern of the heart self-revealed through his own radiance but unrevealed by the ordinary cognitive ways. In this aspect its subsistence is mystical, its concrete reality is directly experienced and felt. Thus, belief in Immortality means only the awakening in man of his true nature as spirit; for it is the spirit alone that has no content in itself, except so far as it may reveal itself through the content of our personality. All seeming changes in the spirit occur only through its association with the personality. The immortal nature can only be realised through the intuitive awakening of spiritual reality.

The concept of change is the concept of death; and the concept of immortality implies the concept of changelessness. The spiritual principle, however it may be enmeshed as it were by the different conditions of our personality, is one in all men. It is universal in its nature not as a mere abstraction but as concrete, spontaneous, free individuality and reality. One of the most fundamental modes of its self-expression must be towards the recognition of the equality of all, freedom of all, and sanctity of all. Every man has an equal right to the development of his capacities and the attainment of happiness. But the religious spirit is not satisfied merely with the recognition of such rights; it calls for the positive development of fellowship and love. Love all men as thyself—is the watchword of Hinduism.

It has been said already that the Upaniṣads teach that joy proceeds from the identification of others with one's self. The recognition of the universality of one's own spiritual self thus implies the outflow of our own joy into others; and this is but another name for love.

The *Viṣṇu Purāṇa* and the *Bhāgavad Gītā*, the two leading gospels of Hindu faith, untiringly emphasise the fact that the intellectual and emotional apperception of all selves as being one with one's own self, is the true worship in religion. Moral science, when abstracted from religion, fails to justify its claims as an exact science. The application of standards in any of their divergent forms fails in logical coherence, and also in explaining the problems of practical morality, which, when their nature is discussed merely from a speculative point of view, present insurmountable difficulties. This is illustrated when it is observed that all pleasure theories contradict themselves by the assumption of qualitative standards, and in the practical impossibility of the calculus of the greatest happiness of the greatest number; rigid theories show themselves to be meaningless on account of the voidness of their content and the contradiction into which they plunge when they deny the place of all emotion on the one hand and are yet forced on the other hand to introduce them by the back door. All social theories of ethics fail on the problem of the circular interdependence of the individual and society, and everywhere the claims of egoism and altruism are left unsettled. The supreme justification of the ethical principle for ever escapes us in our abstract speculations of ethics, because they are treated merely as a normative science. But morality is like a flower that blooms on the plant of religion and realises its true significance when separated from it. Morality presupposes society, and society means the recognition of the fellowship of human beings. If the fundamental fact of religion be the recognition of the spirituality of all, and if this recognition is not merely intellectual or metaphysical, but an emergent fact that arises from the moulding of our entire personality, involving thought, feeling and will, the morality that follows from religion does not involve any splitting of our personality, as is the case even in the most rigorous creed of morals. Thus Kant insists on the opposition of inclinations to will as a defining content of morality which gives rise to many logical and psychological difficulties.

The higher morality which flows from religion is not satisfied with the equal treatment of others, nor in regarding each man as a sufficient end in himself, nor even with an intellectual appreciation of oneness, but only with intense feelings of love, friendship and compassion.

Actions here are no longer separable from the total personality, but are only the external consequences of an inner transformation, in consonance with revelation of the spirit in and through others. Universal friendship, universal charity, universal compassion, imperturbability of temper at the defects of others, and feelings of happiness at the happiness of others (***maitrī, karuṇā, muditā, upekṣā***) are regarded as the cardinal principles of Hindu and Buddhist morality that flows from religion. This is technically called ***brahmavihāra*** or the self-realisation of the highest, the spirit, in and through all others. The sphere of ordinary morality is often limited to particular societies or nations, but the scope of religious morality is unrestricted by the limitations of nations, races, societies, creeds and the like. It proceeds from a positive outflow of love. A truly religious man is in love, peace and friendship with the whole world; for him the obligation of morality has given place to spontaneous sympathy. The difference between art and religion is that while the former is satisfied with sympathy so far as it can be manifested through the limited sensuous contents of artistic creations, the sympathy of religion is the result of the transformation of our whole personality, a religious creation by which we recognise our fellowship with all.

As creative art may have in it an emphasis of the intellectual or the emotional content, so in diverse religious creations also we find the different aspects of our personality emphasised in differing ways. Thus in the philosophic form of religion as taught in the monistic Vedānta of Śaṅkara, the emphasis is on the realisation of the true nature of the spirit as pure consciousness, the one in all. The realisation of this unique reality, infinite and unlimited, is only possible when one wakes within oneself the true philosophic wisdom. But such an awakening is only possible when one succeeds in dissociating oneself from all attachments to the obstructive egoistic and animal functions that separate man from his fellow beings by drawing him to the levels of his lower personality from whence, being still under the bondage of passions, he cannot attain true spiritual freedom. That one Brahman manifests through all and is the one Reality in all is the fundamental tenet of the Vedānta. Religious realisation, therefore, consists in the attainment of that final enlightenment in which the false and impure individuality vanishes in the supreme illumination of the spirit which is one in all. Yoga has a different metaphysical basis. It holds that though the content of pure spirit is the same in all, the life of each individual is presided over by spiritual principles which are only numerically different. Under the influence of these spiritual principles the elements of the personality are continually undergoing change and expressing themselves as experience in association with the external world. The culmination of the evolution of our experiences is the revelation of the religious man as the realisation of the nature of the content of the spiritual principle (Puruṣa) in one's own individuality and in that of others. The process of transformation of one's own personality takes place through the exertion of one's own will by means of psychological exercises in meditation and concentration associated with moral purification of the highest order. On the negative side it involves absolute non-injury as the fundamental creed and on the positive side it emphasises the imperative need for training the mind to the attitude of universal friendship, charity and compassion.

As an aid to this end one should habituate oneself to opposing any tendencies to greed, attachment, or antipathy by engaging oneself in suitable course of thought and meditation so as to control all animal and anti-social passions. The important cardinal virtues are truthfulness, purity and contentment and the surrender to God of all interests in one's own actions. The moral elevation aimed at involves a thorough transformation of one's own nature and personality in the interest of the self-illumination of one's spiritual nature. As a further aid to securing progress the psychological discipline of Yoga, i.e., concentration for the purpose of uprooting all evil tendencies, is recommended. God is acknowledged in the system but plays only a part subordinate to the fundamental religious purpose of the transformation of one's own personality, through which must come the realisation of the supreme spiritual principle. The systems of Yoga and Vedānta form the background of most systems of Indian religion which all utilise the principles in association with other modes of religious experience and discipline.

The spiritual principle in man may recognise its own nature as modifying and transforming the personality, as appreciating the equal individuality of others in thought, action and feelings, and as realising the collective spirituality of all beings as a transcendent immanent principle, which in its pure spirituality transcends the human sphere and yet manifests itself under the specific individual limita-

O.P. 62/49

tions of personalities. The recognition of the transcendent nature of the spirit is the revelation of God in man. Looked at from the transcendent point of view God is our father and we are like sparks from his divine nature. Thus the Upaniṣads teach that we are like the sparks of light from the divine fire or the threads of a web spun by the divine spider out of himself. From another point of view, God is regarded as the inner controller (*antar-yāmin*). If He can modify the entire personality in the interests of spiritual revelation then all the elements of our personality must derive their powers and functions from Him and it is said in the Upaniṣads that all our cognitive and conative senses and even our life functions are derived from Him. Again, from another point of view, our own individuality is already merged and absorbed in Him like rivers in the ocean, like tunes of music in the sound, or like a lump of salt in saline water. In this mystic apprehension of unity the knower and the known vanish in a spiritual enlightenment, and this is regarded as the true immortality of the spirit. Death can only be of the body that changes, but so far as the pure spiritual essence is concerned, there can be no birth and no death, and from this point of view, the mystery of life and death vanishes. With the spiritual moulding of our personality, true immortality is manifested by the inward intuitive revelation of our spiritual nature. But the logical and ontological discussions involved in this religious situation cannot be taken up here as they occupy very large portion of our religious philosophy.

The religious situation herein indicated is admitted in the philosophy of Hindu art, which describes artistic joy as being closely akin to the spiritual realisation of Brahman, the highest, and the identification of spiritual joy with artistic joy. An important modification of the religious situation by the artistic movement is seen when the spiritual situation involved in religion is realised through the intimate terms of human relationship. Thus, according to the Bhāgavata or Vaiṣṇava religion, the heart of the devotee surges from within and fills his whole being with gentle love for his master, father, friend or lover, who is the supreme Lord both of himself and of the universe. The devotee's love for his master is so great that he calls nothing his own. He has offered to God not only all his material possessions, but all his inner attachments also. All his impurities are burnt away by this great love. Within and without he becomes filled with one sweet emotion that renders him dear to everyone, and endears all to him. The image of his Lord fills the world, and his whole being pulsates with divine emotion. The call of his flute springs from the cavern of his heart, from the bamboo groves of grazing cattle, and from fields of golden crops bathed by the glowing rays of the sun he sings the Lord's name in joy and melts in ecstasy. His heart flows out in milk and honey toward all the creatures of his Lord and lover. He has come in touch with the deep infinity of love and being in his Lord he longs continually for him.

To get so much is still to ask for more.
The unfathomed ocean's voice is in his heart,
The Lord's bewitching beauty lights his eyes,
Music enchants, his spirit floats on wings,

His Lord's caressing touch completes the joy.
And, loving thus, the saint awakes in God.
And through Him wakes in man, and, wakening thus,
Senses again in man an awakened God.
So, spiritual progress in a cycle moves
From God to man and back again to God.
Thus is man free to enjoy spontaneous life
Which blooms into a flower, and, blossoming so,
Binds man and God in one sweet, fragrant whole.

In some forms there is an emphasis on the metaphysical consciousness, in others on the determinate controlling of will, and in others again on the outflow of spontaneous love. But all forms of Hindu religion mean a spiritual awakening of the nature in man through an internal transformation of personality, just as art in its varied forms means the creative transformation of a sensuous content for the revelation of the spirit in nature and man. The fellowship of man and the awakening of the spirit are thus the two poles that have determined all religious movements in India.